TRAVESTY OF JUSTICE

THE SHOCKING PROSECUTION OF LIEUTENANT CLINT LORANCE

DON BROWN

WILDBLUE
PRESS

WildBluePress.com

TRAVESTY OF JUSTICE published by:

WILDBLUE PRESS
P.O. Box 102440
Denver, Colorado 80250

WILDBLUE PRESS is registered at the U.S. Patent and Trademark Offices.

ISBN 978-1-948239-11-0   Trade Paperback
ISBN 978-1-942266-10-3   eBook

Interior Formatting by Elijah Toten
www.totencreative.com

To the paratroopers of First Platoon, Charlie
Troop, of the 4th Squadron/73rd Cavalry
Regiment, 4th Brigade Combat Team,
82nd Airborne Division, United States Army
for their Gallant Service in Afghanistan – 2012
"All the Way!"

In memory of:

PFC MARK L KERNER, 82nd Airborne Division
November 19, 1991 ~ March 1, 2015 (age 23)

&

CPL MATTHEW HANES, 82ND Airborne Division
June 27, 1991 ~ August 7, 2015 (age 24)

A Special Salute to:

1LT Don Latino and PFC Samuel Walley
Both Awarded the Purple Heart

With Special Gratitude to

THE UNITED AMERICAN PATRIOTS

For supporting
Our nation's warriors
falsely accused of "war crimes."

To help American soldiers like Clint Lorance,
go to

WWW.UAP.ORG

TRAVESTY OF JUSTICE

THE SHOCKING PROSECUTION OF LIEUTENANT CLINT LORANCE

TABLE OF CONTENTS

INTRODUCTION

LANDMINES, SUICIDE BIKERS AND THE BLOODY WAR IN AFGHANISTAN

On July 2, 2012, two days before Independence Day in America, a young Army lieutenant, a decorated member of the elite 82nd Airborne Division, took charge of his platoon in Kandahar Province, Afghanistan. First Lieutenant Clint Lorance was one of the most decorated junior officers in the United States Army.

With an impressive seven Army Achievement Medals on his chest, most of them earned as an enlisted man, Clint had served overseas on two separate tours before Afghanistan. First, he was assigned to the Eighth Army in Korea in Pusan, where he was often near the dangerous and volatile Demilitarized Zone on the border between North and South Korea. After that, he served in Iraq, during the Iraq War, at Forward Operating Base Kalsu, 20 miles south of Baghdad. During his tour in Iraq, Clint's post came under heavy rocket and mortar fire from the enemy on a daily basis. He often led dangerous convoys outside of the post while in Iraq, frequently drawing rocket fire, mortar fire, and gunfire.

Clint put his life on the line for his country. Many soldiers, coming under the type of constant fire that Clint had endured in Iraq, elected to do their time and get out. That is understandable. Combat is a living hell that most Americans will never be forced to witness up close and personal. For those who served and then got out, their service is no less diminished, and should be greatly appreciated by all Americans.

At the end of his dangerous tour in Iraq, Clint could have left the Army. A number of his buddies did. But Clint elected to stay. Service to his country was in his bloodstream and ran through his veins. Clint Lorance wanted to continue to serve, even if it meant giving his life for America.

The Army recognized his hard work, dedication, and service to his country, and offered him the opportunity to earn a commission as an officer. He responded to the challenge, and entered the Army's Green-to-Gold program, competing to become an officer in the United States Army. Clint excelled in the officer candidate program, soon earned his commission as a second lieutenant in the infantry, and then became a paratrooper in the elite 82nd Airborne Division.

Now, as a young officer, he had been called to serve his country in a third dangerous overseas tour, this time in Afghanistan.

On the morning of July 2nd, Clint had been on the job as platoon leader for only three days when he called his men together at 5:55 a.m. to brief them on the day's mission.

Lorance had been called in to take command of First Platoon, Charlie Company, when the platoon's previous commander, First Lieutenant Dom Latino, was wounded by an exploding improvised exploding device (IED), which blew the hell up when another American soldier stepped on it, a couple of weeks before Clint Lorance would take command. Shrapnel had torn through Latino's face and abdomen, and they rushed him off the battlefield to try and save his life. Like Latino, many of the soldiers in First Platoon had taken a beating from the IEDs. Some were injured, some maimed, others killed.

An IED is a deadly, homemade bomb built by the Taliban, and then hidden in the ground, for the purpose of killing and maiming American soldiers. Between 2008 and 2010, nearly

60 percent of American soldiers who died in Afghanistan were killed by IEDs. Sometimes, these devices were set off remotely, triggered via radio transmitters in the hands of Taliban operatives hiding well out of sight.

Sometimes, a single step on a routine patrol triggered the explosion, as these "pressure plate IEDs" were set off by pressure alone. But whether the IEDs were pressure detonated, or radio triggered, the results proved deadly for American GIs.

In southeastern Afghanistan, where Clint and his men had been deployed, the environment was exceptionally dangerous.

Here's what 4th Brigade Deputy Brigade Commander Col. Scott Halstead, who later testified in the court-martial of Lieutenant Lorance, said, under oath, at trial, about the battlefield conditions in which these paratroopers were operating:

> "Zhari/Maiwand (the district in Kandahar province where the platoon operated) is almost entirely—I mean it's a gigantic minefield ... Our paratroopers were, justifiably so, very cautious. They'd seen many of their Ranger buddies killed and maimed."

In addition to mine-ridden battlefields, the Taliban had been employing another terror tactic to kill Americans. A tactic that was impossible to defend against.

Motorcycles.

The Taliban had begun strapping explosives to their bodies, mounting motorcycles, and then charging toward American troops, blowing themselves up at close range. This became known as a "VBIED attack" for Vehicle Borne Improvised Explosive Device. This tactic gave attackers the dual advantage of 1) engaging in Islamic martyrdom, while 2) murdering Americans and anyone who sympathized with Americans. The tactic of mass-murder-by-motorcycle had increased in recent months, and under suicidal rules of engagement employed by the American military in 2012, self-defense against suicide bikers became an impossible choice.

American troops were hand-strapped from firing, unless they could first determine "hostile intent," which normally meant identifying a weapon on the attacker. Then, after determining the presence of "hostile intent," our soldiers had to analyze the enemy for a potential "hostile act."

The American soldier in 2012 was relegated to the role of battlefield lawyer, forced into a series of mental gymnastics to reach a legal conclusion about whether to fire in self-defense. All this in a war-torn battle zone, in a historically war-torn country, in the ancestral home of the Taliban.

But the Americans could not always identify bombs on fast-approaching motorcycles. Nor could they see bombs under the insurgent's shirt, or hidden within the motorcycle. Motorcycles moved too quickly for positive identification of anything, and life or death often hung upon split-second decisions.

Soldiers were trained to fight, not to play lawyer on the battlefield.

A split-second too long of playing lawyer in a barbaric war zone, then deciding at the last second to refrain from firing against a fast-charging motorcycle, could lead to instant carnage, perhaps multiple deaths for American troops in the motorcycle's path.

But as an American soldier, if you opened fire to defend yourself against what looked like an aggressive motorcycle charge coming at your troops at 40 mph, you had better make damn sure the Taliban was armed. Because if you tried to defend yourself and your troops, and those bodies on the ground after an attempt at self-defense in a war zone are not armed, you had better be ready to face the music with your high command.

By 2012, the same question had grown pervasive throughout American forces in Afghanistan. Would the American chain of command have your back?

Would politically correct rules of engagement, designed to appease the ever-complaining Afghan government of Hamid Karzai, be used to keep Americans from protecting themselves? These questions haunted our troops, and they were questions wrought with life-or-death consequences.

This became the impossible dilemma faced by American ground forces in the 11th year of the Afghan war: defend yourself, and hope like hell that they were armed after you fire; or cross your fingers, and pray that they didn't pull guns and spray you with fire as they passed, toss grenades at you, or blow themselves to hell and back and take you and your buddies with them.

The choice was impossible. But this dilemma had come down from the American high command, which seemed to care more about enforcing politically correct rules of engagement than it cared about the lives of its men.

Even in the weeks before Lieutenant Lorance take over at First Platoon, the Taliban had carried out several high-profile suicide attacks by motorcycle in Afghanistan.

On April 12, 2012, seven American soldiers, members of the Ohio National Guard, had come off the battlefield and retreated into the city of Maimanah, the capital of Farayab Province. They needed respite from the savage war, and visited a park in a more peaceful area of northern Afghanistan.

But in Afghanistan, no place is off limits to the Taliban.

Striking with the surprise of a sudden lightning bolt, their Taliban attacker, mounted on a fast-moving motorcycle, struck out of the blue, a fast-moving human bomb. The explosion killed 10 people, including several of the principal targets, three American soldiers.

Master Sergeant Sgt. Hannon, who died that day, worked for the Department of Veterans Affairs back home as a lawyer serving veterans. With a heart for those who served, including the aging World War II vets, Shawn helped them with their legal needs, putting together wills and health care directives, and giving them advice. Though he could have made tons of money at a private firm, he gave his life to veterans. He was also a great soldier, had been wounded on previous deployment and received the Purple Heart. "If somebody in the world needed help, he'd be there," one of his co-workers told the *Military Times*. Shawn left behind a wife, Jamie, and a son, Evan, who was 9 months old.

Master Sgt. Jeffrey J. Rieck left behind a 15-year-old son, Joel. At a military funeral in Columbus 12 days after the fatal motorcycle attack, Joel accepted the American flag that had been draped on his father's casket from Maj. Gen. Deborah Ashenhurst, the Ohio Guard's commanding officer, who knelt before the boy on one knee.

Capt. Nick Rozanzki, 36, had been married to Jennifer for five years. Their two young daughters are Emma Kathryn and Anna Elizabeth. Nick had been a marathon runner, and an avid soccer player and coach. Volunteering large amounts of time to young people, Nick coached for 15 years for Eagles Soccer Club.

In that one motorcycle attack, two wives lost their husbands, and four children lost their fathers.

The Army calls the weapon that killed these men a "suicide vehicle-borne improvised explosive device." Translated from military-ese to English, it means "motorcycle with a bomb, and impossible to detect before it blows the hell up."

On June 6, 2012, three weeks before Lt. Lorance took over First Platoon, the Taliban carried out another motorcycle attack, this time outside the Kandahar Air Field used by the U.S. Air Force to keep logistics, supplies and reinforcements supplied to the U.S. Army. The suicide motorcyclist charged into a populated area often frequented by American troops.

The massive explosion killed 22 people, and wounded 50. Fortunately, no Americans were in the crowd at the time of the attack, and the "talibiker" killed mostly civilians. But the bloody carnage sent a clear message to all: "If you are an American soldier, or if you work with or near American servicemen, you are a target."

The increase in suicide-bomb-by-motorcycle had sent shock waves throughout U.S. forces in Afghanistan. Against this backdrop, Clint Lorance took command of his platoon on June 29, 2012, determined that none of his boys would be shipped home in body bags. In that noble cause, the lieutenant would succeed.

But it would cost him his freedom.

CHAPTER 1

"All rise!"

The military judge, Col. Kirsten V.C. Brunson, U.S. Army, Judge Advocate General's Corps, cloaked in a black robe, stepped into the courtroom and surveyed the scene before her. It had been a long trial, and now, the military jury was about to render its verdict.

Under the soft-white glow of four massive globe lights hanging from the ceiling, the courtroom was packed with a small army of military officers, civilian court personnel, and civilian onlookers. Every face was tense, every eye glued on the judge. The silence, broken only by the solitary cry of the bailiff, was deafening.

Stately dark mahogany desks and barrister rails set against the red burgundy carpet provided a stark contrast to the red-hot tension that now filled the room.

To Judge Brunson's left, when facing the front of the courtroom and the large dark paneled "bench" where the judge is seated, the military jury, or "members" as they are called in the military justice system, had taken their places. Some glanced at the accused. Others looked away, to deliberately avoid eye contact.

"Please be seated."

he was accused of killing, and never even saw an alleged victim. Still, the Army had charged him with attempted murder and double murder.

Lorance, the prosecutors claimed, ordered men in his platoon to fire on a motorcycle in a Taliban-infested battle zone in southeastern Afghanistan. At the time of the order, the motorcycle had charged his platoon at a high rate of speed, on a rural dirt road that had been controlled by Taliban forces. Both sides of the road had coiled barbed wire to prevent anyone from entering it.

Signs were placed, in English and Afghan, restricting the roads in the area to only police and military. But coming down a road controlled by the Taliban, the motorcycle kept speeding toward the point where lead elements of the American platoon crossed the road. And, there was not one rider on the motorcycle. There were not two riders on it. But rather, there were three riders on the single red motorcycle.

Lorance knew that the Taliban had used motorcycles as a weapon in suicide missions to blow up Americans in blood-strewn carnages. The prior incidents at Kandahar Airfield and the "talibiker" attack in Farayab Provence provided evidence of the Taliban's suicide-by-motorcycle tactics.

In addition, the month before Lorance arrived, in June of 2012, First Platoon had been battered by the enemy. Four of its 40 men were killed or seriously wounded by land mines, IEDs, or rifle fire. Unidentified and unseen Taliban snipers had fired on the platoon every day. The casualties were so bad, and the landmines so thick, that at the end of June, the Army had pulled First Platoon back off the battlefield for five days for emotional counseling and therapy away from the fighting, and to spend time with "combat stress specialists."

Now, First Platoon had returned to the battlefront, with Lt. Lorance as its new leader. Under the most difficult, dangerous and bloody circumstances imaginable, Clint Lorance's main goal was to keep his men out of body bags, and to keep them from losing limbs and becoming bloody human stumps. American soldiers had suffered enough carnage.

The morning of July 2 promised more burning heat. The searing temperatures, which had eclipsed 100 degrees for 26 out of the last 30 days, had reached 100 degrees by 6 a.m., nearly an hour before they pushed off on their patrol.

After Lt. Lorance conducted his pre-mission briefing around 6:30 a.m., at 6:55 a.m., the platoon left its post on an armed patrol through rows of grape fields and into a Taliban-infested village.

Because the landmines were thick, they were forced to move out from their post in a tight single file, one man behind the other, with mine sweepers out front to detect for lethal bombs in the ground. A step too far to the left or to the right could set off IEDs powerful enough to take out multiple men in a single blast. The plan called for them to move out from their forward operating base, to the west, first through heavily vegetated grape fields, where visibility proved difficult.

They would move through the grape berms for several hundred yards, then turn north, cutting across the grape rows into the small village, known as Sarenzai, where they would move through the back of mud-hut building and then turn and move along the single dirt road through the village. There, they would sweep the village for Taliban operatives, before turning right on the dirt road to head back to their post. Their march pattern resembled a giant fishhook, out into the fields, then looping up into the village, then the spear of the platoon hooking back to the right, down the main road, back toward base.

That was the plan, anyway.

On the route planned for the morning of July 2, the men of First Platoon would cross over much of the same ground that had gotten so many Americans killed or mutilated in recent days. Even after five days of respite and counseling common every day in Washington. But it got worse with the rain. Every time.

Veterans Day had come to Washington, marking Barack Obama's first Veterans Day as president. Despite the dreary weather, nearly 5,000 Americans, including a mix of freedom-loving patriots and curious onlookers, had gathered at Arlington, many hoping to honor the fallen, and some hoping to catch a glimpse of the new commander in chief.

By 11 a.m., temperatures had dipped to 46 degrees. Orange and russet leaves had fallen from trees, scattered all over the rain-soaked lanes of Constitution Avenue that were cleared of all traffic by D.C. police to make way for the black Suburbans and black Cadillacs in the fast-moving presidential motorcade that zoomed along the wide boulevard from the White House, past the Lincoln Memorial, and onto the Memorial Bridge for the short drive into Virginia and into the green hills of the cemetery.

The rains stopped at 11:20, raising the hopes of the hundreds of spectators at the Tomb of the Unknown Soldier awaiting the presidential wreath-laying ceremony. But at 11:30, light rain started again.

At the eastern steps of the Memorial Amphitheater that faced the great marble crypt with a foggy view of Washington off in the distance behind it, splashes of black-and-blue umbrellas had sprung in the visitor's section. Below, the presidential party, including First Lady Michelle Obama, Second Lady Dr. Jill Biden, and Veterans Affairs Secretary General Eric Shinseki, stood single file facing the monument. Trim soldiers in dress navy jackets and lighter blue trousers held black canopy umbrellas for Mrs. Obama, Dr. Biden, and Secretary Shinseki.

As the sentinel guarding the tomb stepped into the small, green booth to make way for commencement of the ceremonies, President Obama, wearing a black overcoat, white shirt, and light blue tie, stepped forward into the spray of light rain. Obama turned to his left, accepting from a lone soldier the large green wreath with red, white and blue flowers and ribbons.

The president held onto the front of the wreath for a second, and with the back of it still being supported by the soldier, took seven steps forward and laid it on a white, wrought-iron stand in front of the tomb. He bowed his head, in a moment of silence.

When he turned around and walked back to his position next to Maj. Gen. Karl Horst, beside the black mat used by the honor guards to patrol and guard the tomb 24 hours a day, the Army bugler to the president's left began a slow rendition of "Taps." Military members saluted. Civilians, including the president, placed their right hands over their hearts.

Moments later, the wreath-laying ceremony ended. The presidential party turned and walked up the eastern steps to the circular amphitheater, to the sound of "Ruffles and Flourishes" by the U.S. Air Force Band, where several thousand had gathered to hear the president's remarks.

The service had ended by noon, and the crowd dissipated.

The president was not ready to return to the White House. Not yet, anyway.

As the crowd thinned out, Obama requested a private walk-through of the freshest graves in Arlington—in Section 60—set aside for Americans who had given their lives in Iraq and Afghanistan. Accompanied by Brig. Gen. Horst, commander of the Military District of Washington, Obama took a quiet walk among the graves, alone with the general, quietly, and in thought.

As the first lady and a small handful of others followed at a respectful distance behind the president and the general, the names of the fallen rose from the graves as Obama walked past the narrow, white tombstones—their lives and stories crying to him out in an unforgettable silence.

The president passed by the grave of Green Beret Sgt. 1st Class Bradley S. Bohle, 29, who died on Sept. 16, 2009, on his second deployment to Afghanistan, when his vehicle rolled over an IED. The violent blast killed Brad along with two of his fellow soldiers that day. He left behind a wife, herself an Army veteran, and three young daughters.

Then came the grave of Sgt. Jason T. Palmerton, a Green Beret from Auburn, Neb., who died on July 23, 2009, at age 29, in Qal'eh-Yegaz, Afghanistan, of gunshot wounds, when his unit came under fire while on foot patrol.

Obama walked right beside Sgt. Palmerton's grave. And while many of the headstones of Christian soldiers bore a simple cross, in block design, Palmerton's bore a thinner cross with a larger flame swooping up the left side, the sign of the Holy Spirit, and the symbol of the United Methodist Church.

Sgt. Palmerton left behind a fiancée and his parents, Denise Brown of Auburn and Steve Palmerton of Norman, Okla. He also left behind three sisters.

Then came a gravestone that stopped the president in his tracks. The simple inscription reflected heroism that was larger than life.

ROSS ANDREW McGINNIS

MEDAL OF HONOR

SPC US ARMY

JUNE 14, 1987

DEC 4, 2006

BRONZE STAR

PURPLE HEART

OPERATION

IRAQI FREEDOM

Nineteen years old. Still a teenager. Cut down before the prime of his life even began. Not even the president could wrap his mind and his thoughts around such a young man lying in the grave before him.

Obama kneeled down by the grave, with the first lady, Horst and two other soldiers standing behind him, giving him quiet space with the young hero.

A miniature American flag had been stuck in the ground to the right of the grave marker. Two freshly cut roses, one red and one white, stood in a small vase on the ground to the left.

Obama lingered for a moment, then placed a presidential coin on the grass in front of the gravestone, between the flowers and the American flag.

Five months before President Obama had been elected, on June 2, 2008, President George W. Bush had signed a citation honoring McGinnis for his service to the nation:

OFFICIAL CITATION

The President of the United States of America, authorized by Act of Congress, June 2, 2008, has awarded in the name of Congress the Medal of Honor to

Private First Class Ross A. McGinnis
United States Army

For conspicuous gallantry and intrepidity at the risk of his life above and beyond the call of duty:

Private First Class Ross A. McGinnis distinguished himself by acts of gallantry and intrepidity above and beyond the call of duty while serving as an M2 .50-caliber Machine Gunner, First Platoon, C Company, 1ˢᵗ Battalion, 26ᵗʰ Infantry Regiment, in connection with combat operations against an armed enemy in Adhamiyah, Northeast Baghdad, Iraq, on 4 December 2006.

That afternoon his platoon was conducting combat control operations in an effort to reduce and control sectarian violence in the area. While Private McGinnis was manning the M2 .50-caliber

Machine Gun, a fragmentation grenade thrown by an insurgent fell through the gunner's hatch into the vehicle. Reacting quickly, he yelled "grenade," allowing all four members of his crew to prepare for the grenade's blast. Then, rather than leaping from the gunner's hatch to safety, Private McGinnis made the courageous decision to protect his crew. In a selfless act of bravery, in which he was mortally wounded, Private McGinnis covered the live grenade, pinning it between his body and the vehicle and absorbing most of the explosion.

Private McGinnis' gallant action directly saved four men from certain serious injury or death. Private First Class McGinnis' extraordinary heroism and selflessness at the cost of his own life, above and beyond the call of duty, are in keeping with the highest traditions of the military service and reflect great credit upon himself, his unit, and the United States Army.

Ross left behind his mother and father, who accepted the Medal of Honor on his behalf, and two sisters.

Ten years before Ross McGinnis was born, Billy Joel had written the lyrics in his 1977 smash hit that captured the nation. And now, those words seemed all too real to describe Ross and other young men and women, struck down in foreign lands, just like him.

Aw, but they never told you the price that you pay
For things that you might have done
Only the good die young.

President Obama returned to the White House that afternoon, haunted by his walk among the graves of the men of Afghanistan and Iraq, and more determined than ever to end the war, as soon as possible. That afternoon, in the White

House Situation Room, the president received a briefing on the status of military operations in Afghanistan.

But everything about the briefing had shown a continuous replenishment of troops on a rotational basis, matching the number of troops continuously withdrawn. To the president, the plan was a revolving door, with no end in sight.

Obama summoned in his military advisors to demand advice on how to end the war, and how to end it quickly. His walk at Arlington would lead to a three-month review in search of an exit strategy for getting the military out of Afghanistan. During that review, one man wielded the most influence over the president: General Stanley A. McChrystal.

Legend had it that McChrystal, a trim four-star general known for his rigid personal discipline and keen intellect, ran seven miles a day and ate only one meal. Born into a tradition-rich military family at Fort Leavenworth, Kan., McChrystal's father served as a two-star general, and his brother a full-bird colonel.

The president trusted McChrystal, and the general's political affiliation as a registered Democrat did not hurt matters. In June of 2009, Obama appointed him as commander of the International Security Assistance Force or ISAF, the NATO-led military operation in Afghanistan that had been established by the U.N. Security Council by resolution in December of 2001. In other words, McChrystal commanded all U.S. and coalition forces in Afghanistan.

Obama wanted to drawdown from Afghanistan immediately. The graves he had seen in Arlington haunted him. He wanted no more Bradley S. Bohles. No more Jason Palmertons. No more Ross McGinnises. He wanted these young men alive and with their families. No more graves at Arlington.

But McChrystal's advice on how to accomplish that conflicted with Obama's original vision for withdrawal. Too quick a drawdown, McChrystal argued, would be dangerous—not only to American troops, but to America's

Afghan allies, who had fought shoulder-to-shoulder with American troops since 2001.

To safely end the war, McChrystal later argued, we must drastically *increase* troop totals, not decrease troops. The increase should come rapidly, to completely destroy the Taliban. Then, and only then, could the war be safely ended.

McChrystal's request for an additional 40,000 troops seemed counterintuitive to the president's initial basic instincts. But the more Obama learned about the consequences of a rapid drawdown, the more he warmed to the idea of a robust, if temporary buildup. Working with Defense Sec. Robert M. Gates, who agreed with McChrystal's advice, at the end of the 90-day review following the president's walk in Arlington, a new Afghan War Strategy was born.

In the White House, the strategy became known as "escalate then exit."

But to the troops in Afghanistan, to America's allies, and to the rest of the world, the strategy became known, simply, as "the surge."

The three-month review that had birthed the surge led to a three-year buildup that would entangle the American military more than ever, and send young men like Ross McGinnis and Clint Lorance into the deepest, most dangerous places in the world.

How ironic that "the surge" had been birthed from a long, sad walk on a cold Veterans Day amongst the graves of Arlington.

American lives matter.

CHAPTER 3

THE SHOOTING OF CORPORAL MATTHEW HANES
VILLAGE OF SARENZAI,
KANDAHAR PROVINCE, AFGHANISTAN
JUNE 23, 2012

It was the third year of the surge, and they had been without an officer for 10 days now. But still, the war raged on. Still, they had to fight. Either they would take the fight to the enemy, or the enemy would take the fight to them. There was no in between.

This was Taliban country, the most dangerous place in the world for any American. It was the height of the "fighting season," the hot weather months. And although these American paratroopers had superior weapons, they were greatly outnumbered and surrounded by Taliban insurgents, all who wanted them dead. Meanwhile, the Taliban grew and spread like a malignant cancer. It had to be kept in check.

So they had to get up and get moving early, even in oppressive heat, to clear the area around Strong Point Payenzai, lest the Taliban choke in on their position like a hangman slipping a noose over a condemned man's neck.

They got up, readied their weapons, studied their mission for the day, and by sunrise were moving single file out into the battlefield adjacent to their Strong Point. It was hot as hell outside, maybe even hotter.

Like a great blowtorch in the sky, by midmorning, the sun beat down on them, pounding them with merciless rays that heated their bodies and zapped their strength.

These were the men of First Platoon, 4/73 Cavalry, 82nd Airborne Division, U.S. Army. Today, they were still without an officer leading them into combat. It had been that way for 10 days, when their platoon leader, Lt. Dom Latino, was wounded on June 13, when another soldier, Pvt. First Class Mark Kerner, had stepped on a hidden landmine buried in the dirt.

In five days, they would be under the command of their new platoon leader, Clint Lorance. But for the time being, they would be led into battle by their platoon sergeant, Sgt. First Class Keith Ayers. An experienced paratrooper with multiple combat tours under his belt, SFC Ayers was one of the toughest soldiers in the 82nd Airborne Division. The platoon was in good hands as it awaited the arrival of its new lieutenant.

In the third year of the surge, this small band of paratroopers had been sent to the tip of the American military spear. They had pressed onward into the edge of hell itself, deeper into the heart of Taliban country than any other members of the United States military. They had reached the hottest, bloodiest, and deadliest place on the planet for anyone who did not embrace the Taliban's version of radical Islam.

When the surge began, in December of 2009, it began with a clear military goal: Crush the Taliban with overwhelming force and then get the heck out of Dodge. The idea had merit. It had worked in Iraq. Why not Afghanistan, too?

But with the best-laid plans of mice and men, the simple goal of the surge, laid down nearly three years before, had gone awry. In contrast to the goal of defeating the Taliban with overwhelming force, the goal became watered-down over a period of less than three years.

The force and rules of engagement brought by First Platoon to the Zhari District of Kandahar Province in June of 2012 was, by design, underwhelming. But not from lack of training, or inferior equipment, or a lack of bravery. In all those areas, the paratroopers were superior to their Taliban opponents.

It was a matter of numbers.

Forty American soldiers in a single platoon surrounded by thousands of Taliban operatives, all of whom blended into the landscape, with the home-field advantage in terrain and the population, does not make for overwhelming odds for the good guys.

The original surge goal of crushing the Taliban had been watered down into myriad different sub-objectives. Now, the goal was simply to "degrade" the Taliban (not "crush" it), in part by recruiting and training local Afghans from the local population to rise up and to protect themselves against the Taliban. Then came yet another objective. These troops were here to "protect the local population," a far cry from the original goal from over a decade earlier, to single-handedly punish and destroy the terrorist organization responsible for bringing down the Twin Towers and sending an airplane full of innocent civilians crashing into the Pentagon. Their job had morphed one-third policeman, one-third international diplomat, and one-third soldier—when they were only trained to be paratroopers.

Against this backdrop, the president's announcement of a definite pullout date, a move criticized by many as a major strategic blunder, would undermine the purpose of the surge. On June 22, 2011, President Obama entered the East Room, alone, smartly dressed in a black suit, white starched shirt, and gray tie. On the left lapel of his black suit, he wore a small American flag.

"Starting next month," the president said, "we will be able to remove 10,000 of our troops from Afghanistan by the end of this year, and we will bring home a total of 33,000 troops by next summer, fully recovering the surge I announced at West Point. After this initial reduction, our troops will continue coming home at a steady pace as Afghan security forces move into the lead. Our mission will change from combat to support. By 2014, this process of transition will be complete, and the Afghan people will be responsible for their own security."

The announcement came out of the blue, unexpected by the entire country and catching the military off guard. The sudden drawdown announcement was counter-intuitive to the "surge."

The president had approached the podium and, with the television cameras of the national press rolling, announced that American forces would be out of Afghanistan by 2014. Aside from the fact that this never happened, the sudden announcement set off a ripple effect.

The president's thinking and his motivation for making an announcement that undercut the U.S. "surge" strategy to destroy the Taliban remains unclear to this day. Obama, who had been moved by the graves of men and women who had died in Afghanistan, had in one announcement created a situation far more dangerous than it had ever been in the 10 years of the Afghan Civil War. Whether he realized the danger that he created is impossible to say. But Americans serving in Afghanistan would soon pay the price.

Not only did the announcement give hope and encouragement to radical Islamists operating in Afghanistan, but the person most rattled by the announcement was the American-installed president of Afghanistan, Hamid Karzai. Up until now, Karzai had been propped up by American military power.

With the Americans gone, Karzai might not survive. So he started negotiations with the Taliban, and even discussed bringing the Taliban into his cabinet. During the Karzai-Taliban negotiation, after Obama's announcement in 2011, the Taliban complained to Karzai about the American military. The U.S. military had been devastatingly effective at killing Taliban, and the Taliban sought advantage.

To appease the Taliban, Karzai complained to Obama, claiming that the American military had killed too many "civilians." But in fairness to Karzai, and as will be discussed in more detail, it was not just the Afghan president negotiating with the Taliban in the 2011 to 2012 timeframe.

On Sept. 16, 2011, the United States endorsed plans by the Taliban to open a political headquarters in Qatar. The next month, October, four months after President Obama's unilateral withdrawal announcement, Secretary of State Hillary Clinton stated that the U.S. would enter negotiations with Taliban leader Mullah Omar. And by February of 2012, President Hamid Karzai confirmed direct U.S.-Afghan negotiations with the Taliban.

To appease Karzai, who now sought to appease the savage Taliban, with whom the United States was now negotiating, the U.S. military tightened the rules of engagement, making it much more difficult for U.S. forces to fire in a war zone. On the flipside, the tightened rules of engagement made it much easier for the Taliban to kill Americans. The effect: the United States elevated the importance of enemy lives over American lives.

Then, to make matters worse, came the added "nation-building" objectives imposed upon the military.

U.S. paratroopers, including First Platoon, and Green Beret Special Forces units were dispatched out to the deadliest, most remote Taliban strongholds in the world to try and recruit Afghan nationals to fight the Taliban.

The problem with that assignment: the Taliban and the locals all looked alike, and many of the locals recruited either had sympathy to the Taliban, or subversively assisted the Taliban after being recruited. Making things even more challenging, many times, the Taliban would pose as cooperative villagers to befriend the Americans, only to kill them another time.

But First Platoon could give a rat's ass about geopolitical strategy at the moment. The men of the platoon, working under unbearable conditions, had two goals. One, to carry out their mission, and two, to come home alive.

All day long, for the past 30 days, the sun had burned their lips, their hands, their noses, and their foreheads. Under the hot cover of their uniforms, sweat poured from their backs, their stomachs, and their armpits. With heat trapped inside their Kevlar battle helmets scorching their heads, sweat rolled from their foreheads onto their noses and into their eyes, sometimes forcing them to blink hard or to wipe their eyes with their hands to regain their visual gaze.

A dozen bottled waters a day would not replenish their sweat drain, nor give them shade, nor give them full respite from the heat. The constant sweat coupled with the dirt of deployment and the lack of daily showers often made for uncomfortable rashes, abrasions, and sores all over their bodies.

Nothing drains a man's strength like constant, pulsating, 100-degree sunshine, pounding a man's head, shoulders, and neck, for hours and hours, with no end in sight. Add to the heat the daily sight of men getting their legs blown off and of best buddies transformed by explosions into instant bloody, human stumps.

How could men operate under such conditions?

Who would do so, voluntarily? Except an American soldier.

Kandahar Province was the hottest damn place on the face of the Earth. And for Americans operating there, the stress of war, a war that now had lasted 11 years, magnified the impact of the searing heat.

In the last week, only once had the high temperatures not clipped 100 degrees. During the "cool front" on Sunday, June 19, noontime highs only reached 97 degrees. Every other day, the midday sun had baked well above the century mark.

In the three-day stretch from June 20–22, the consecutive highs had reached 109, 106, and 106 degrees. The whole month of June had been a broiling oven.

Today, June 23, would bring another 100-degree-plus scorcher. In fact, when the sun rose at 6 a.m., the temperature had clipped 90 degrees.

While the men of First Platoon prepared to make another dangerous combat patrol through the Taliban-infested Village of Sarenzai, a few miles back off the front lines, Lieutenant Clint Lorance reported to his position at the Brigade Tactical Operations Center or TOC, where he worked as liaison officer for 4th Squadron to the 73rd Cavalry Regiment, spoken in military parlance as "4/73 Cav." Clint had served as one of several liaison officers for 4/73 since arriving in Afghanistan from Fort Bragg in February.

So far, since deploying to Afghanistan, Clint had worked in an air-conditioned environment at 4th Brigade Headquarters, away from the fighting. This allowed him to brave some of the mid-day heat, as brigade HQ had some of the best field air-conditioners assigned to the Army.

As a liaison officer or LNO, in the brigade's Tactical Operations Center, Clint's job involved monitoring and reporting significant acts in the battlefield, and serving as the liaison between the squadron and brigade. But his current behind-the-lines job in the Brigade Ops center did not reflect his full experience as a combat soldier. As a former enlisted man before becoming an officer, Clint had been deployed to combat zones before, in Iraq, and had served in the Demilitarized Zone in South Korea.

As a young soldier, Clint stood out as a star among his peers, and in the eyes of the officers in his chain of command. His performance had been so exemplary that the Army selected him for its coveted Green-to-Gold program, which paved the way for him to become an officer.

Thus, unlike most young lieutenants taking charge of a combat platoon for the first time, who had little or no prior service experience, Clint had served in Iraq, in a war zone, and carried into battle more experience than most young officers.

While he excelled in his job as a liaison officer at the battalion operations center, Clint Lorance was a soldier's soldier. His place was with his men, on the battlefield, in war, and in peace. In a matter of days, he would detach from Brigade Headquarters and take command of First Platoon after Dom Latino was wounded in action, bringing with him a determination to keep safe every man with whose life he would be entrusted.

Meanwhile, in early June of 2012, the Army sent First Platoon to a small, remote American outpost called Strong Point Payenzai, on the outskirts of the rural village of Sarenzai.

The village of Sarenzai is located in the Zhari District of Kandahar Province, in southeastern Afghanistan, near the Pakistani border. The Zhari District is referred to as "the ancestral home of the Taliban," and this platoon of the 82nd Airborne Division, First Platoon of Charlie Troop, had been sent there to establish a military front line right in the middle of Taliban country.

A month of hell had produced constant enemy fire against the paratroopers. Not a day passed that they were not shot at, as they had patrolled the grape fields and hot, dusty roads around Sarenzai village. The end of June had not come fast enough.

Not only had their platoon leader, Lt. Latino, been wounded and taken out of battle by a massive land mine, but one of their most beloved soldiers, Corp. Matthew Hanes, had taken a bullet through the neck by a Taliban sniper hiding somewhere in the vicinity of the village.

Corp. Hanes, a minesweeper from York, Pa., was out in front of the American patrol that morning, operating a hand-held minesweeper, checking for mines and IEDs planted in the ground. As he swept the ground to the left, and the right, taking cautious steps forward as he swept, the rest of First Platoon followed him in a tight, single file.

Though American combat squads prefer to spread from left to right as they advance across the ground in combat, in the Zhari district, because so many bombs were in the ground, that became impossible. Single file was mandatory. By contrast, the few villagers in the remote area did not need a minesweeper—they apparently knew where the deadly IEDs had been laid.

But if any of the Americans stepped outside the limited sweep of Matt Hanes' "mine-hound," a lethal blast might take out half the platoon. So they moved in a tight, single file holding their breath, and keeping their eyes peeled.

It was a dangerous mission, with Matthew in the most vulnerable spot in the Platoon, for two reasons. First, if his handheld minesweeper missed a bomb out front, he would be the first to step on it. Second, because he moved at the front of the column, "on point," he became the most vulnerable target for sniper fire from the enemy.

By midmorning that day, with the burning sun high overhead, the sharp sound of rifle fire cracked the air. In Afghanistan, the sound of rifle fire was not unusual. Gunfire in the Zhari District was as common as the songbirds chirping at dawn back in America. But when Matthew collapsed to the ground, writhing in pain, struggling to breathe, with blood gushing from his throat, the men of First Platoon knew that their friend was in serious trouble.

Corp. Matt Hanes had taken a bullet through the front of his neck that shattered his vertebrae. He lay on that battlefield, blood gushing from his neck and throat, tortured by pain under the searing sun, bleeding to death, dying. For the men who saw him lying on the ground, it became a stunning, surrealistic moment, frozen in time, that they would never forget. But the men of First Platoon did not panic. American paratroopers don't panic. Instead, they rushed to secure their position around their fallen comrade.

An Army medic named Joseph Fjeldheim sprung to action, and supported by the boys of First Platoon, charged over to Matthew, oblivious that the sniper was still out there, and that he, Fjeldheim, was now in the sniper's gunsights. Fjeldheim did not care at the moment whether he got shot, or not. He had to do everything he could for his friend, and the situation looked bleak. Matthew struggled to breathe and could not sustain massive blood flow for long. The oppressive heat only made Matt's situation worse.

Fjeldheim worked like hell to save Matthew that day, to stop his bleeding, to numb his pain, to prevent him from coding beyond reach. Under the searing hot sun, with the temperature hovering at 100 degrees, as the soldiers of First Platoon gathered around, Joe Fjeldheim worked, and worked, and worked some more. "Stay with me, Matt! Stay with me!"

With sweat dripping from every inch of his body, Fjeldheim got his friend stabilized. Hanging to life by a string, Matthew Hanes was shipped off the battlefield, still breathing, but paralyzed from the waist down. He would never walk again.

Three years later, on his Facebook page in the weeks before he died, in 2015, Corp. Matthew Hanes penned these words, a loving tribute to the men of First Platoon with whom he served, and to his friend, Joseph Fjeldheim, an unsung American hero:

"Three years ago, today, my life changed drastically. I shouldn't be here, but I had the best men I've ever had that honor of knowing there with me. And they went above and beyond, doing what was needed to keep me alive.

"I don't remember a single detail of that day, but I know that my best friend and the best damn medic out there, Joseph Fjeldheim, worked his ass off and saved my life. And the rest of 1 Charlie was there to assist. I owe you all a debt for saving my life that day, every other day in Afghanistan, and giving me the willpower to continue fighting until the day comes, I'm able to call this injury a thing of the past. There is no greater love than that which I have for you all!"

Matthew Hanes, gunned down on June 23, 2012, never should have been in the position that he had been placed in—out in a Taliban-infested war zone, on a nation-building assignment, with his hands strapped by rules of engagement that did not place Americans first, walking through a minefield, exposed to sniper fire.

Three years later, in August of 2015, Corp. Matthew Hanes died in York, Pa., from a blood clot related to the gunshot wound in his neck by a Taliban sniper at Sarenzai, Afghanistan.

They held Matt's funeral service at the Memorial Hall West at the York Fairgrounds, surrounding his white casket with American flags, and adorning it with red roses.

Afterwards, a thunderous motorcycle procession rocked the silent streets of York. The booms from the squadrons of Harleys echoed through the streets and the buildings of the town. They were the men of the Patriot Guards, the Warrior Brotherhood and American Legion Riders. They had come from all over the country, with American flags on flagpoles strapped to their motorcycles, to honor the fallen young hero. They moved out slowly, the Stars and Stripes flapping in the breeze behind each bike, leading Matthew's white hearse through the streets of York, as hundreds of patriots lined the funeral route to pay their respects to the young corporal.

Others came, too, from afar. Some 40 members of First Platoon came hundreds of miles, many from Fort Bragg, to honor their comrade. Matthew Hanes had saved their lives many times, they all acknowledged, by stepping out in front of their unit and finding dangerous mines and IEDs that could have killed any of them in an instant.

Brian Bynes, who had served with Matt in Afghanistan, drove all the way from Chicago. "He saved our lives every day," Bynes told the local press.

Joseph Fjeldheim, the heroic Army medic who saved Matt's life that day, was there, in full dress uniform.

Before they laid him into the ground, Betty M. Frey, a family friend who spoke at the funeral, recalled Matt's dream to be cured of his paralysis, and return again as a soldier in the U.S. Army:

"His desire and his love was the military. And that's all he wanted to do ... to get back to the military."

Moments later, under sunny, blue skies, and standing on the lush, green grass of southern Pennsylvania, against a sweet, cool afternoon breeze and the sounds of chirping sparrows, a U.S. Army honor guard fired shots into the air, as they lowered Matt's casket with full military honors at the Mount Rose Cemetery in York.

Matt never made it back to the Army, as he desperately wanted. But his country will never forget him.

On June 28, 2012, five days after Matthew Hanes was shot on the battlefield, Clint Lorance was scheduled to take command of First Platoon, the same platoon that surrounded Matt and worked so hard to save him on the battlefield. His job would be to take them back into combat, to the same battlefield that would take Matthew Hanes' life.

Lorance was determined. What happened to Matt Hanes would not happen to his soldiers.

"Never again."

CHAPTER 4

The small forward combat post known as Strong Point Payenzai, the home of First Platoon in Afghanistan in 2012, had been set up in a rural, remote, Taliban-infested area of the Zhari District, at the southeast corner of a grape field bordering the village Sarenzai. The American post at Payenzai had been erected as a makeshift fortress and, viewed from the air, showed the configuration of a triangle.

But because it had the configuration and the khaki-like color of the most popular snack food ever sold by the Frito Lay Corp., many of the American paratroopers nicknamed it "The Dorito." For indeed, from the air, the Strong Point did resemble a giant Dorito, and the name stuck. Though officially known as Strong Point Payenzai, even intelligence officials at other posts began referring to it as "The Dorito" as a shorthanded nickname.

At each corner of the triangle of "The Dorito," an observation tower rose 20 feet into the air. American soldiers from First Platoon manned two of the towers. The third was manned by soldiers of the Afghan National Army, who were, in theory, allies of the United States in the American war on terror.

The fortress walls that connected each of the towers had been built by combat engineers using HESCO units. In many ways, a HESCO unit is like a high-tech sandbag, except that it is much bigger, much stronger, and capable of providing superior protection.

First used in the first Gulf War in 1991, a HESCO unit is a large, empty box with fortified sides, approximately 7 feet tall and 5 feet wide. Of course, the walls on the HESCO boxes are not made of cardboard, but rather a heavy-duty fabric liner with a collapsible wire mesh.

To establish a secure perimeter for American troops in hostile Taliban regions, combat engineers had set these hollow boxes along a line to create the foundation for a long, buttressed wall, then using graders, filled these units up with rock and gravel, and stacked them beside each other, until a huge, protective triangle making up the outer walls of the fortress was in place. Finally, once these rock-filled protective walls were in place in a triangular configuration, the interior of the triangle became the remote living spaces and headquarters for First Platoon on the battlefront. The platoon lived in large "Alaska tents," inside the HESCO walls.

These walls, now filled with rock, gravel and dirt, each weighing well over 12,000 pounds, were able to take mortars, rockets and small-arms fire from the outside and provide safety and protection for the soldiers on the inside from an all-out frontal assault from the Taliban. On top of the triangular walls, to prevent the enemy from trying to scale over the top, the Army mounted massive amounts of coiled barbed wire, called "concertina wire" also referred to as "c-wire." Nobody could crawl over the thick c-wire without getting bloodied up like a loaf of sliced salami.

Inside the only entrance to the fortress, to prevent unauthorized entry by Taliban or villagers sympathetic to the Taliban, the paratroopers had established an entry control point, manned 24 hours a day. A sergeant supervised the

ECP security team, and at the entrance, a manned gun truck carried either a .50-caliber machine gun or a .240-caliber machine gun, capable of wiping out unauthorized intruders. During the court-martial of Lt. Lorance, Spec. James Oliver Twist, a cavalry scout in First Platoon, described the purpose of the c-wire as a means of protecting the troops at Payenzai:

> Defense Counsel: "And why did you—if you know—why did you have concertina wire in the area where you have it? Why was it there?"
>
> Spec. Twist: "Just in case the enemy decided to stroll up the road in the middle of the night and we didn't see 'em. Like just—if—if it happened to be a low—low visible night and we didn't want an enemy being able to stroll through—stroll through the ECP and come inside and kill or hurt any of us."
>
> Defense Counsel: "And so, you agree that the reason we had the c-wire there (was) to protect friendly forces?"
>
> Spec. Twist: "Yes."

Once inside, the compound featured sparse living quarters, in tents, for the 40 members of the platoon.

Later, when Clint arrived, a 40-foot pole rose above the camp, with a long-range camera to monitor the grape fields and the village nearby. The platoon also used an unmanned aerial vehicle (UAV), which is a drone with a mounted camera, sometimes flown to monitor enemy movement in the area. Clint brought both the UAV and the sky camera to the platoon when he arrived. He also established an operations center, where the soldiers communicated up the chain of command. The drone, the sky camera and the operations center were not established at the Strong Point until Clint arrived.

With the HESCO walls in place, the c-wire strung all over the place, and with armed guards at the entrance, on the towers and on gun truck manning .50-caliber machine guns to back up the armed guards, the inside of the Strong Point was relatively secure. The problem wasn't the inside of the Strong Point, but, rather, the hyper-dangerous environment outside the HESCO walls.

By June 24, 2012, the day after the Taliban gunned down Cpl. Matthew Hanes, after Lt. Latino had been wounded by an IED and evacuated, after two other paratroopers had been seriously wounded by IEDs, and after having gotten shot at every day for 30 days, with rules of engagement that often would not permit firing back, morale at First Platoon had taken a dip.

Since Lt. Latino had been medevacked out, Sgt. First Class Keith Ayers had stepped in admirably, as platoon sergeant, and continued taking his men out on patrols through Sarenzai. A seasoned, decorated combat veteran, Ayers was one of the best damn soldiers in the U.S. Army, and one of its finest NCO leaders. But even the best leadership cannot mitigate unadulterated danger from an enemy that often can't be seen, or looks like the local population, or hides bombs in the ground, then disappears behind the rocks like a bunch of scampering cowards.

Each and every day on patrol they continued to draw enemy fire, with bullets whizzing by their heads. They were hand-strapped by new, restrictive rules on returning that fire.

June 24, the day after the Taliban shot Corp. Hanes, the temperature at sunrise just after 6 a.m. had risen to 104 degrees. By noontime, the mercury had shot up to 111 degrees, making temperatures almost unbearable.

Four men had gone down in the last 30 days. And by June 24, a combination of the heat, the constant gunfire, the stress of walking every day through a minefield, and the all-too-fresh memory of Matt Hanes bleeding on the ground, struggling for his life, weighed on the entire platoon.

Here's how Spec. Twist described the platoon's mind frame at the time:

"I mean, there's a lot of stuff going on at that time. I mean, my buddy had just been blown up like a month earlier—actually exactly like a month earlier or pretty much. And, you know, a lot of my friends had gotten hurt and I was just—I was nervous."

Spec. Twist then testified about the platoon's morale, answering questions from Lt. Lorance's civilian defense attorney, Guy Womack, at the time.

Womack: "Okay. Would it be fair to say that morale was pretty low...?"

Spec. Twist: "It wasn't—it wasn't ridiculously low, but—I would say that we were—we hadn't taken a casualty until June, like, from our platoon. And so, we—we were hit by it. But I think we still wanted to do our job. It was just—we were wondering, you know—probably just wanted to change some things (about) how we were operating."

Womack: "And by changing the way you operated, you wanted to be more aggressive with the enemy. Correct?"

Spec. Twist: "I think we wanted to be more careful with our minesweeping so we didn't step on any more IEDs or, you know, be a little bit more guarded, I guess—be a little bit more vigilant, not aggressive."

Womack: "Well, when I say aggressive, I mean you wanted someone to make sure that the platoon took the steps to safeguard the members of the platoon, correct?"

Spec. Twist: "Yes."

Womack: "You wanted to bring everyone else back that you could—back home?"

Spec. Twist: "Yes."

Spec. Twist's testimony could not have been clearer. The platoon's morale had taken a hit, troops did not want to "step on any more IEDs," wanted to be "more guarded" and "more vigilant."

The memories were too fresh, and too clear for them all. In one massive blast, Lt. Latino took peppering shrapnel wounds to his abdomen, limbs, eyes, and face. In another blast, Pvt. First Class Samuel Walley lost his left arm below the elbow, his right leg below the knee, and incurred serious soft tissue damage to his left leg.

On June 13, Pvt. First Class Mark Kerner, from Albany, Ore., also stepped on an IED and sustained serious injuries in his thighs and buttocks. The same IED explosion that took out their platoon leader, Lt. Dom Latino. (And like Matthew Hanes, Mark Kerner also died in 2015). Then came the terrible, fresh memory of Matthew Hanes being shot in the throat, lying on the battlefield, bleeding, and struggling for his life.

The brigade decided to pull First Platoon off the battlefield, for a few days. So, the night of June 26 would be the platoon's last night at Strong Point Payenzai, at least for a few days.

Next stop, Strong Point Gariban to regroup, recoup and rest, before returning to Payenzai and to the battlefield.

They would soon meet their new platoon leader, Lt. Clint Lorance.

CHAPTER 5

Their long, 15-hour flight from Pope Airfield at Fort Bragg to Manas Air Base in Kyrgyzstan, aboard the tightly packed quarters of the huge C-17 Globemaster, was almost over. Many of these paratroopers were too young to appreciate the twisted irony of the first leg of their journey to Afghanistan. They were flying from a U.S. Army airfield in the United States, to another American air base, located in a country that 30 years ago, had been a communist republic of the Soviet Union, America's longtime cold-war adversary.

Kyrgyzstan is a mountainous, Islamic landlocked country in Central Asia that gained independence from the crumbling vestiges of the Soviet Union in August of 1991. Ten years later, by December of 2001, Kyrgyzstan had floated far enough from the old Soviet orbit that it signed a lease with the United States to allow the presence of an American air base, to be operated by the 376th Air Expeditionary Wing. Manas Air Base, located outside the Kyrgyzstan capital of Bishkek, and 1,450 miles northeast of Kandahar, had become as a transit point to move troops in and out of Afghanistan during the Afghan war.

As the big bird circled above for final approach, it passed over the massive snow-capped peaks of the Kyrgyz Ala-Too

Mountain Range, a stark contrast to the flat, rolling grounds full of loblolly pines around Fort Bragg. The first destination for the elite 82nd Airborne on its way to Afghanistan was nothing like the sandhills of North Carolina.

From the wall of the cabin behind the cockpit, all the way back to the tail of the aircraft, paratroopers were jammed in tight seats of five abreast, with less than an inch between each seat. In addition, along each inside wall of the aircraft, another row of seats had been jammed together on the walls, where windows would be found on a commercial aircraft. Soldiers lucky enough to get one of these seats sat with their backs to the aircraft wall, with their knees pointed to the inside of the cabin. An aisle, running the length of the aircraft, separated the soldiers with their backs to the walls, from the soldiers who sat five abreast across the middle of the cabin.

Many of these paratroopers had left behind wives, girlfriends, and fiancées, all of whom would be on their minds tonight. Hopefully, they would see them again in another year, if they survived that long.

The face of death is cruel and cold. Many of these young soldiers on their first deployment had never faced death before. The combat vets among them, including Clint Lorance, had seen it up close and personal, in Iraq.

Seconds later, the giant military transport touched down on Asian soil. The paratroopers started stirring, anxious to get the hell off the plane. It was nice to get out of the crowded aircraft to stretch. But as they stepped off the bird, one by one, for their brief stopover in Kyrgyzstan before their last leg into the warzone, the freezing, frigid weather of Bishkek's cold winds slapped them in the face. With high temperatures on Feb. 14 never rising above 25 degrees, and on the 15th never topping 28, the frigid temperatures pointed to the frigid reality of cold death that many of them would soon face in a very hot place, some 1,400 miles to the south.

A week later, Feb. 21, the paratroopers crammed back onto the C-17 for the final leg to Afghanistan. This time, the final flight to Kandahar would last only two hours, if even that. It would be a short flight from the extreme cold to the malevolent hot of southern Afghanistan.

The evergreen pines they had left behind in the sandhills of North Carolina around Fort Bragg, and the frigid snow-capped mountains surrounding them now would soon give way to real sand, and to real danger.

For the few who could see outside the aircraft, the huge Kandahar Airfield, located outside Afghanistan's second-largest city, took on the light brown color of sand, almost like a chameleon blending into the landscape. From the air, the borders of the air base resembled the borders of the state of Idaho and out to the left, the long airstrip ran adjacent to what would be the Oregon border. Beside the airfields, peppered throughout the base, were dozens of sand-colored Quonset huts, a sure sign of a huge military presence.

In the middle of the base, a large, round, body of chocolate-colored water sat under the mid-February sun. Some of the paratroopers who had been here before knew it well. The infamous "poo pond." A huge, round lake of sewage in the middle of the base and the source of the putrid, noxious shit-smell that at times floated all over the base, even at times into the terminals of the international airport. Such was the flavor of the City of Kandahar, where raw sewage ran in open ditches all over the city, and under hot, hundred-degree sunshine in the summer, even under the call to Muslim prayer, spewing forth fecal odors strong enough to make westerners not accustomed to it gag and want to vomit.

The larger bases, such as Kandahar Airfield, or "KAF" as the Americans called it, were generally more secure than many of the combat outposts way out in the cancerous heart of Taliban country.

But in Afghanistan, danger pervaded everywhere. On the air base where they were about to land, only three weeks before, a suicide bomber in a car outside the main gate set off a trunk full of explosives, killing seven civilians. The Taliban had been targeting United States forces. Another bomb had been set off outside Kandahar Airfield a few days before that.

As the plane dropped in its controlled descent towards the runway, Clint Lorance went through his mental checklist. Six months earlier, a Taliban rocket-propelled grenade (RPG) had taken out a CH-47 helicopter, codenamed Extortion 17 in Wardak Province, killing 17 U.S. Navy SEALs.

Not even American aircraft on approach were guaranteed safety in this place.

Clint Lorance turned his thoughts from danger, and from RPGs or shoulder-launched missiles that might target the aircraft. He was an American Army officer, his only focus on the mission at hand, his brain ticking through the next steps:

Touch down in Kandahar. Secure gear. In process. Then report to the helo pad to catch a flight to his ultimate duty station, Forward Operating Base Pasab.

He sat back, breathed in deeply as the plane slowly dropped, and dropped some more. A moment later, touch down. They had arrived in hell.

It was difficult not to exhale that sigh of relief. A safe touch down on a flight into an active war zone was always cause for gratitude that no one had fired an RPG, or a surface-to-air missile at the plane.

Moments after taxiing down the runway, Clint stepped out into the Afghan weather for the first time. The mild temperature of 64 degrees felt like what they left behind at Fort Bragg. In the distance, the brown, jagged peaks of the Chilzina Mountains rose above the horizon, somewhere to the west. Seven years earlier, in 2005, at the White Sands Missile Range in southern New Mexico, Clint had participated in the annual re-enactment of the Bataan Death

March. Afghanistan, on first blush from the tarmac of the air base, bore a slight resemblance to the New Mexico desert, with the Chilzina Mountains resembling the limestone San Andreas Mountains.

Clint's ultimate duty station, Forward Operating Base Pasab, was out to the west, in the direction of the mountains. That was all he knew. And there was no more time to think.

He had to get to his next ride, a U.S. Army Blackhawk helicopter revved up and ready to take off for Pasab. Clint slung his gear over his back, and jogged across the tarmac to the waiting helicopter. After Clint boarded, then belted in his seat, the chopper lifted off, turned and started on a straight course, flying out toward his next duty station.

Clint took a final look down at the Kandahar Airfield. Next time he saw this place, he would be a suspect for murder. Although he did not know it yet, Afghanistan would become a country that would change his life forever.

CHAPTER 6

The story of the Army's ultimate decision to prosecute Lt. Clint Lorance cannot be explained or understood outside the context of a major tragedy that occurred fewer than two months after his arrival in Afghanistan.

The Kandahar massacre.

The international press called it the most gruesome act of mass homicide against civilians ever committed by a single soldier of the U.S. military. It would later serve as an excuse for the Army railroading Clint Lorance on cooked-up murder charges.

On the morning of March 11, 2012, within an hour after midnight, 16 Afghan civilians living in two rural villages in the midst of a Taliban-infested warzone were shot to death, allegedly by an American soldier, Staff Sgt. Robert Bales, who snapped, believing he was executing a mission against the Taliban.

Bales, on his fourth combat tour, was stationed at a remote outpost in Kandahar Province in the heart of thick Taliban activity in the country. Bales arrived in December of 2011 at this small post, only a few miles from where Lorance's First Platoon would soon operate. Every day after arriving on base, Bales and his men had been shot at and subjected to constant mortar fire. But these soldiers' biggest fear was not the enemy that they could see or the bullets whizzing by their heads.

Their greatest fear was the hidden weapon called an IED that they oftentimes never saw until after they were maimed, or their brothers-in-arms were dead. These IEDs were disguised, often hidden under the grounds where American soldiers operated and were hard to detect. They were lethal booby-traps, explosives set off by Taliban detonators. They tore off the legs and limbs of American soldiers, flipped Humvees upside down, blew holes through steel-armored troop carriers, and sent dismembered arms, legs, torsos and charred victims home in body bags.

In early 2012, Bales' platoon supported a small unit of Green Berets in the most dangerous area of Afghanistan. In the dark hours after midnight of March 11, 2012, Bales saw lights crisscrossing the sky to the north and south of the American observation post. The flashlight beams in the night were communication signals used by Taliban as they planted landmines, to be set off against Americans the next day.

Bales reported this to his superiors, but no one listened. Determined not to lose any more of his buddies to IEDs set by these Taliban bastards, he grabbed his M-4 rifle and his pistol, then set out on a one-man mission to take care of the problem. Bales fired in the dark, his war-torn mind thinking that he was firing into a Taliban nest.

In the end, there were 16 dead Afghans, including women and children.

The event caused an immediate international firestorm, with the Afghans, including President Karzai, demanding immediate justice against Bales in the streets, Sharia-law style. The U.S. military, and the Army in particular, had a public relations nightmare on hand. Secretary of Defense Leon Panetta fueled the fire by sending his personal jet to Afghanistan to scoop up Bales in the middle of the night.

The rest is history.

In Bales' defense, he was on his fourth combat tour, suffered from post-traumatic stress disorder (PTSD) and had been given a diagnosis by the Army of traumatic brain injury *prior to* being assigned to the remote, dangerous outpost in the midst of Taliban-infested territory. The traumatic brain injury had been caused by Bales having been "blown up" by IEDs nine times in a 10-year span, in which IEDs had gone off and slammed his head against steel on multiple occasions.

Bales had taken an Army-administered mind-altering anti-malarial drug called mefloquine, known to cause permanent injury to the brain, and to cause suicidal ideations, homicidal ideations, hallucinations, permanent psychosis, and memory loss.

Bales' brain injuries, both from bombs and mefloquine, contributed largely to his actions. But Bales' condition was hidden from public view in the cacophony of international outrage and bad press against the Army.

As a direct result of the Kandahar massacre, the Army needed to prove to Karzai and others that civilian casualties would not be tolerated. Any soldiers found to have inflicted civilian casualties would be dealt with severely.

Clint Lorance would become the Army's first chance to make a point.

Lorance would become a sacrificial scalp for the Army to hand to Karzai to prove how tough it would be on soldiers whose orders caused civilian deaths.

Meanwhile, the Taliban vowed to retaliate against America and its allies.

This retaliation would come through motorcycle attacks.

CHAPTER 7

While the Kandahar massacre created an embarrassment for the U.S. Army, it started a public relations nightmare for the Afghan government. "The government favors the Americans over the people," its critics howled, using the massacre as exhibit #1.

To try and soften the criticism, two days after the Kandahar massacre, the pro-American Karzai government, under fire from harsh critics that it could not protect Afghan civilians from casualties inflicted by troops, sent a high-level delegation to visit with the locals and to attend a memorial service within the Panjwai District.

The remote, dusty village of Belandi sat at the closest crossroads nearest to the site of the shootings, some 40 miles southwest of the provincial capital at Kandahar City. While President Karzai would not personally attend the event, for security reasons, his appointed delegation included his two brothers, including his oldest brother, Qayum Karzai, rumored to be a presidential candidate to replace Hamid. The delegation also included Shah Wali Karzai, the president's younger brother, whom Karzai had appointed as head of Kandahar's provincial council only eight months earlier, in July of 2011, after the president's popular half-brother,

Ahmed Wali Karzai, had been shot in the head and killed by a local police commander.

Karzai's father, Abdul Ahad Karzai, had become a popular tribal leader in Kandahar. After the Taliban assassinated his father in 1999, President Karzai and his brothers took a stand against the Taliban's savagery. The Karzais' opposition to the Taliban explains why the U.S. government installed Hamid Karzai as president after the American invasion in 2001.

The president's half-brother, Ahmed, became chairman of the Kandahar Provincial Council in 2005. Ahmed would survive nine assassination attempts by the Taliban, and was loved and respected by tribal leaders.

But in Taliban country, Ahmed Karzai's luck would only last so long. Just as they murdered his father, the Taliban murdered Ahmed, too, gunning him down on July 12, 2011, with a single shot to the head.

Because of his immense popularity amongst the locals in Kandahar Province, Ahmed Karzai's funeral produced a huge, emotional outpouring, the type reserved for a popular head of state.

Thus, by sending his brother, Shah Wali, who had replaced his beloved half-brother Ahmed, to the scene of the Kandahar massacre, President Karzai hoped to reduce the inflamed emotions of the situation. In addition to his two brothers, the presidential delegation included the chief of staff of the Afghan Army, General Shir Muhammad Karami, and the governor of Kandahar Province, Dr. Tooryalai Wesa. Also among those gathered at the small local mosque were members of the American press corps, including reporters from *The New York Times*.

The visit by the governmental delegation started on rough footing, as Gov. Wesa told villagers that Bales was mentally ill and a sick, lone-wolf soldier, not representative of the American Army. The villagers screamed in response and shouted the governor down. They accused him of protecting the American Army instead of the citizens of Kandahar.

After the public verbal berating by local villagers, the delegation stepped into a local mosque to console family members. But as soon as the service ended, and seconds after the Karzai brothers stepped out of the mosque, the Taliban struck.

Speeding into town on motorcycles, the Talban opened fire on the delegations. The Afghan National Army fired back, killing three of the motorcycle riders.

But the Taliban motorcycle riders shot one of the Karzai bodyguards in the head, killing him instantly. Security forces whisked the Karzai brothers, the governor and general to safety. The Taliban had struck and killed, with motorcycles. The tactic, ambush-by-motorcycle, had been used for years by the Taliban, and was on the rise as a means of ambush, attack and suicide.

New York Times reporters Taimoor Shah and Matthew Rosenberg covered the assassination attempt, on March 13, 2012:

> PANJWAI, Afghanistan — Militants riding motorcycles attacked a high-level Afghan government delegation during a memorial service on Tuesday in the village where an American soldier is said to have killed 16 people, mostly children and women, in a door-to-door rampage two days earlier.
>
> The Tuesday assault, on a mosque in the Panjwai district of Kandahar Province, left at least one Afghan soldier dead and punctured the calm that had largely prevailed in Afghanistan since the massacre.

Note the mode of attack described in the *NYT* report: "Militants riding motorcycles."

At Pasab, where Clint Lorance served as a squadron liaison officer to 4th Brigade Combat Team, news of the motorcycle attacks by the Taliban in the nearby Panjwai District dominated the conversation for days. Nevertheless, under pressure from the international community and the Afghan government, the United States emphasized its determination to eliminate what it called CIVCAS, the acronym for civilian causalities.

These events, the Kandahar massacre and the Taliban retaliation by motorcycle against the Karzai delegation, occurred three months before Clint would take command of First Platoon. Three months would pass before Matthew Hanes would be shot in the neck. Three months would pass before Lt. Dom Latino, Pvt. First Class Samuel Walley and Pvt. First Class Mark Kerner would be taken out by land mines. And another three months would pass before Clint Lorance would become a sacrificial lamb for the Obama Administration to hand back to the Afghans for the unfortunate events of the Kandahar massacre.

CHAPTER 8

MAYMANA, FARYAB PROVINCE
THE SECOND RETALIATORY
MOTORCYCLE STRIKE
THE ATTACK ON THE BUCKEYE BRIGADE
APRIL 4, 2012

In the Spring of 2012, as the surge began winding down, a heavy load of the direct fighting against the Taliban had been carried out by Special Operations Forces, such as U.S. Navy SEALs and U.S. Army Rangers, alongside the elite 82nd and 101st Airborne Divisions. Out of Afghanistan's 34 provinces, much of that fighting took place in the southern and eastern part of Afghanistan, including Kandahar, Nangarhar, Logar, and Paktia provinces.

Much of the heaviest fighting came along these provinces on the Afghan-Pakistani border. The Taliban would often attack, then retreat across the border into Pakistan for safety.

But it was not just SEALs, rangers, paratroopers and U.S. Marines taking the fight to the enemy on the ground in Afghanistan. The Afghan War, the longest war in American history, was fought by Americans of all stripes, including reservists, National Guard members, and regular infantry, all who volunteered to make, if necessary, the ultimate sacrifice for their country.

These Americans included the proud 37th Infantry Combat Brigade of the Ohio National Guard. The largest combat arms unit in the Ohio Army National Guard, the 37th Infantry Brigade Combat Team traces its lineage back to 37th Infantry

Division. Reorganized as an infantry brigade combat team, it became known as the "Buckeye Brigade." And as much as the sousaphone that dots the eye at halftime of Buckeye football games in the famed "Horseshoe" during the great "Script March" at Ohio Stadium, the Buckeye Brigade is one of the great treasures of Ohio.

The men and women of the Buckeye Brigade served out of a love of their great state, and out of love of country. The Buckeye Brigade traces its roots back to World War I, and wears on the left sleeve, to proudly identify itself as a unit, a large garnet or black O (garnet for dress uniforms and black for service uniforms) symbolizing the state of Ohio.

Their blood ran red, white and blue, along with a tinge of Buckeye garnet and gray.

In April of 2012, elements of the Buckeye Brigade had been deployed to northern Afghanistan, to Faryab Province, on the north side of the country. Like most of Afghanistan, rural Faryab Province consisted of a thousand small tribal villages dotting the countryside.

Its capital, Maymana, was a Third World agrarian city of 75,000 residents at the foot of the Torkestan Mountain Range. Small in comparison to many provincial capital cities—Kandahar had a population of more than 500,000— Maymana's proximity to the Maymana River made the lands around it rich, fertile, and green in comparison to the much harsher desert climate of Kandahar in the south. Vegetable exchanges and markets flourished in the capital, brought in from farmers in the surrounding countryside.

The population of the capital included a mix of international ethnicities, including Uzbek, Tajik, Turkmen, and Baluch.

The Pashtun population, the ethnic group historically noted as Afghan and the overall majority population of Kandahar, was a minority here. This made Faryban's ethnic mix unlike much of the other regions of Afghanistan.

No province of Afghanistan could be considered safe, or outside of the reach of the Taliban's strike. And while Faryab had in the past been controlled by Taliban invaders, and had been racked by heavy fighting in the Afghan Civil War in the 1990s, by the spring of 2012, most of the fighting in this province died down, as the American invasion had pushed much of the Taliban to the southern and eastern provinces bordering Pakistan. The American command considered Faryab Province to be among the least risky, for western soldiers, of Afghanistan's 34 provinces.

The ISAF military command headquartered in Maymana was called the Provincial Reconstruction Team or PRT, and consisted of troops from Norway, Latvia, Macedonia, Iceland, and the United States. American allies Norway and Germany rotated command of forces in Faryab Province, and much of the military load in the 2010–12 timeframe had been carried by Norwegian soldiers.

Most of the NATO troops in Faryab at the time were Norwegian, who proved to be very popular with the locals.

The proud Buckeye Brigade had been dispatched from Columbus to provide support for the PRT in the capital of Faryab Province, to provide stability in the province, and to quell any insurgencies that could arise.

The morning of April 4, 2012, brought sunny skies and temperature swings that ranged from the mid-50s at midnight to the mid-80s around noon.

Despite the ever-present knowledge that danger always lurks beneath the Afghan surface, the small city presented a sense of security. And despite the smelly, open-sewage ditches—so common throughout Afghanistan—and thousands of shanties piled alongside gravel streets and roads, there remained a certain peaceful charm about the vitality of open-air markets, where live chickens might be bartered for beans, or clothes for a rusty gardening tool.

Faryab Province's lush, green look that time of year, with evergreen pines along the streets and in the parks of the capital city, provided a view that many ISAF forces did not enjoy in the vast swaths of desert in other parts of the country. With spring in the air, under deep-blue sunny skies, 10 members of the Buckeye Brigade—all close friends— decided to walk to a local park to enjoy a few minutes of sunshine.

After all, part of their duties in supporting the Norwegian-led PRT included providing security on the streets. A NATO visible security presence, even in a local park, could provide stability to the region.

National guardsmen are called "citizen soldiers" because, for most of the year, they are civilians with full-time jobs, attending school, or taking care of their families. Guardsmen drill two days a month, then spend two weeks on active duty in the summer and sometimes, in wartime, get called to active duty, even for extended periods of time. When they come home, they go back to their families and their civilian jobs, and the cycle begins again.

Sgt. First Class Shawn Hannon, 44, of Grove City, Ohio, had been deployed all over the world with the Ohio National Guard, all the while maintaining his job back home in Columbus. In his military service, Shawn had served in Iraq, where he had been awarded the Bronze Star for heroic service. He had been injured in combat on a previous tour, and received the Purple Heart for his wounds.

Unlike regular members of the Army, National Guardsmen serve at home as well, in the United States, stepping forward during times of domestic disasters. Shawn had deployed to Mississippi in 2005 when the Gulf Coast was hit by Hurricane Katrina and before that, he deployed to Florida in 1992 during Hurricane Andrew, which took 44 lives and left 1.5 million Floridians without power for days. Shawn had also received the Ohio Distinguished Service Medal, which is awarded to a small number of the Ohio National Guard who "set themselves apart through service by placing themselves in grave danger."

In his civilian job, Shawn Hannon was a lawyer. But he was a lawyer unlike most other lawyers, declining a commission to the prestigious JAG Corps. Instead, Shawn threw his life's work into serving veterans, as chief legal officer for the Ohio Department of Veterans Services. He volunteered for the most dangerous position possible as an infantryman. He attended jump school at Fort Benning and qualified to be a paratrooper. Shawn had devoted much of his life to serving veterans, his beloved Buckeye State, and his country.

Only family meant more to Shawn, and that meant his sweet wife, Jamie, and their 9-month-old-son, Evan. Shawn could not wait to get back to see Evan again, to teach him how to play soccer, and to watch him grow up.

As the clock approached noon, Shawn and his fellow guardsmen approached the park near the main business district of town, the warm sun and gentle breeze bringing with it a sense of serenity.

A few moments later, the Taliban motorcycle rider spotted them, and revved his engine. The rumble of the fast-moving motorcycle, coming out of nowhere, broke the peace. Then came the violent blast that shook the earth.

Screams cut through the air. Sirens blared.

Three guardsmen lay dead in the street. Seven others were injured.

Shawn Hannon lay dead on the streets of Maymana, Afghanistan.

Within moments of the explosion, photographs of the dead, of American blood glistening under the sun, were blasted over the internet.

The Taliban took credit. This attack in the park marked its second motorcycle strike since the Kandahar massacre.

Within the next two weeks, Shawn was buried with full military honors in his beloved native state of Ohio.

Also buried were his friends and fellow members of the Buckeye Brigade, Master Sgt. Jeffrey J. Rieck and Capt.

Nick Rozanzki, all three killed by a motorcycle bombing attack.

Months later, Lt. Clint Lorance would be prosecuted, for murder, for ordering his men to fire on a fast-moving motorcycle that had been bearing down on his platoon, in a Taliban hellhole-of-a-battlefield that was the most dangerous place on Earth.

CHAPTER 9

D-Day had again arrived in the United States. All across America, in small towns and larger cities, Americans stopped to give pause to the 67th anniversary of the greatest and most daring amphibious and airborne invasion in the history of the United States, onto the booby-trapped beaches and up the steep cliffs of Normandy, France. The invasion has been carried out largely by the United States First Army, which included the vaunted 82nd Airborne Division, that parachuted in behind the lines before American, British, and Canadian troops hit the beaches. The Greatest Generation, America's greatest treasure, its "pride of our nation" as President Roosevelt noted while announcing the invasion on the radio that morning, was dying away.

Now, another generation of Americans was at war, in another part of the world, against a different type of enemy, the likes of which the Greatest Generation never saw. One of the links to those two wars was the 82nd Airborne Division, which had been in Normandy, and now, was in Afghanistan.

At Strong Point Payenzai, where elements of the 82nd Airborne were encamped, Lt. Dom Latino still had command of First Platoon. Spec. Matt Hanes still had use of his legs, and Pvt. First Class Samuel Walley had not yet had his leg and arm blown off, and was yet to lose his leg. Pvt. First Class Mark Kerner had not yet been injured by a land mine.

Lt. Clint Lorance, another member of the 82nd Airborne, had reported for duty at Brigade Headquarters, reviewing intelligence reports for the men in the field, to warn them of the impending dangers they faced from the enemy.

The men in Afghanistan—Lorance, Latino, Hanes, Walley and others—all carried within their hearts a reverence for the Greatest Generation, and for their older brothers in the 82nd who had served in France and Germany. But in the great heat of the blistering sun, and in the ferocious danger of the battlefield, the newest generation of American warriors could not focus on honoring the Greatest Generation as much as they would have liked. On this D-Day, they could only focus on staying alive.

And that's the way the Greatest Generation would have wanted it.

War was hell. It was a hell that spanned the generations that only a warrior could understand.

At sunrise, in the red-hot Kandahar province, the temperature had clipped 91 degrees. For the native Afghans lined up outside Kandahar Airfield, the summer temperatures had long ago become as normal as the smelly, open-sewer ditches. The stench from the sewer pond on the base, the flies buzzing in and out of the waste in the ditches, and the sweat drops rolling from their faces became afterthoughts.

For many Third World countries, the presence of the U.S. military brought economic opportunities for the locals to feed their families and put clothes on their childrens' backs. These Afghans were not warriors like Lorance, Latino and Hanes. But by their work on the American air base, or through their trade with the air base, they supported the American war effort against the hated Taliban.

For these Afghans, some standing in line, many waiting in trucks to be cleared through security to get on base, feeding their families meant more to them than buying into the strictest Sharia-Islamic philosophy being peddled by the Taliban. And thus, the Taliban hated them, because of their willingness to suck on the American sow.

On both sides of the crowded road leading to the base, a busy, indigenous marketplace had cropped up, the spinoff of American capitalism in a hostile, foreign land. Merchants along the road operated out of open-air toothpick-like structures, held together by two-by-fours, or wooden poles, whatever scrap wood the merchants could pull together. Most had a sand-colored canvas tarp serving as a makeshift roof to mute the blistering effects of the mid-day sun.

By the high-water mark of the military surge, the U.S. had spent $650 on each man, woman and child living in the city of Kandahar. And that's just an average. The street vendors and contractors did much better than even that.

The economic boom around the American Kandahar Airfield made this the most profitable section of the Afghanistan's second-largest city. Backed-up traffic jams, a blend of horns honking, blaring and beeping, and an excited chorus of auctioneers and bidders trying to get base-goers to buy their wares, created a profitable synergy for local merchants. Truck drivers, cars waiting to get on base, men standing in line, all had money from their work with the Americans, money they could spend with merchants before entering the base. The economic spinoff from the NATO base spun money into the hands of these poor merchants each and every morning, through their roadside stands for the sale of fruits and vegetables, garments and shoes, tarpaulins, meat sizzling on grills, even secondhand mobile phones, and of course, Afghan carpets and knock-off DVDs from "Bollywood."

As the street vendors competed for dollars outside the main gates, inside the base, four Afghan provincial governors were at this moment meeting with American military officials, discussing security in the wake of the Kandahar massacre.

Outside the base, as a vibrant micro-economy created by American money boomed amongst Islamic Afghans bitten by a capitalistic fervor, the fires of resentment burned, far hotter than the scorching sun, in the hearts of thousands who hated the Americans.

Kandahar city, and the rural Kandahar Province, was the birthplace of the Taliban. The Taliban, when it defeated other mujahedeen tribal leaders in the Afghan civil war in 1996, had moved the Afghan capital from Kabul to Kandahar. Eleven months before this D-Day of 2012, Uri Friedman wrote an article in *The Atlantic* titled, "Kandahar Has Become the Afghan Assassination Capital," published on July 27, 2011.

Friedman's assessment was on mark.

Two weeks after President Karzai's brother had been assassinated, on July 27, 2011, another Afghan official, the mayor of Kandahar, Ghulam Haider Hamidi, was assassinated by a Taliban suicide bomber who had strapped explosives inside his clothes.

While these politicians, such as the mayor and the president's brother, had acquiesced to the American invasion of Afghanistan, and the American war against the Taliban, they also acquiesced to and even enjoyed the American money infused into Kandahar. The Sharia-purist Taliban hated the Americans with a vengeance, and hated fellow Afghans who did business with them.

Out of view of the chatter and activity, ready to squeeze into the tightly populated makeshift market, the Taliban rider waited. He would enter the target area at the exact right moment.

The time had come. The rider saw his opening. *"Allahu Akbar!"*

The insurgent hit the throttle, rushing his bike into the crowded lanes between the street leading to the air base, and the mélange of street vendors with their hands held out, hoping to make an extra dollar.

The thunder of the loud explosion brought glory to Allah!

Blood sprayed all over the streets. Car horns blared in instinctive reaction to the thunderous blast. Screams pierced the hot morning air.

Men and women on the street, with many women wearing Islamic garb, ran around in desperate, confused circles, trying to determine what had happened. Within seconds, reality hit. Bleeding, dismembered corpses lay all over the street, with rivers of blood glistening under the morning sun. Screams turned to wailing as family members and co-workers rushed through the bloody scene to check on their loved ones. The acrid smell of burned flesh filled the air.

As the first wave of shock and horror flooded the marketplace, another blast rocked the air. The Taliban struck again. A third blast sent steel, fire, and shrapnel in a thousand different directions.

Within moments of these massive strikes outside the air base, the shrill sound of sirens blended into the screaming, crying, and wailing. Another blood-soaked scene in Kandahar province had been set off by coordinated motorcycle attacks.

Blood and tears are not contained within the boundaries of any one nation, or within the doctrine of any single religion.

Three successive blasts within a matter of seconds had drawn the entire city's attention to the gates outside the air base.

The Taliban had hoped to kill Americans waiting outside the air base. In this goal, they had failed. Only by the grace of God were no Americans going home in body bags. At least not this time.

But the Taliban had indiscriminately murdered 22 Afghan citizens, including innocent women and children, and injured 50 others. To put the blast in perspective, the Taliban had, in one swoop, killed more Afghans in this suicide-motorcycle-attack than Staff Sgt. Robert Bales had allegedly killed during the Kandahar massacre.

Not that murder mattered to the Taliban, as Islamic Sharia law called for murder as a means of purging the Earth of infidels for anyone not submitting to Islam. Anyone working with the infidel swine Americans, including Afghan citizens who would sell their souls to Satan to make corrupt money generated by the United States military presence, would be targeted along with their American puppet masters. The use of the fast-moving motorcycles would continue as a method of attack against the infidels.

News of the bloody motorcycle attack spread throughout Kandahar. At 4th Brigade Headquarters, where Lt. Lorance worked as liaison duty officer, the latest attack by motorcycle dominated the conversation among the officers. The bloody strike outside the gates of Kandahar Airfield marked the third retaliatory motorcycle strike by the Taliban since the Kandahar massacre. They'd gotten lucky this time that no Americans were killed. But it was not a matter of if, but when the Taliban struck again, and by motorcycle. Everyone in the U.S. military knew this.

Unfortunately, the U.S. military had begun to employ tightened rules of engagement, partially in response to the Kandahar massacre, and partially in response to pressure being applied by the Karzai Administration. However, the Taliban did not operate under these rules, and these ROEs would make it impossible to defend American troops against sudden motorcycle attacks by the Taliban. Under the new rules, any American forces who felt threatened by fast-moving motorcycles approaching them would have to apply a two-part, legal battlefield analysis before deciding to fire.

First, the soldier would have to decide whether the fast-approaching motorcycle displayed a "hostile intent." Secondly, after making the determination that the fast-moving motorcycle displayed a "hostile intent," the American soldier then had to make a battlefield determination as to whether the fast-moving inbound motorcycle constituted a "hostile act." If, and only if, the American soldier made a battlefield determination of first, a "hostile intent," and then, a "hostile act," the American soldier would be free to defend himself. If you can't figure it out in a split-second, and if you're wrong, and do nothing, prepare to die, be blinded, lose an arm, or have your legs blown off.

Of course, by the time this one-step, two-step determination was made, and by the time the American soldier somehow figures it out that a hostile act was on the way, in most cases, the Taliban motorcyclist will have blown himself up and killed Americans with him. Just ask the Buckeye Brigade in Faryab Province, a few weeks earlier.

In other words, these foolish, politically correct rules of engagement required American troops to sit back and commit suicide.

Against this dangerous backdrop, First Platoon operated from its forward position, deep within Taliban country at Strong Point Payenzai. First Platoon, the same platoon that Lt. Lorance would take command of in less than one month, even as blood spilled outside Kandahar Airfield, was now on the battlefield drawing heavy fire from the Taliban each and every day.

On this D-Day in Afghanistan, Lt. Clint Lorance remained on his post at Pasab, still unaware that in a little over a week, he would receive orders to take over as platoon leader of First Platoon.

And the Taliban was not finished. Many more strikes were on the way.

Soon, an even bigger disaster would strike.

CHAPTER 10

"Lorance, you need to get yourself a set of new boots."

Clint had been sitting at his desk, monitoring the computer screen for raw intelligence and collecting information from the battlefield, when the words came booming from over his shoulder. Clint turned around and saw his squadron commander, Lt. Col. Jeffrey Howard, standing there in full battle gear.

At first, a moment of temporary confusion set in.

New boots?

As liaison officer at Pasab, part of Clint's duties included monitoring all the movements of the squadron, including the combat movement of the two platoons in the squadron, and also the movements of the squadron commander, Lieutenant Colonel Howard. Thus, Clint knew that Lt. Col. Howard was en route to brigade headquarters at Pasab via motorized convoy.

But the colonel coming to Pasab from Sia Choy did not mean that Clint expected to see him. The colonel often came to speak with the brigade commander, Colonel Bryan Mennes. So, Lt. Col. Howard's voice booming over Clint's shoulder surprised him. Clint stood and exchanged a firm handshake with his boss, who he was always happy to see, even on short notice, while processing what the colonel had meant about "new boots."

Then, Clint knew.

Two days earlier, Lt. Dom Latino had been evacuated off the battlefield from the near fatal-explosion by the IED. The blast sprayed dangerous shrapnel into his abdomen, nearly takings his life. First Platoon lost its platoon leader.

The next man in line, logically, to become platoon leader was Lt. Clint Lorance.

Clint had served admirably in Iraq and had earned his way to a commission from the ranks of the enlisted. Clint knew First Platoon better than any other officer in the Army.

In one sense, he knew the platoon so well because each and every day, he had been monitoring intelligence traffic and presenting battle reports up the chain of command about the military status of First Platoon in the field. He knew that Lt. Latino had gone down. He knew that Pvt. First Class Mark Kerner had gone down. He also knew that Pvt. First Class Samuel Walley lost his left arm below the elbow, and his right leg below the knee. Corp. Matthew Hanes had not yet been shot in the throat and paralyzed. Clint knew that First Platoon had taken a beating in the field.

While Clint knew all about First Platoon, in another sense, he did not know them at all. He had not met the paratroopers of the platoon, and did not know them personally. The call now, to assume command, generated mixed emotions. Every soldier in the Army, especially every junior infantry officer, worked toward becoming a commander of men in combat in the field.

Clint longed to command his own platoon. But his heart hurt for Lt. Latino, a man who he did not know, and he prayed that the man he replaced would live.

He felt for these men of First Platoon, and would do everything in his power to ensure that none of them would be removed from the battlefield in body bags, and put in a flag-draped box in the back of a C-17 for a long flight back to Dover Air Base.

He resolved then and there. No American deaths on his watch. Not in his platoon.

The call to command had come sooner than he expected. Clint was more than ready. To protect his men, and carry out their military mission, he had to focus on the dangers at hand. One of those dangers: classified reports revealed the increasing suicide motorcycle attacks by the Taliban.

The massive motorcycle suicide attack by the Taliban outside the Kandahar Airfield a little over one week ago, on June 6, remained one of the top topics of conversation at Brigade Headquarters at Pasab. Clint knew, from his access to intelligence reports, that managing the problem of suicide riders on motorcycles, and managing the dangerous problem of IEDs planted all in the ground, would be among the major challenges to helping these men live.

"Yes, sir, I am ready," he said to Lt. Col. Howard.

The Army, including the vaunted 82nd Airborne Division, operated under a philosophy of "next man up." Clint Lorance, the young officer who worked his way up from the enlisted ranks, born in Oklahoma and who grew up in Texas, had been called into combat, to lead paratroopers in combat, in the most dangerous battlefield in the world.

No sense of fear would stop him, and he had no hesitation. Clint had a job to do, and he would carry it to the best of his ability.

Still, now that the call had come, he needed some time to gather his thoughts, to prepare himself mentally. Since he arrived at Pasab on a Blackhawk helicopter last February, his limited view of Afghanistan to date had consisted of the short time spent at Kandahar Airfield, and then four months inside the walls of Pasab. Fortified by HESCO walls all around, Pasab protected dozens of Quonset huts where hundreds of American troops lived and worked in a variety of missions supporting other troops in the field.

The post featured a helicopter pad, with almost daily flights in and out of Kandahar Airfield or other battlefield locations, to support or defend troops under fire, often described by the Army as "troops in contact." A large blimp flew overhead all the time, armed with an aerial camera, used for surveillance to warn the Army of danger congregating outside the walls of the base.

The safest place within the province may have been inside the walls of Pasab. While these thick HESCO walls did not stop mortar or rocket attacks from flying into the base, the inside grounds of the Strong Point were without IEDs to worry about and were relatively safe from sniper fire from the outside.

Every day since his arrival, Clint had followed a strict physical fitness regimen, which included jogging around the inside perimeter of the base.

Now that he had been ordered to leave, he decided to go out and take another jog. The sun had baked the base all day long. No one escaped the heat, ever. But later in the day, it was like the oven had been turned down from broil to bake.

Clint picked up the pace as he rounded the southern perimeter just inside the HESCO walls. Sweat dripped from his face and his body as he sprinted through the thick, hot air, his rushing blood pounding at his ears.

His call to duty raced through his mind with each additional lap around the base. Soon, he would head to the bloodiest front of the battlefield of the war. Clint was eager to leave the safer conditions found inside the compound, go stare danger in the face and take the battle to the enemy. This was his call as a soldier. This is why he had become a paratrooper.

CHAPTER 11

After nine years in the Army, Clint had learned that many things needing to get done on a day-to-day basis in the military were managed by simply "asking around." The asking-around technique, when put in practice, sometimes resulted in additional duct tape for stabilizing a worn-out power cord for a laptop, additional bullets for target practice at the range, or even an additional box of baby wipes for a "field shower." Yes, baby wipes were the prime means of cleaning the skin in the sultry Afghan afternoon. Or sometimes, the technique led to bartering for missing uniform parts. Maybe a good conduct medal for a belt buckle. Or a fresh, crisply starched uniform shirt for a promise to buy a round of beer.

Clint asked around Pasab and found out that a logistics convoy would be headed out to Combat Outpost Sia Choy.

As if he did not already know the answer to the question, Clint approached the sergeant overseeing logistics for the convoy that was still being assembled inside the walls of the compound, not far from the main gate.

"Where are we headed, sergeant?"

"Sia Choy," came the response.

Perfect.

"Got any extra room for some supplies for my new platoon?"

More asking around.

"Don't see why not, L.T.," the sergeant asked. "Whatcha got?"

"Mainly a few boxes. We've got a UAV for my new platoon, and some other stuff. Right over there."

The sergeant nodded. "I'll get my guys on it, L.T."

A few minutes later, rectangular boxes, all sizes and the shape of wooden coffins that he scrounged up for his new platoon, with tons of supplies, including the most important supply of all, the new UAV that would fly aerial surveillance before patrols, were being loaded onto the convoy. *Good.*

One last logistical detail remained. "You got a place I can hitch a ride, sergeant?"

"That one, sir." The sergeant pointed to a sand-colored, four-wheel MATV, the Army's acronym for Multipurpose All-Terrain Vehicle.

Designed to absorb most IED blasts, the MATV carried a crew of four, plus a gunner, who operated a .50-caliber machinegun from a mounted turret position on top of the vehicle.

The vehicle's interior had two front seats and two back seats. They directed Clint to the right-rear passenger seat on the backside opposite side from the driver. As they cranked their engines one by one, the rumbling of the convoy's engines permeated the air, pouring exhaust from their tailpipes. And then, they started rolling out.

CHAPTER 12

The MATV, now jam-packed with five soldiers in desert battle fatigues, rolled through the front gate of Pasab, and onto the road outside of the base. The military convoy turned left as soon as it hit the main road.

This marked the first time Clint had gone beyond the walls of the fortified American military compound in Afghanistan. He let that thought sink in. He had landed at heavily fortified Kandahar Airfield, and then took a helicopter to Pasab, which is also heavily fortified. But these two heavily fortified outposts were all of Afghanistan that he had seen, until now.

Leaning back in his seat and attempting to relax his body and his constant thoughts, Clint noted the sights before him, through the window of the MATV as the convoy rolled out. A vibrant marketplace, full of colors and flowers, with Afghan merchants trading their wares, had been set up outside the base. That made sense. American money attracted even rudimentary capitalism.

An active marketplace had also sprung up outside Kandahar Airfield, which had been struck by a Taliban motorcycle suicide rider just two weeks, earlier on June 6.

In Afghanistan, even the most innocent of sites, like a colorful outdoor bazaar, could instantly become rivers of running blood and bodies strewn on the streets.

CHAPTER 13

As the convoy rolled farther away from the main gates of Pasab, leaving the colorful marketplace with Afghan merchants in the rear view, large light poles dotted the road outside the base, stretching hundreds of yards beyond the main gate.

But as they got farther from the base, the roadsides became vacant. No one was in sight for miles. In some places, the landscape was a desert, but in other places, there was normal vegetation, with grass, with a splattering of trees and flowers here and there.

The light poles around the entrance of the base had disappeared.

Most of rural Afghanistan had no light poles at all, because much of rural Afghanistan has no electricity. The road stretched across a desolate, desert-looking area that reminded Clint of parts of southwest Oklahoma, a dry-looking, prairie-like landscape, with mountains off in the distance.

The seven military vehicles in the convoy formed a tight, straight line, rolling down the highway. Just in front of Clint's MATV, a semi-truck towed a flatbed trailer, with a bulldozer chained onto the trailer. They added the bulldozer, Clint was told, because the Army Corps of Engineers was building a road out in the Kandahar battle space somewhere. Road building starts with minesweepers and bulldozers.

The last views of Pasab had disappeared into the distance awhile back, and the gunner assigned to Clint's vehicle had climbed up top, manning his .50-caliber machine gun. Clint and the other soldiers were all armed, but the .50-cal overhead provided an additional sense of security.

Despite the growing threat of Taliban suicide bikers, the greatest danger to American troops in Afghanistan remained IEDs. These merciless weapons had taken American lives both in the battlefield and on roads as well.

Even though Clint's MATV was classified as "blast-resistant," and while its protective armor provided superior protection over regular vehicles, the Taliban had become more sophisticated with powerful IEDs planted along roadsides. On occasions, IED blasts had destroyed some of the most blast-resistant American vehicles. And even if the vehicle weren't totally destroyed by an IED, the blasts often flipped the vehicles over, sometimes killing the troops inside.

The convoy picked up speed, now headed west, along Highway 1, out toward the rural battlefront of Kandahar Province.

Highway 1, also known as the "Ring Road," made a huge loop all the way around the perimeter of the country. Huge chunks of it remained incomplete. But the link from Kandahar's capital at Kandahar City to Qalat, capital of the neighboring province in Zabul, which ran past Pasab, was complete.

As the main highway connecting various cities within the country, part of the U.S. military's job was to maintain "Highway 1" as the main traffic artery for moving U.S. troops and equipment by ground. The road was largely devoid of bumps and potholes, and Clint's convoy rolled along on it at a quick pace.

His mission would be executed not only under dangerous military conditions, but also under oppressive heat. By 6 a.m., temperatures had climbed to 93 degrees, and the forecast called for the temperature to eclipse 100 degrees by noon. But the color of the Afghan sky above the convoy did not change with the heat, and was as deep blue as some of the cold Texas Januarys that Clint had endured as a teenager.

But one thing about the Afghan sky differed from Texas. About every two miles, large blimps floated up in the air, several hundred feet above the road. Each resembled the famous Goodyear blimp that covered so many sporting events around the United States. The Army called them Aerostats, and one had remained airborne above Pasab every second for the last five months during Clint's time there.

The United States had dotted the airspace over the roadways with Aerostats for many miles stretching beyond Pasab. These floating blimps created an extraterrestrial look, like squadrons of alien spacecraft hovering overhead, ready to zap people up out of cars and take them away to a faraway galaxy—nothing like the clear, open skies back home in Texas. But Clint felt relieved knowing that American cameras on board the blimps could detect sinister Taliban activity, including the roadside bomb activity.

The convoy rolled on, picking up speed, deeper into Kandahar Province. No one in Clint's MATV said anything. But everyone knew that Kandahar was the heart of Taliban country.

Thankfully, the American blimps were overhead to keep an eye on things. But who knew if they would be floating out above the fields, out to the left and the right? The overhead surveillance for those spaces would be left to remote-control drones and U.S. military helicopters.

Because so much American military traffic moved back and forth on Highway 1, if the Taliban could ever get to it, it could inflict considerable damage. They had managed to infiltrate the highway a few times, planting roadside bombs that had exploded and killed allied troops, even in blast-protective vehicles.

The American blimps high above the roads had helped. But the blimps could not detect a jihadist who strapped bombs under his clothing and mounted a motorcycle, determined to detonate himself on top of American vehicles along the roadway. The blimps did not stop the Taliban motorcycle rider from driving his motorcycle into a crowded market, killing more than 20 people and injuring another 50.

Nor could the overhead surveillance see explosives hidden in vehicles moving along the highway near the convoy. Any car on the road that wasn't American was a potential rolling bomb.

Clint tried not to think about all that. Though the sun burned hot, the bright blue sky brought about a refreshing reminder of the beauty of life, and of the great and noble cause for which the U.S. Army was here, to stop radical Islamic terror from spreading across the oceans to the shores of the United States.

CHAPTER 14

ENTERING TALIBAN COUNTRY

Clint couldn't see the speedometer from the back-right passengers' side. But they must have been doing 50 mph. Maybe faster. In some ways, the faster the speed, the better.

At as they rolled across rural Kandahar Province, nothing showed the danger around them. No signs proclaimed that they were entering the heart of Taliban country. If any of the soldiers riding with Clint were worried, they all wore good poker faces.

Moments later, the landscape changed.

Colors.

All in the fields.

The fields were ablaze with the colors of the rainbow. The chromatic blur outside the fast-moving convoy flashed streaks of yellow, pink, white and green, from an ocean of thousands of colorful flowers, swaying in the breeze.

The landscape had gone from southwestern scruff to Holland in the springtime. The flowers sat atop lush green stalks, which were waist-high, half the size of a cornstalk or a full-grown rose bush. How could such beauty appear in an area that was so deadly? It was almost like the beautiful flowers were a casket spray at a funeral. Except most of the men who might die in the convoy would get an American flag draped over their caskets. No flowery casket sprays for soldiers.

Afghanistan leads the world in opium production. Most of the heroin causing addiction and death by overdose in the United States comes from these fields. The flowers swaying in the breeze, as beautiful as they were, were more deadly than beautiful.

These poppy bulbs formed the largest part of Afghanistan's economy. Both the Taliban, intent on killing Americans, and the average farmer wearing a white robe, which also happens to be the uniform of the Taliban, would kill for the right to control these fields.

Not only did heroin addiction made these flowers deadly, but money received from the heroin production bought bombs that killed American soldiers. The opium crop funded the Taliban's war chest to purchase weapons, bombs and other instruments of terror. Kandahar Province, along with neighboring Helmand Province, produced more opium than any other provinces in the largest opium-producing country in the world.

Why, then, would the U.S. Army turn a blind eye to these deadly flowers?

Wouldn't it be simpler to destroy the opium in the fields, and thus destroy the illicit drug trade in the United States? Would destroying the opium fields not eliminate the principal source of money to the Taliban, so hell-bent on killing Americans?

These questions have been asked and debated ad nauseam.

At first, the answer might seem simple. Wipe out Afghanistan's opium poppy, and much of the world's drug problems are solved. Not only that, but wiping out the opium poppy would quell conspiracy theorists who claimed that both Bush and Obama sent troops to Afghanistan to protect the drug trade.

But, as usual, complex problems complicate seemingly simple solutions.

First off, there are legitimate medicinal millions for opium. Not only that, Afghan farmers needed the poppy to make a living. Just as thousands of Americans are addicted to opioids, so is the Afghan economy. Destroy the opium, and Afghanistan loses its economic sustenance.

The Army opted for a different tactic. Rather than destroying opium fields, it began interrogating the farmers about who bought the opium. From there, the Army tried, sometimes, to track down the purchasers. If the purchasers were Taliban, and if they could be tracked down, the Army could deal with them.

The technique had proved partially effective. Sometimes the Afghan farmers led American troops to Taliban purchasers. And other times, the farmers were not cooperative, leading to a dead end.

Under the new Obama negotiation strategy, American troops had other missions on their mind aside from the opium problem. Obama's famously announced drawdown, announced in June of 2011, changed the Army's entire strategic approach. Now at the top of the Army's agenda: turning operational control of the country over to the Afghan National Army.

All this opium-strategy stuff was beyond Clint's pay grade, and the last thing on his mind. His focus was on the survival of his troops. Not opium poppy.

Thirty minutes after they left Pasab, the vehicles started slowing down.

A moment later, a slow left turn off Highway 1 redirected the convoy to the south, onto a gravel road. The convoy was now moving from under the direct camera of the overhead blimps to less aerial protection. That meant greater danger of ambush and IEDs.

As they turned onto the gravel road, the convoy kicked up rocks and dust in its wake. The flatbed with the heavy bulldozer became the biggest dust generator. Like campfires emitting smoke signals to the enemy in the Wild West, the dust plumes increased their visibility from afar to Taliban that might be in the area.

Clint scanned the fields outside the convoy. So far, nothing. No signs of danger. No visible militants, not Taliban, and, thank God, no IEDs.

Combat Outpost Sia Choy could not be far away.

They rolled down the gravel road for another mile or so, and the convoy slowed down. Clint looked up and saw it for the first time.

Sia Choy.

CHAPTER 15

COMBAT OUTPOST SIA CHOY
A FINAL STOP BEFORE HELL

Sia Choy.

Unlike Pasab, located back and away from the battle zone, which had never sustained an attack in the months Clint had been there, Sia Choy displayed multiple blast holes and bullet holes in its outer HESCO shell. Signs of multiple rocket and mortar attacks appeared everywhere. Deep craters marked the ground where the enemy's rockets and mortars had landed in the stiff, dry dirt around the base. The areas around Sia Choy reminded Clint of the last battle zone he had been in: Iraq.

Clint had seen all these horrors before. He had experienced many incoming mortar rounds, seen big crater blasts around the roads, seen bullet holes in the walls. He had seen houses blown to pieces, and kids walking around on one leg. He had seen cars burning in the streets.

Yes, Clint had seen the ugly face of war. But in Iraq. Not yet in Afghanistan. Combat Outpost Sia Choy at this moment gave him his first personal taste of a war zone in yet another country.

Off in the distance, several white Aerostat blimps hung in the air, tethered to the ground by steel cables. The sight of the blimps offered a reassurance that America had kept eyes in the sky. On the other hand, the Aerostats had not prevented the blast holes at this outpost.

Here marked the beginning of Clint's opportunity, finally, and responsibility to carry out his duties as an infantry officer. To serve and lead and protect the men who worked for him and below him, in the chain of command. He wanted to be at Payenzai. But Payenzai would have to wait a day or so. First things first.

The convoy finally stopped in front of the main gates of the outpost and Clint hopped out into the hot sun. He stretched his legs, his eyes searching the ground with each step. White rocks were scattered on the ground, outside the base. Perhaps they were used to keep all the dust down.

A moment later, loud thunder of motorized rotor blades roared from inside the post. A Blackhawk helicopter lifted slowly above the c-wire atop outer HESCO walls. Clint felt the wind from its rotors, and the *thwock-thwock-thwock* of its engine made it impossible to hear anything else. The chopper cleared the top of the guard towers, pivoted in the sky, dipped its nose, and then flew off to the north, out of sight.

A helo base close to his Strong Point and close to his platoon might prove invaluable later on. Clint made a mental note. Air power was a great asset, especially in a war zone.

He walked quickly toward to the main gate; loose, powdery sand substance puffed up around his boots. The soldiers called this "moondust." It was dustier than the more tightly packed ground inside Pasab.

At the highly guarded security checkpoint at Sia Choy, soldiers armed with M-4 carbine rifles crawled all over the place. A .50-caliber machine gun backed up the initial security detail. Anyone trying to penetrate the perimeter of this post without authority would pay a heavy price.

When he cleared security and stepped into the compound, he saw a more militarized presence than Pasab. Weapons displayed everywhere. Soldiers on a tighter edge. Given its closer proximity to the Taliban battlefield, and all the bullet and rocket holes Clint had seen outside the gate, that made sense.

Clint's time here at Sia Choy, in the central Zhari District of Kandahar Province, would be short, by design. Maybe two days at most. The Sia Choy leg was in part to check in with his squadron commander, LTC Howard and to execute paperwork. The Army was all about paperwork. Especially for any change of duty station. But the sooner he could get in and get out, the better.

Time to get on with it.

CHAPTER 16

By midnight, as Thursday the 28th of June rolled into Friday the 29th, the temperature outside at Sia Choy had dropped to a near week-long low of 79 degrees. For late June, in southern Afghanistan, anything in the mid-70s was a cold front. One might assume that more comfortable weather would translate to better sleeping conditions.

Not for Clint.

Not tonight.

Clint's mind raced like a propjet, locked and loaded on the mission that would begin tomorrow. Like a master chess player game-planning multiple moves, his swirling thoughts about the next couple of days had made sleep a challenge. He had replayed the mental checklist in his mind perhaps a dozen times between 10 p.m. and 2 a.m.

He thought about how he would handle his first meeting with his men at Strong Point Payenzai, and looked forward to implementing his drone policy, convinced that the shoulder-launched UAV would give his men better protection, on a constant basis.

While U.S. Army helicopters were helpful, when they were available, the choppers could not be everywhere all the time. And in some ways, calling in helicopters for air support was like calling the police back home.

If a crime has been committed, or if a crime was in progress, the police, when called, would sometimes show up quickly. Sometimes after the fact. Sometimes, they got there quicker than at other times, depending on whether they were distracted by other calls, or how far away they might have been when called. The police, like Army aviation, in most cases were called in reaction to trouble.

The UAV, by contrast would allow the platoon to be pro-active, to get assets and cameras in the air, before a mission ever began. Returning to the police-at-home analogy, having the UAV in the air at all times during combat operations would almost be like having a permanent police officer assigned for 24-hour protection against criminals. And from Clint's perspective, ground troops should always have air support, and the closer in the air support, the better. And even with the new drone, he would still have the ability to call in Army helos.

As Clint twisted in the rack, with nervous sweat beads forming on his forehead, he thought about another new policy that he would bring to Payenzai: a permanent dog team for bomb sniffing and detection. The Army's combat dogs, trained to sniff out bombs not visible to the human eye, could provide another valuable asset to help, to supplement the mine hound, and discover hidden explosives just under the dirt, hard to detect by the human eye.

After the shooting of Cpl. Hanes, Clint needed to find another soldier to serve as mine hound. This was the most dangerous job in the patrol, as this soldier shuffled out in front of the patrols with the handheld, electronically sensitive minesweeper. The mine hound was the first line of defense against hidden IEDs and booby-trap bombs planted in the ground. Now, a new dog-sniffing team added to the patrol would provide additional protection, in addition to the mine hound, against IED explosions and death related to IEDs.

Arranging for the dog team had taken some heavy-duty backroom wheeling and dealing. Here, Clint's experience as liaison officer paid off.

The canine bomb-sniffing unit, or "dog unit," for this battle space around Payenzai was headquartered at Pasab. An Air Force technical sergeant who Clint had befriended ran the unit. When Clint got the word that he was taking First Platoon, he sought out the technical sergeant, and arranged to bring a dog and a dog handler with him in the convoy.

"Hey, tech sergeant. I'm heading down to Kandahar to take over a platoon. No matter what you might hear from other officers, I want to make sure that I have a dog unit with my platoon at all times. Are we clear on that?"

"Yes, sir. Roger that, sir. When do you ship out, sir?"

"Next week, tech sergeant. Can you make it happen?"

"Yes, sir, lieutenant. I'll have a dog and handler ready to roll when you're ready, sir."

And with that conversation, a dog and a dog handler would be in place for additional protection against IEDs and landmines.

In many ways, Clint started his command of First Platoon even before he had met the troops. He was determined that his platoon would never be in the field without an operational UAV, and at least one dog and dog handler in the battle space, working alongside the mine hound, to seek out and destroy hidden IEDs in the ground before anyone else got their legs blown off.

He looked forward to sharing these new measures with his men, and hoped that the additional protective measures would be well received and help boost morale. Once he arrived on the ground at Payenzai, he would conduct an initial overview of the situation to determine if any further protective measures needed to be implemented.

After he had replayed a thousand mental scenarios in his mind during the course of the night, the Afghan horizon gave way to the rising sun.

Any semblance of cooler temperatures from the midnight before had melted with the red-hot sunrise. By 5:42 a.m. when the sun finally crested over the eastern horizon, the temperature had reached 99 degrees.

The day would bring another red-hot scorcher. But Clint did not have the weather on his mind. He jumped out of the rack, got in uniform, and was ready to push off to his next destination, company headquarters at Strong Point Gariban.

With his duties at the battalion headquarters now complete, Clint hitched another ride, this time on a logistics convoy, for the drive from battalion headquarters at Sia Choy to company headquarters at Gariban.

The baking heat felt like a blast of hot air escaping from his mother's oven door, wide open just before it was time to remove the turkey on Thanksgiving Day.

Wiping sweat from his forehead under 108-degree temperatures, Clint stepped through the gates of the Strong Point that would be the headquarters for his company, and most importantly, from his standpoint, the final stop-off point before he got to be with his men.

Viewed from the outside, Strong Point Gariban, like Combat Outpost Sia Choy, displayed ample evidence of war damage. Craters, mortar holes, bullet holes, all reflected heavy enemy fire in the recent past. The Department of Defense News Services featured Gariban when insurgents attacked it with an 82-mm weapon. In that case, when coalition forces returned fire, the insurgents tried escaping by motorcycle. U.S. helicopters opened fire and killed one of the insurgents on the motorcycle with a Hellfire missile.

The attack on Gariban had provided more evidence of insurgents using motorcycles both during surprise attacks and then, using them as getaway vehicles while engaging U.S. forces. As proven most recently by the massive motorcycle attack at the gates of Kandahar Airfield earlier this month, the motorcycle problem was a growing threat, confirming intelligence reports that Clint had seen while working as liaison officer at Pasab. Next to the ongoing threat of IEDs, surprise attacks by motorcycle had become the greatest threat to U.S. forces in Afghanistan.

After clearing the heavy security at the main checkpoint, Clint stepped into the interior of the post. Gariban had a smaller, almost charming feel about it. At first, he could not put his finger on the reason for this. Then, it hit him.

The outer barrier of the post had been built around a small Afghan village. The mud huts of the village contained within the parameters of the post gave it more of a village-like feel. The inside of Gariban had a tight feel to it, in part because of the native buildings that were already there, squeezed up beside the American tents that were pitched for housing the American troops.

Gariban was also home to Second Platoon, which was the sister platoon to First Platoon, the outfit that Clint would take command of, hopefully, as soon as tomorrow. Capt. Patrick Swanson, who was the company commander, or "troop commander," held direct command over the platoon leaders of First and Second Platoons.

Clint looked forward to meeting his new company commander and working with him during his transition as platoon leader for First Platoon.

Clint did not know Captain Swanson well. The two officers had exchanged emails and had limited communications while Clint worked at brigade headquarters. During that time, Swanson was interested in the brigade commander's perception of his company.

Of course, as liaison officer, Clint had been in the best position of anybody to know how Chainsaw Company (the military unit directly above First Platoon in the chain of command) was viewed at brigade headquarters. Every day, Clint had interacted with the brigade commander himself, Col. Mennes.

Clint's reports to Capt. Swanson about his company's performance had been positive. Clint had told Swanson that the brigade commander rarely questioned any of Chainsaw Company's decision-making, which was good news for Swanson. Put another way, because Clint had brought good news for Capt. Swanson, he hoped that some of the goodwill generated might translate over into the start of a good relationship with his new immediate boss in the chain of command.

They were both junior officers in the 82nd Airborne Division, their prospective pathways having led them along different routes to their commissions. West Point grads were the crème de la crème of the U.S. Army.

Clint's route to a commission, the Green-to-Gold program, was the most blue-collar route for an enlisted man to become an officer. But at the end of the day in the structure of the Army, rank counted more than the educational pedigree. And West Point or no West Point, Capt. Swanson nevertheless outranked Clint.

Swanson in many ways was a unique individual, with a bit of a complex personality.

The captain exuded a laid-back aura, and in some ways, resembled a yacht club captain or a late-morning golfer at the country club. Swanson presented a bit of an aristocratic air. Nothing wrong with that, but it marked a distinctive trait about Swanson that made him different from some of the other officers. In stark contrast, for example, Lt. Col. Howard, Swanson's immediate boss, could come across as impetuous, forward, and aggressive in his personality.

Swanson was polar-end opposite of Howard. So chill was the captain that if one did not know better, one might conclude that the captain was on marijuana. Of course, had that been the case, the captain would not have lasted as long as he had in the 82nd Airborne Division. Swanson was "Captain Chill." As a West Pointer, Swanson belonged to a club unto itself, which oftentimes is said to enjoy a different standard of judgment from officers who are not West Point grads.

However, despite the different route they took in becoming officers, they shared some important commonalities. Both were about the same age. They both served in Iraq at about the same time, and had seen combat in Iraq. Swanson was a battle-hardened veteran and also had commanded a platoon, with the 10th Mountain Division.

With dark brown hair and a chiseled jawline, Swanson could have been the poster boy for an Army recruiting campaign. Having graduated from West Point in 2006, Swanson took over as company commander of Chainsaw Company in July of 2011, and had nearly a year of combat under his belt, first in Maiwand District, and then later in the Zhari District of Kandahar province. Both Maiwand and Zhari were among the most Taliban-infested districts of Kandahar province.

As he had done at Sia Choy, Clint found Capt. Swanson in the company commanders' tent, came to attention, saluted, and reported for duty.

They exchanged pleasantries, and chatted for a few minutes, trying to get to know one another a little bit better. Although Capt. Swanson and Lt. Col. Howard brought different personalities to the table, Swanson, like Howard, commanded respect.

Before they got down to business, the captain sprung surprising news.

"Clint, your platoon is here on base, right now, at Gariban."

Had Clint heard, that right? "Say again, sir?"

"We pulled them off the battlefield. They needed a break from the pounding they've taken. We're calling it a safety stand-down. Some of the guys need to get some counseling before we send them back out. The chaplain has been available for them, and some have been talking to the chaplain. You can meet them starting today."

The news hit Clint by surprise. Lt. Col. Howard, for whatever reason, had elected not to give him a heads up on the situation. Maybe that explained the colonel's somewhat surprising decision to throw him out of the Tactical Operations Center at Sia Choy.

The shooting of Cpl. Matthew Hanes, six days earlier, had hit the platoon hard and had been the deciding factor that triggered the company's decision to pull them back off the battlefield

"If the platoon is here," Clint asked, "who's manning the store at Strong Point Payenzai?"

"We've got replacements down there from the headquarters and headquarters troop defending the post until you take your platoon back down there tomorrow," Swanson said. "Let's first go over our agenda for the next week, including mission planning, then you can start meeting your men, beginning with Sgt. First Class Keith Ayers."

"Roger that." Clint felt sad that the morale of his men had been rocked so hard that they needed to be pulled off the battlefield for therapy, after just 30 days. On the other hand, he felt grateful to meet them a day early.

Clint spent about an hour with Swanson discussing the transition and specific battle plans to be implemented when Clint took command of the platoon, an event that now would occur within the next two hours.

These battle plans would put them in mortal danger every second they stepped outside the barriers of their Strong Point, and into the countryside and the villages surrounding it. Their job would be to dodge oceans of landmines, avoid sniper attacks from unknown positions, and somehow survive against kamikaze motorcycle attacks. And oh, by the way, on top of all that, their job also would be to recruit native Afghans to join the Afghan police force to fight the Taliban, and somehow, to establish goodwill in community relations.

Clint knew the mission. But Swanson, as a good company commander, had to lay it out again anyway. They discussed First Platoon's assignments for each day for the next week, which would involve dangerous patrols in the area around the Strong Point. At the end of the week, they would meet again and discuss planning for the following week.

His heart pounded with excitement at the prospect of soon meeting his men. In one sense, the transition should be smoother than might normally be expected, because in Clint's former role as liaison officer, he already knew intricate details of both platoons that were under Captain Swanson's command.

On the other hand, Clint did not know the men. It wasn't that Capt. Swanson had been around the members of the platoon on a 24-hour basis and knew them well. However, he did have a better bird's-eye view of the men than Clint. Swanson had met regularly with the former platoon leader, Lt. Latino, and the platoon sergeant, Sgt. First Class Keith Ayers.

Capt. Swanson, like Clint, had been concerned about heavy battlefield casualties suffered by the platoon, and wanted to take extra steps to beef up discipline in an effort to try and cut down on soldiers getting shot and losing their arms and legs. Swanson never mentioned a morale problem in the platoon. He didn't have to.

The morale problem was not indigenous to First Platoon. The morale problem extended across the board to all platoons. It stemmed from the tight, suicidal rules of engagement, from the Army's new mission of serving as national police force for the Afghans, and from the un-soldier-like role of becoming recruiters for members the Afghan military and police force.

The tightened rules, requiring battlefield lawyering at the moment of attack, made it much more difficult for soldiers to defend themselves. The strict rules had gotten so many Americans killed or had their limbs blown off, that Col. Mennes' suspicions were spot on. Platoons were not anxious to patrol in heavily infested minefields, or get blown up by kamikaze riders on motorcycles. Many platoon commanders did not want to march their men through these death fields,

running a high risk of having someone's legs or knees blown off or their guts spilled all over the ground.

This reality, this no-win situation imposed by increasingly restrictive rules of engagement, had placed company commanders such as Capt. Swanson in a tight box. They needed to get their men out into the field, to keep the Taliban in check, but knew full well that the platoon leaders were oftentimes looking for excuses not to go on patrol.

Capt. Swanson made himself clear. He expected a higher level of self-discipline from First Platoon, and exhorted Clint to improve platoon discipline, mainly for the men's safety moving forward.

Clint did not take Swanson's comments as criticism of the former platoon leader, Lt. Latino, or the platoon sergeant, Sgt. First Class Ayers. Both were excellent soldiers. Latino, like Swanson, was a West Point man. And Ayers' reputation as one of the finest NCOs in the Army preceded him.

In the absence of an officer, Ayers had taken control of First Platoon and led it for two consecutive weeks, since Latino's injury. Keith Ayers had done a masterful job keeping the guys together.

Clint worried that Ayers, as platoon sergeant, might have been too hard on himself about some of the injuries to the guys in First Platoon, most recently Matthew Hanes. But Clint wanted to make sure that Ayers did not blame himself. He knew, full well, even before meeting his new platoon sergeant, that Ayers had led these guys in the most dangerous battlefield in the world in 2012. No one could have done better. As soon as he finished up with Capt. Swanson, Ayers would be his first call, and then he would meet the rest of his men.

Clint promised Capt. Swanson that he would speak to each of his men as soon as he could, to try to instill a fresh vision for a higher disciplinary awareness.

CHAPTER 17

MEETING THE TROOPS
THE FIRST NIGHT AT GARIBAN

As soon as he had broken from his meeting with Capt. Swanson, Clint headed straight to the tent of his new platoon sergeant, Sgt. First Class Keith Ayers. Before he stepped into the tent, he wanted to get this right.

Establishing rapport between a platoon leader and the platoon sergeant is crucial because there is no relationship that is more important in a combat platoon. The platoon sergeant is often a seasoned combat veteran with several tours under his belt. The platoon leader, by contrast, is often a younger lieutenant, though in command of the platoon and over the platoon sergeant in the chain of command, who has either just gotten out of West Point, Officer Candidate School, or some Army ROTC program at a major university, which are the typical paths to a commission in the Army.

A good platoon leader must rely on his platoon sergeant, should respect his platoon sergeant, and should heed the advice of the platoon sergeant, especially during times of combat when the platoon sergeant ordinarily has seen much more combat than the platoon leader has ever seen. But, at the end of the day, the platoon leader is in command of the platoon.

Sometimes this creates an inherent tension, because the platoon sergeant is oftentimes the most valuable member and the most experienced member of the platoon, and the entire platoon knows it. Yet the platoon, in some cases, is under the command of an officer with little or no combat experience.

Clint knew this. Undoubtedly, Sgt. First Class Ayers also knew this. So did every man in the platoon. Ayers had been with the platoon since August of 2011. Clint was coming in cold turkey. Therefore, Clint wanted the relationship off on the right foot.

He needed to show an immediate level of respect to Keith Ayers, both for his position as platoon sergeant and based upon his combat experience.

Clint was eager to show his respect to Keith Ayers. But he also needed to establish clear, but respectful chain of authority, giving the clear signal that the platoon leader would be in command of the platoon.

Hopefully, one factor would make this transition a bit easier than under normal circumstances. Clint was not coming in as some "butter-bar" second lieutenant with no experience. First off, Clint was a first lieutenant, not a second lieutenant. The bar on his collar was silver, and on the chest of his battle dress uniform, black. He carried more experience and a higher rank than a typical second lieutenant who had never seen action. He lived through combat on his previous tour in Iraq.

He did not possess the same level of direct hand-to-hand combat experience that Ayers had. But at least Ayers wasn't dealing with someone who had never taken cover from inbound rockets or incoming mortar rounds, or someone who had never been shot at before or had never seen death along the side of the street or bodies strewn across the battlefield.

Clint was not concerned about any of this. He knew what he had to do.

A few moments later, he arrived at the entrance of his platoon sergeant's tent. Ayers was about 6 feet tall, slender—maybe 170 pounds on a good day—with a physique that resembled that of a distance runner. He was Caucasian, but dark-complexioned—the obvious result of hours in the hot, brutal sun.

Ayers was a little taller than Swanson, and looked more battle-tested than the captain. From the rugged contour of his chin, to the callousness of his palms revealed when they shook hands, Keith Ayers bore the look of a seasoned warrior, of a man who had served his country on multiple tours. Of that there was no doubt.

Ayers welcomed Clint, respectfully, but looked a bit tired in the face. Then again, maybe not. Then again, maybe so. Clint wasn't sure. But if Ayers were tired, he had reason to be. The man had been through hell and back in the last month. Even still, everything about Ayers showed strength and resolve. Ayers was gracious and professional. Obviously, Clint was not the First Platoon leader that Ayers had broken in.

Now, where to start?

After their hellos, Clint at first decided to share with Ayers Capt. Swanson's concerns about the need to improve platoon discipline. By citing Swanson's directives, Clint hoped to avoid the appearance that he was personally criticizing Sgt. Ayers or the platoon. Although he agreed with the captain's recommendation, by making it clear that this was the captain's directive, Clint wanted Ayers to know that both the platoon leader (Lorance), and the platoon sergeant (Ayers), were both under orders by the company captain to improve platoon discipline. This would give them a common objective to take on together, to work together as common members of a team, and to achieve together.

Nah. Clint hesitated.

That could wait. One of the marks of good leadership is the flexibility to change one's mind at the last second, if instincts so require. After what Ayers and his men had been through, Clint decided to wait until they got to their ultimate duty station to go over the discipline checklist that

Capt. Swanson had given him. The last thing that this good soldier needed was the impression that anyone was trying to pile on him. It is much easier to play armchair quarterback than to play quarterback. He tried a different tact.

"Hey, Sgt. Ayers. You look like you could eat a couple more sandwiches." It was the perfect icebreaker.

The chain of command was concerned about issues such as soldiers out of uniform, soldiers not shaving, or soldiers not always adhering to strict military regulations and standards that improved the unit's mental sharpness. A lot of these details could wait. First things first.

Clint could deal with all that in the days to come. But for now, having his platoon sergeant back him up would be a valuable asset. After all, Ayers knew all the guys. Clint knew none of them. Not yet, anyway. This meeting, first and foremost, was about establishing a good rapport with his new platoon sergeant.

Then came the main point that Clint wanted to emphasize. How to approach this? He went straight to the point.

"Sgt. Ayers, I want none of our platoon members brought home in body bags. I want nobody else medevacked out, like Lt. Latino. I want no soldiers with their legs and arms blown off by land mines, like PFC Walley. I want nobody with shrapnel blown into his stomach, like PFC Kerner."

Clint avoided mentioning Matthew Hanes. The shooting was still too fresh on everyone's mind, and Clint did not want Ayers to think in any way that he was responsible for what happened to Hanes. Because Ayers was not responsible. What happened to Hanes was a product of restrictive rules of engagement, and a change in American war strategy that called on American troops to become much more passive and less aggressive against the Taliban.

"Yes, sir." Ayers nodded in respectful agreement. Of course he did. Who wanted more wounded soldiers? Who wanted more soldiers killed or getting their arms or legs blown off?

Yet, why did Clint sense that Ayers might not have been as confident in this goal? Ayers did not disagree, with the goal, at least not openly. In fact, he agreed, and was respectful and cooperative about it. Maybe Clint was imagining that Ayers seemed skeptical. Maybe the skepticism, if real and not imagined, came from all the bloodshed the sergeant had seen in the battlefields around Payenzai in the last month. Perhaps it came from seeing First Platoon shot at every day. Either way, Ayers had earned his stripes.

"One other thing, sergeant."

"Yes, sir?"

"I would like to meet my men."

"Yes, sir. When would you like to begin to meet them?"

"Immediately."

"Right away, sir."

One by one, Ayers introduced Clint around to the men of First Platoon. Clint spent about 30 minutes with each man, finding out where they were from, what they like to do, and just trying to get to know them as best as he could in such a short timeframe.

After a while, Clint excused Ayers, as the sergeant needed some sleep, but kept searching his men out all night long. Some were pulling guard duty, even up on the lookout towers at the Strong Point. Clint found them all, sacrificing all sleep that night, but he wanted them to know that he was there for them, that he cared about them, and was going to bring them home alive. He spent most of the night walking from one lookout tower to the other, until just before sunrise, he had touched base with them all.

Tomorrow, they would return to Payenzai. Then, 30 days after that, if they all survived, they would return home to Fort Bragg.

It had been a long night, and with Clint's adrenaline exhausted, fatigue had started to set in. He checked his watch. Maybe he could catch a few minutes of sleep before daybreak. He needed some rest, that was for sure, if even a

CHAPTER 18

THE RETURN TO PAYENZAI
JULY 30, 2012

The sun rose above the eastern Afghan horizon at 5:05 that morning, and with it, cloudless skies and no break from the merciless heat. Another day from hell was on the way.

One by one, they rolled out of their racks. Some had managed to get a little shuteye. Others had not. Today, they would return to the fields of death.

What was on their minds as they prepared to return to Payenzai?

They had spent the last five days at Gariban getting battle fatigue counseling, sequestered in the relative safety of the post and its fortified walls. No worries inside Gariban about stepping on a landmine and getting their legs blown off, or about having someone shoot them through the head or through the neck from out of nowhere. Now, that was about to change. Again.

Each one of them experienced different emotions, each man with his own perception about what happened. But perhaps Payenzai could be best described by Sgt. First Class Ayers, who talked about it in detail, at Clint's court-martial at Fort Bragg in 2013.

> "Prior to Lieutenant Lorance arriving, we only had one relationship in the village of Payenzai and that was the farmer that lived directly south of our strong point. Most of the rest of the compounds in

that village were abandoned and occupied by the Taliban. We had never been able to really go far into the village of Payenzai due to the high IED threat in there. It was an abandoned village. Every time we went into an abandoned village in the area something bad happened, so he was pretty much the only person we talked to in that village."

When a veteran, seasoned platoon sergeant such as Keith Ayers described the village that they were heading to as, "every time we go there, something bad happens," one can imagine the emotional psyche of the young 18-, 19- and 20-year-old soldiers who were experiencing combat for the first time.

But now was not the time to worry. Nor was it the time for hesitation.

Whether they had slept or not, the men of First Platoon had a full day ahead of them. Clint had discussed the logistics of their return to the Strong Point with Sgt. First Class Ayers the night before, and even though about a mile separated the two bases, they decided that the return could not be accomplished in one single movement. Moving the platoon back to the Strong Point would take most of the day.

Part of that reason dealt with logistics. It will be best not to march the platoon through the intense heat, which presented a constant health hazard. With the temperature at sunrise at 100 degrees, and a noontime high predicted to reach 108 degrees, even on routine combat patrols, the heat proved problematic. Men could drop on a dime to dehydration and heat exhaustion. If not properly managed, heat could kill like the Taliban.

Therefore, better to move them by vehicle, to avoid prolonged heat exposure.

They were also concerned about Taliban snipers.

A long march through the heat from Gariban to Payenzai would leave the entire platoon open to pot shots from

Taliban gunmen hiding behind rocks, somewhere in the trees, or behind a bush, not visible to the naked eye at first blush. No one saw where the sniper shot came from that felled Matthew Hanes and Clint wanted to avoid a replay of that tragedy.

And then, the risk of IEDs along the roadside remained a concern. While the company had worked hard to keep the roadway clear between Gariban and Payenzai, and had strung c-wire along the road to protect the route, nothing was guaranteed.

The Taliban planted bombs in the ground at night, under the cover of darkness. Even with Aerostats in the sky, the Taliban continued planting IEDs that killed and maimed Americans. First Lt. Latino, Pvt. First Class Walley and Pvt. First Class Kerner were all evidence of the Taliban's continued success in planting bombs all in the ground, despite improved surveillance from American air cover.

Both Clint and Sgt. First Class Ayers agreed. They would transport the platoon back to Payenzai, piecemeal, by armored vehicle.

But this plan presented a logistical challenge. The platoon had only three armored vehicles. One had to remain at Payenzai, to provide for armed defense against potential Taliban strikes. The second need to be stationed in the road, between both strong points, to deter the Taliban from trying to plant mines in the road during the troop transport process back to Payenzai.

That left one armored vehicle available for the platoon for transport. The vehicle, like the MATV that Clint rode from Pasab two days earlier, could carry between four and five soldiers on each trip. Multiple trips would be required during the day to transport the entire platoon.

Clint decided to ride in the first vehicle with the first group of soldiers to the base, to begin to set up and establish things as he saw fit. Sgt. First Class Ayers would ride in the last vehicle out, to make sure that no one had been left behind.

Clint checked his watch. *6 a.m.* He looked up at his men, and gave his first command of the day.

"Okay, guys, it's time. First group to the vehicle. Time to roll. Let's go."

And with that order, First Platoon began its move back to the fields of hell.

For many of them, Hanes, Latino, Walley and Kerner weighed on their minds. For others, their stomachs knotted. The order brought lumps to their throats. They knew what was out there—the most barbaric, murderous face of radical Islam in its most brutal form. No greater evil existed anywhere in the world.

But paratroopers had no time to fear. Only to obey their orders from their superiors, and carry out their duty to their country. And give their all, as duty required.

CHAPTER 19

The armored vehicle, a MATV carrying First Platoon's new commander and four other members of the platoon, cleared through the fortified checkpoint at the main entrance of Payenzai.

As the MATV rolled to a stop inside the triangular-walled HESCO fortress, Clint hopped out and accepted salutes from the soldiers of Chainsaw Troop (Charlie Company) who had maintained security for the last few days while First Platoon had been recuperating at Gariban. He returned their salutes, thanked them for their service, and then commenced a self-guided inspection of the remote Strong Point that would be under his command for the remainder of his tour in Afghanistan, which would end in a little over 30 days.

With Sgt. First Class Ayers still back at Gariban, overseeing the transport, Clint had brought along with him in the first group of soldiers transported back a senior NCO named Staff Sgt. Chris Murray. Murray was the next senior NCO in the platoon, under Keith Ayers.

In the few hours that he had at Gariban, Clint had conducted a quick assessment of all his men the night before. One man who stood out, in addition to Keith Ayers, was Staff Sgt. Chris Murray. Standing at about 5 feet 9 inches, Murray wasn't as tall as most of the other soldiers in the platoon.

But he looked to be in great physical shape, maybe the best physical shape in the platoon. Murray wore a stoic look on his face, and bore a focused intensity about him that would carry him as a long way as a soldier, as long as he wanted to stay in the Army.

As he met each of his soldiers at Gariban the night before, Clint spent a few minutes with each of them to ask about their long-term hopes and goals. Many had not given much thought about the future. Perhaps that is understandable for young men between 19 and 24 years old, whose main goal at the moment was getting out of Afghanistan alive.

But when Clint popped the question to Staff Sgt. Murray, Chris Murray knew what he wanted to do. "I'm going to finish this tour and hope to enter the Special Forces Program at Fort Bragg, sir!"

Clint knew what that meant. Staff Sgt. Murray wanted to finish this combat tour in Afghanistan, and then go back to Fort Bragg to train to become the most elite of elite in the U.S. Army Special Forces, to become a Green Beret.

Staff Sgt. Chris Murray was a highly motivated soldier, and it showed from the beginning. Because he was highly motivated himself, Clint loved working with other motivated soldiers. Motivated soldiers could create monumental results. Clint knew from the beginning that he and Chris Murray would get along great, even in the short time that they would have together.

First Platoon was scheduled to be deployed at Payenzai for three more weeks. After that, they would head back to Kandahar Airfield, where they would out-process, and then fly back to Fort Bragg to rejoin their families. Then, their tour would be over. If Clint could keep these guys alive for another three weeks, his job would be done, and his sole mission accomplished. With two excellent and motivated in NCOs like Keith Ayers and Chris Murray at his side, Clint felt confident that he could get the job done.

As Clint and Staff Sgt. Murray inspected the grounds, walking in the intense morning heat to examine the compound for security purposes, one of the first things on Clint's agenda was to meet with the Afghan National Army, or ANA contingent stationed at Payenzai. Clint's need to meet with the Afghan platoon leader could be traced back to President Obama's surprise announcement on June 22, 2011, that the United States would pull out of Afghanistan and turn the fight over to the Afghan National Army. They called it "Afghan in the Lead."

Up until that point, everything about the war had been run, prosecuted, and controlled by the U.S. military. But with Obama's instructions to turn military operations back over to Afghanistan, even before the Taliban had been defeated, the U.S. Army had come up with ways of transitioning that turnover back to the Afghan National Army, leading to the birth of the "Afghan in the Lead" program.

Under "Afghan in the Lead," local American commanders devised strategies to begin transitioning control and prosecution of the war to the Afghans.

In the Zhari District of Kandahar Province, here's what that meant for Clint's paratroopers. Although the troopers of the 82nd Airborne would still provide the bulk of the firepower for combat patrols into dangerous sectors controlled by the Taliban, members of the Afghan National Army would start taking a more active role in the missions, particularly foot patrols through the countryside. In the case of the missions by First Platoon, that meant that the Afghans had to take the physical lead, by marching out in front of the single-file combat patrols, out in front of the Americans, into the mine-infested battlefields as they prosecuted the war against the Taliban.

Clint checked his watch. Today was June 30. Tomorrow, July 1, was their first scheduled mission with the Afghan National Army into the villages around Payenzai. Therefore, they had some mutual planning to do, and Clint needed to meet with the platoon leaders from the Afghan National Army today in order to plan for tomorrow's first mission. Because Ayers had not yet returned from Gariban, Clint took Chris Murray to the meeting with the ANA to discuss mission planning.

As it turned out, however, this meeting would go above and beyond a simple briefing for the next day's combat patrol, commencing July 1. The Afghans had one concern on their minds, above all else.

Motorcycles.

The African National Army had come under increasing attack by Taliban operatives on motorcycles, and the ANA platoon leaders wanted to express their concerns to Lt. Lorance and Staff Sgt. Murray.

To understand the Afghans' deep concerns over motorcycle attacks, let us consider the verbatim transcript of SSG's Murray's sworn testimony at Lieutenant Lorance's court-martial. The testimonial exchange set forth below is between Captain William Miller, the Army JAG officer and assistant prosecutor in the case, and Staff Sgt. Murray, who was answering questions under oath. Testimony took place in the military courtroom in Fort Bragg on July 30, 2013.

> Capt. William Miller, Military Prosecutor: "Did you attend a meeting on 30 June with Lieutenant Lorance and the ANA?"
>
> Staff Sgt. Murray: "Yes, I did."
>
> Miller: "Can you describe what happened at that meeting?"
>
> Murray: "At that meeting—it was a mission brief for the next day's mission. It was myself, an interpreter, the ANA platoon sergeant, and Lieutenant Lorance. I just briefed the mission for the next day; the interpreter obviously interpreting for me. Lieutenant Lorance was there. I briefed

the mission, giving the idea, the concept … what we're going to do.

"And then after I was done briefing the ANA platoon sergeant and the interpreter had a back-and-forth; it seemed to last two or three minutes. And basically, when they were done the interpreter interpreted to me and Lieutenant Lorance, who said that the platoon sergeant said that a lot of their soldiers—ANA—had been killed by guys on motorcycles recently. And that they were going to be firing at guys on motorcycles. And at the end of that it was just, you know—Lieutenant Lorance said, okay, good. And that was it."

Therefore, from the testimony of Staff Sgt. Murray, it is clear that the Afghan National Army platoon sergeant had one thing on his mind.

Death by motorcycle.

Many soldiers in the Afghan National Army had been killed by Taliban insurgents using motorcycles. This was becoming an increasing problem, and the ANA, which was loyal to President Karzai, wanted to put a stop to it. The ANA made it clear to that if they were going to be leading the platoons into the battlefield, that if another motorcycle approached at high rates of speed, the Afghans would be firing, in order to protect themselves. As will later be seen, this is exactly what the ANA would do (open fire on a motorcycle) within two days of this very meeting.

CHAPTER 20

By the middle of the afternoon, as the final armored vehicle mission rolled in from Gariban, a new synergy flowed at Payenzai. As his men were setting up tents and new equipment that they had brought back with them from Gariban, Clint wanted to keep his men optimistic, to keep their heads up, and give them reason for hope.

"Three more weeks, gentlemen. Just 30 more days and we head home." Clint reminded them that if they would hang tight with him, if they would follow the higher level of safety standards and protective measures he was about to impose, they would all go home to their families, and within the month.

As the men gathered in the midst of the Strong Point, preparing for commencement of battlefield patrols, which would begin tomorrow, Clint announced five new measures that he, as a new platoon leader, would impose that had not been employed before, all in an effort to keep them safe and alive.

The first of these five measures was securing the new platoon drone. Clint had pulled some big-time strings back at Pasab, just before he left, and made arrangements to bring the drone, complete with aerial surveillance camera, with him to Payenzai. The drone would give them an opportunity to keep a better eye on the movements of the enemy in the battlefield, and help them to head off disaster before it struck.

On the afternoon the 30th, once the entire platoon had arrived, the men gathered around the center courtyard area inside the Strong Point, focusing on the new drone that Clint had somehow managed to snarf away from Pasab.

First Platoon's new drone was classified as an RQ-20 "PUMA" built by AeroVironment Corp. in Simi Valley, Calif. About 4 feet long, with a wingspan of about 9 feet, the drone resembled a miniature Cessna, single-engine aircraft. With a single, battery-powered propeller in the nose of the aircraft, it could be launched by hand, and then flown by ground-based remote control.

The PUMA carried both an electro-optical and an infrared camera for remote monitoring of everything on the ground, both during the daytime and also at night. It could fly up to nine miles from its launch point, and could climb up to 10,000 feet. The PUMA could hang in the air for a maximum of two hours, without a re-charge, before it had to land. When its mission was complete, the navigational system was programmed to return to a GPS-selected landing spot on the ground.

Clint acquiring the drone was a major coup for the platoon. No other platoons in the area had one, and the price tag on this baby? A cool $250,000.

Contacts. Clint had them.

Hopefully, the damn thing would work. If so, they were in business.

"Okay, guys," Clint said, "let's keep it over the air space right above the Strong Point here. If it goes down outside the walls of the Strong Point, I don't want to go outside the walls looking for it. Not today, anyway." He looked at his men. "Let's see what we have. Anybody wanna try to fly this thing?"

Spec. Todd Fitzgerald, a young paratrooper from Tennessee, stepped up to the plate, and got the job.

"Okay, let's do it," Clint said.

They cranked the battery-powered engine, which buzzed almost like a bumblebee, and then, taking a running start, tossed the drone into the air. A moment later, it nosed up into the sky, climbing high above the Strong Point. The sight of the small, unmanned American aircraft flying circles over the top of the base, soaring like an eagle against the blue afternoon sky, sent a jolt of excitement through the men.

Maybe the drone could have saved Matthew Hanes. They would never know. It would've given them a better opportunity to spot the position of the enemy sniper, and perhaps chance to take him out before he could have gotten off a shot. The drone gave them more reason for hope that they could come back alive. And Clint had laid down the law. He would to take no missions out on combat patrol unless a drone was launched in advance.

The drone landed from its test flight, and they moved on to Clint's second new protective measure, the erecting the sky camera.

While the HESCO barriers that made up the three triangular outer walls of the post ranged anywhere from 7 to 10 feet high, depending on the amount of steel-barbed c-wire that had been bolted on top, the highest points at Payenzai were the three guard towers, each located at the three "points of the triangle" of the HESCO walls. The guard towers, two of which were manned by paratroopers in the 82nd Airborne, with the Afghan National Army manning the third, provided a high ground for defensive fire in the event that the post came under siege by Taliban insurgents.

The observation decks on top of the guard towers rose about 30 feet off the ground. This height gave the platoon the best position to look out over the village of Payenzai, and to monitor the village and the dirt roads and grape fields around the Strong Point for enemy activity. Even still, two or three soldiers at the top of the guard tower have their limitations.

And when it got dark, visibility became more difficult, even through night vision goggles, with their limited range.

Clint wanted something better for his men. He had envisioned a high rise, supercharged camera when Lt. Col. Howard first appointed him as the next platoon leader back at Pasab. But wanting something like that, and pulling it off in this era of strict Obama budget cuts against the military, might be easier said than done.

Clint got lucky to find the UAV back at Pasab. But his quest for a tower camera looked less promising. He had rolled out of the Strong Point on June 27 still without camera in hand, and without a definite plan on how to make this happen. His luck got no better at Sia Choy. No sky cams, anywhere in sight.

So far, Clint's "asking around" technique that had worked so well in securing the Puma UAV for the platoon, had so far fallen flat on its face in this quest for a tower cam.

But Clint believed in the old axiom that "the third time is a charm," and he also believed in the words of wisdom for the from the great Georgetown basketball coach, John Thompson, who once said that, "Luck follows those who work hard."

He would not take "no" for an answer, and would push until somehow, some way, he found a sky camera for his men.

Then, pay dirt! Well, maybe.

When he learned that an extra Cerberus camera, along with a telescoping pole used for a mounting tower, happened to be lying around, unused, at Gariban, for Clint, Christmas could be coming in July.

The Army's Cerberus surveillance camera tower was a versatile combat tool that used perimeter ground radar to detect and track potential attackers. It used motion detection software that could pick up movement outside of the base, and track the image of a target inbound toward the base. Even better, the camera could switch to infrared at night, and monitor Taliban who might be approaching the Strong Point under the cover of darkness.

In many ways, the system is like a super camera, an all-seeing "eye in the sky" that functions even at night, which would give First Platoon a tremendous tactical advantage over any Taliban operatives outside the walls of Payenzai, or attempting to plant bombs on the grounds where American troops will be operating.

If Clint could get his hands on this baby.

The camera would sit atop a telescoping pole about 40 to 50 feet into the sky, which means it would rise above all of the walls and even the three surveillance towers at Payenzai. In this way, the men of the platoon would be protected by a superior detection system, on multiple fronts, in comparison to the guards maintaining visual lookout on top of the towers.

Like cockroaches scrambling out from under a large rock, the Taliban flourished at night. The Taliban planted IEDs in the ground at night. In fact, the IEDs that took out Lt. Latino, Pvt. First Class Walley and Kerner most likely had been planted at night.

The Cerberus camera system would give First Platoon the opportunity to fight back against the Taliban's nocturnal activities. Using high-powered infrared cameras, the system could monitor large swaths of ground around the Strong Point at night. If the Taliban tried to plant bombs over the next two to three weeks, during the remaining time of First Platoon's deployment, this Cerberus camera would allow the paratroopers to lock and load, and to take care of business.

Clint wanted this system so bad for his men that he could almost taste it.

But just because he had discovered the camera system in storage at Gariban, that did not mean he could grab it and take the system to Payenzai. The system was a powerful tool, undoubtedly in high demand.

Only one man stood in the way of his grabbing the camera for First Platoon, Capt. Swanson. And nothing would stop Clint from making a pitch.

Making a beeline back to the captain's tent, he found Swanson in the middle of some paperwork.

"You wanted to see me, Clint?" the captain asked, his voice as chill as a cup of crushed ice in a Slushee from a 7-Eleven store.

"Sir, I want to ask you about the Cerberus camera system that I found. Nobody seems to be using it."

Swanson looked at him. Clint continued.

"Well, sir, I was wondering if anybody else was planning to use it with the next three weeks."

"You wanna take the system with you to Payenzai?"

"Roger that, sir. That would be great. Thank you, sir."

"Go for it."

It was that easy. And with that, he had acquired a second powerful tool for defending and protecting his men, one just as powerful, probably even more so, than the UAV, which had to be recharged after two hours. The Cerberus camera offered 24/7 surveillance.

Sometimes, maybe it helps to have a laid-back captain.

Clint smiled at the thought of it.

He smiled again on the afternoon of the 30th, as he stood out in the midst of the Payenzai compound, about to deploy the new camera system for his platoon. "Okay, men! Let's get this tower in the air. Let's get this baby up and operational. Move it!"

He stepped back, crossed his arms, and watched his men pushing up the 40-foot telescope tower, like a giant finger pointed to the sky, with the powerful Cerberus camera mounted on top. It reminded him of the Marines raising the flag on Iwo Jima, some 67 years ago, when they took Mount Suribachi to establish the high ground against the Japanese.

Now, here in the Zhari District, with the UAV that he had acquired, and now the "super eye" in the sky, the men of First Platoon would establish the "high ground" against the Taliban. And the high ground was one of the greatest advantages in war.

A definite excitement and confidence now permeated the air. Good. These men had needed a morale boost. But they still had work to do. Clint yanked his shirt off in the middle of the heat, and then jumped in to help his men put up a new tent in the center of the base, which would serve as the platoon's new command post.

The new command post marked the third concrete step, in addition to the drone and the "eye in the sky," that Clint had ordered to protect his men and improve their chances to survive in the final three weeks of their deployment.

Up until now, First Platoon did not have an established command post headquarters tent at Payenzai. But now, from inside the new command post, not only would Clint engage in battle planning with his senior NCOs, and issue orders for his platoon, but they would also monitor the images from the new UAV flying over the battle space, and would monitor images and information from the new tower camera, as they kept close track and monitored Taliban positions and movements outside the base.

By late in the afternoon of the 30th, the first three protective steps that Clint had brought to first platoon were now in place. The UAV was ready to fly. The eye in the sky camera sat atop the 40-foot tower, ready to conduct surveillance. And the command post tent was now in place, ready to serve as the central nerve center of operations once combat began.

Tomorrow morning, the final two pieces would be added to the new, battle-ready look of First Platoon. The new, bomb-sniffing dog team that Clint brought from Pasab would be stepping off on patrol with them at about 6 a.m., with dogs capable of sniffing out and detecting bombs buried several inches deep into the ground. And then, once their patrol got under way, new air support from U.S. helicopters would enter the area, a new addition that Clint had made arrangements for in order to beef up aerial surveillance.

Clint checked this watch. It was late afternoon, and he had not slept in several days. He knew that he needed sleep, but there was no time for sleep. Tonight, he had to meet with his platoon sergeants and squad leaders to discuss tomorrow's battle plans.

He hoped to catch an hour or two of shuteye before pushing off for tomorrow's combat patrol.

If they were not attacked tonight, tomorrow they would be in battle. It would be a new month, and a new start. Survive the month, and then go home.

CHAPTER 21

July.

The month had finally arrived that their tour in Afghanistan would come to an end.

July.

If they could survive July, they could return home to their families, spouses, fathers, mothers, and children. July had arrived, and so had their final month in hell.

Eight days had passed since Cpl. Matthew Hanes had been shot in the throat by a Taliban sniper who remained at large. The sting of the shooting remained so fresh that it felt like it happened yesterday. For the men of First Platoon who were there, the image of their beloved mine hound, lying unconscious under the hot sun, bleeding from his throat, appearing on the cusp of immediate death, lingered like a gaping wound.

And in other ways, the eight days since the shooting seemed like an eternity both to the men of First Platoon, and to its new commander, Lt. Clint Lorance.

Now, they had to return to battle. They had to put the shooting behind them and find a way to make it through the next three weeks. The shooting occurred in June, just over a week ago. But July had arrived. A new month. Perhaps a new beginning. Perhaps a fresh opportunity to do things differently. Perhaps the end of American bloodshed, and then they go home. Three more weeks.

At 3:58 in the morning, Clint opened his eyes for the final time that night. He had tossed and twisted, and turned some more, battling for even a little bit of sleep leading up to the big day. And maybe, in fact, he had dozed for 30 minutes here, or napped for 15 minutes there. But the adrenaline flowing in his body and the cortisol seeping into his bloodstream set off rapid-fire checklists that kept flashing through his mind.

If Clint had a weakness, it was all think and no play. He was thinking all the time, even at night, and the mental gymnastics would not cooperate with his body's need for rest.

July 1.

He had thought about it all night.

July 1 meant two things. First, today marked day one of the "Afghan in the Lead" program. So in addition to all the logistical issues related to taking his own men back out into the minefields, he would also have to coordinate with the Afghans, to make sure that the Afghan National Army was in the right place, as it led the American platoon out into potential battle.

Something about the Afghans leading the Americans made Clint nervous. In the war on terror in Afghanistan, the Afghan National Army had not always proven to be the most reliable military partner to the U.S. Army.

But, aside from the "Afghan in the Lead" policy starting today, July had another significant meaning.

Each day, he knew, between now and Aug. 1 would be a calendar-marking exercise. If they could make it through the month of July …

Outside this war-torn hellhole called Afghanistan, the rest of the world marched on. Divorces, weddings, inaugurations, and deaths made the international headlines.

Yesterday, Mohammed Morsi had been sworn in as president of Egypt. The controversial actor Alec Baldwin married his girlfriend, Hilaria Thomas, at St. Patrick's Cathedral in New York City. Philadelphia Eagles quarterback Michael Vick and Jade Jagger, the daughter of rock star Mick Jagger, had gotten married in Miami and London, respectively.

Vicious storms had ripped through the midwestern United States, through Ohio, Virginia and Maryland, killing 13 Americans. The day before, on June 29, movie stars Tom Cruise and Katie Holmes finalized their divorce.

In Great Britain, the Wimbledon tennis championships had been under way for a week, scheduled to be completed one week from today, on July 8.

But none of that mattered to a single man in the First Platoon. Right now, the next three weeks would determine whether they lived, or died. Finishing their mission, then going home alive. That was all that mattered to them, and it was all that mattered to their new platoon leader, Lt. Clint Lorance.

In skivvies and a brown T-shirt, Clint hopped off the cot, got into his uniform, grabbed his canteen and his razor, and stepped outside the Alaska tent, into the early-morning dark. He unscrewed the canteen, poured cold water on his hand, slapped the water on his face, and started to shave.

With each stroke of a cold, wet blade scraping against his neck and under his chin, he replayed every aspect of the day's battle plan.

Their mission on July 1 would send them on patrol to search out an abandoned village about two kilometers north of the Strong Point. Clint had been briefed about this village, known as the village of Mullah Shin Gul, by the troop commander, Capt. Swanson, and also by the senior noncommissioned officers in the platoon who had concerns about Mullah Shin Gul. Intelligence had shown that the Taliban would launch attacks against First Platoon, and then retreat to this abandoned village, where they would hide out, and wait for the next attack.

By all accounts, the natives who lived in the village had fled and abandoned it for fear of the Taliban. With the village abandoned and left to the Taliban, perhaps the sniper who shot Matthew Hanes may have fled there, and might even still be there.

Their mission would be akin to the cavalry in the Old West, searching an abandoned ghost town occupied by outlaws. Except that these radical Muslim outlaws called the Taliban were far more vicious than the worst of any of the outlaws of the Old West in America.

And if they found Taliban, Clint would wipe them out. They would pay for what they had done to Hanes, and the other members of the platoon, if they got unlucky enough to be in the village when First Platoon arrived.

The target village sat between two dirt roads that ran due north of the Strong Point. These roads, which ran parallel to each other on a north-south axis, were identified as Old Chilliwack Road and New Chilliwack Road. Signs were placed all along these roads instructing civilians to keep off of them, and restricting them only to military and police units. The light traffic on either road that was not military traffic was usually Taliban, and especially Old Chilliwack Road, which will come into play later, as this was the road that the motorcycles were on, the next morning, just before Clint ordered members of his platoon to open fire.

But today, Clint would take his platoon to the abandoned village, but not   over either one of the roads. They would, instead, cross by foot over the open ground, across grape fields, and over open land between the Strong Point and the village. In this way, their approach would less likely be detected by the enemy. Or so they hoped. Of course, the danger of cutting across open grape fields and rows of open ground was obvious. The ground was thickly planted with IEDs.

The thing about combat was this: No soldier, not even an officer, is ever guaranteed survival at the end of the day.

Clint was here, after all, shaving at the sink and about to step into dangerous Taliban country, because his predecessor, Lt. Latino, had stepped on a hidden IED and gotten shrapnel blown into his stomach.

Latino was lucky to survive. It was possible, even today, that Clint might not be so lucky. War was a lethally dangerous affair. For any soldier, including a platoon leader, every second in a battle zone could be his last second on Earth.

The enemy recognized officers in the field, and officers were a higher-priority target than even enlisted soldiers, fulfilling a long-held maxim in warfare: kill the officer, decapitate the leadership, and the troops will scramble in confusion. Whether that maxim is true is another question.

These paratroopers were among the finest soldiers in the world, and First Platoon had carried on its military mission under the capable leadership of Sgt. First Class Ayers, for two weeks, in the absence on officer.

Even still, whether that kill-the-officer maxim was totally true, perception becomes reality. The higher the rank, the greater the target value for the enemy. The Taliban knew that the single black bar that Clint wore on his uniform chest and on his helmet marked him as target No. 1 in the field.

Clint had long ago resolved he was willing to give his life for his country, and to give his life for his men. If that happened today, then so be it. Beyond that, he never thought about dying. The constant possibility of death came with the territory.

Much better to focus his mind on his mission.

He scraped the razor across his chin. *Almost done.*

As the quarterback on the football field must be aware of where every player is it at every moment, on every play, today, Clint would have to keep his mind in the game, accounting for all his men in battle, at every moment they were outside the Strong Point. He would have to think about where every man was, about every man's job, and monitor constant updates as the day progressed.

And as the coach of a football team breaks his unit up into three squads, consisting of offense, defense, and special teams, so, too, had First Platoon been broken up into three units to carry out its mission. These units, which rotated between each of the three squads every day, included 1) foot patrol, 2) force security, and 3) quick reactionary forces.

All three units were crucial to the platoon's ability to carry out its mission, to defeat the Taliban, and to survive until the next day.

Force Security Squad. The squad responsible for maintaining force security had the responsibility of protecting the Strong Point against enemy intruders, to make sure that all entry points into the encampment remained secure, and to monitor both the drone and the new sky camera that Clint had been responsible for bringing to the platoon. The force security squad was headed by the sergeant of the guard who reported to Clint and who rotated every day as the squad assignments also rotated each day.

Quick Reactionary Force. The squad assigned to quick reactionary force duty remained on emergency standby, to back up either the foot patrol or force security squads in the event of an emergency. For example, if the unit on foot patrol were pinned down by the enemy, or if Taliban tried breaching the walls at the Strong Point, then the quick reactionary force would swing into action. If no emergency situations arose during the day, then the quick reactionary force could use the day as down time, to rest, in preparation for the next day, when they would return to foot patrol.

Foot Patrol. Of the three squad assignments, foot patrol was by far the most dangerous. Each of the squads, every three days, would go on an assigned foot patrol route outside the base, or sometimes referred to as "outside the wire." The phrase "outside the wire," referred to stepping outside the c-wire, meaning that the men would open up the coiled-up barbed wire that had been strung around the post and along the roads to create an obstacle against the Taliban coming in. They would step out, by foot, into the dangerous booby-trapped roads and fields, where they would search for Taliban operatives.

These were the guys, on foot patrol, most likely to step on landmines, get blown up by IEDs, or get shot by Taliban snipers. Latino, Walley, Hanes, and Kerner had all been taken out while on foot patrol. Under Clint's planned rotating assignment system, every paratrooper would go on foot patrol duty every third day.

There was one exception to that every third-day rotational assignment. Clint Lorance, the platoon leader, would go on foot patrol duty every day, therefore tripling the level of personal danger that he would be facing himself, as compared to the danger faced by his men. This, the highest-ranking member of the platoon, becomes target No. 1 for any enemy, especially the Taliban.

Clint finished shaving and then headed over to the mess tent, where one of the sergeants had managed to fire up some hot coffee. He needed a shot of caffeine, so he poured water from his canteen and replaced it with hot steaming coffee. *Perfect.* Black and strong. The first swig helped jolt him a bit more.

Next stop, the new command post. Clint wanted to check in with the overnight duty sergeant to see if anything had happened while he was asleep. This is where the new overnight camera would prove beneficial, because its infrared radar capabilities would provide protection in the dark.

He assumed that the night had gone well, lest they would have awoken him. Still, his morning routine as long as they remained in Afghanistan would be to check the command post first thing.

"What do you have for me, sergeant?"

"Quiet all night long, sir." The sergeant turned around and looked up at Clint. "Camera works great. All quiet, sir. If anything was out there, we'd have seen it. Or heard it."

"Great news, sergeant." Clint took a swig of hot, black coffee. "Maybe the calm before the storm, but I'll take it." He checked his watch. Almost 4:30 a.m. Sunrise came at 5:05, about 35 minutes from now.

Time for the UAV launch, the next pre-deployment item under Clint's stepped-up security plan. Clint wanted the bird up at first light, to get a visual inspection of the ground below. The drone would fly in pre-mission reconnaissance in the hour or so before the mission stepped off from the Strong Point. It would broadcast live streams back to the command tent so that Clint and his senior noncommissioned officers could see what they would be facing once they moved outside of the Strong Point. By Clint's instruction, the UAV would fly over the general route of the squad's planned foot patrol into Taliban territory.

By 5:30 a.m., the drone was airborne, headed north from the Strong Point, across the thick grape rows, and out toward the suspected Taliban village. Inside the command post, Clint huddled with his platoon sergeant, Sgt. First Class Keith Ayers, and with Staff Sgt. Chris Murray, who would be the patrol leader on the morning's mission.

They squeezed in around the small computer screen, watching aerial images of the dangerous Afghan landscape. The drone first passed over the east-west running dirt road, called Old Cornerbrook, off the northern boundary of the Strong Point. Though not visible from the camera angle, this road ran to the western entrance of the village of Payenzai, where Matthew Hanes had been shot and would be the destination for tomorrow's patrol.

But as Old Cornerbrook Road passed out of view, the landscape below resembled an odd combination of the ocean and mounds of leaves. The appearance of long grape rows and thick grape fields early in the morning looked almost like rolling swells on the ocean. The color of the leaves from the grape vines and bushes at this time of morning, moments after sunrise, looked to be a dark green. In between the long lines of grape vines and bushes, ran narrow rows of dirt, separating the vines.

The long grape rows stretched from east to west. But the squad's destination was due north.

The platoon would have to physically climb across each of these rows, one by one. Their journey would be a hot, arduous, dangerous task. And when they were in the bottom of the rows, sometimes this created visibility problems. The height of the grape rows, which often exceeded 8 feet, made visibility from the bottom of the row almost impossible. The Taliban could, in theory, be on the other side, and you would never know until you came over the top.

The Taliban occasionally planted IEDs in the grape rows, even if that meant taking out Afghans, just to kill Americans. When you hopped over the grape mound and down into the trench on the other side of the row, you could step right on an IED.

Another danger would come when they moved out of the grape fields and across more open ground. At that point, they would become susceptible to sniper fire.

The UAV footage showed no signs of active Taliban or anyone else in the area of the morning's proposed foot patrol down below. But IEDs under the ground would not be visible from the aerial camera aboard the UAV. The absence of Taliban, for the first leg of the mission, was a positive sign, as Clint remained concerned about sniper fire.

The pre-mission briefing with Ayers and Murray gave Clint even more confidence in his senior NCOs. Clint was grateful to have Murray at his side today, and that Ayers would be on tomorrow's patrol. "Okay, guys, let's brief the men and get this show on the road."

Clint put on his helmet, stepped out of the tent and headed over toward where his men stood, waiting for him.

Per standard procedure, First Platoon would receive two briefings before stepping out from "under the wire" and into the battle zone. The first of the two briefings was given the night before the mission, by the officer in charge. Clint had delivered that briefing last night, when he explained that the mission of moving north to the village Mullah Shin Gul was to look for Taliban hanging out, and if necessary, to destroy a Taliban stronghold.

The second pre-mission briefing, referred to as "the patrol brief," commenced moments before the mission began. The sergeant-in-charge of the patrol would deliver the patrol brief. Clint crossed his arms, stepped back, and turned the show over to Sgt. Murray.

Murray began the briefing without hesitation, and with a crisp and professional cadence, went into meticulous detail about each and every plan and contingency plan that the platoon might be required to execute within the next two hours.

"Okay, men, any questions?"

A few hands went up. Most of the questions were about the new changes Clint had brought to the platoon, how the UAV flights would work with the helicopters and about the dog teams. A couple asked about the new "Afghan in the Lead" program.

Murray's responses were short, concise, and on mark. The man was all business. "Anything else?"

Clint checked his watch. Fifteen minutes till showtime.

"Line 'em up, sergeant."

"Roger that, sir."

"Okay, line up! Let's line up!"

Murray moved up and down the line of the squad, barking orders, and making sure the men were assembling in a tight single-file formation, spaced about 15 feet apart. This process was known as the Formation and Order of Movement, or FOOM. The tight, single-file formation kept everyone in tight step behind the mine detection operator, known as the "mine hound," at the front of the line, who swept the ground for IEDs. The platoon's last mine hound, Cpl. Matthew Hanes, had been shot in the neck. Today would mark their first mission with a new mine hound.

But sometimes, the mine detector misses. Thus, the 15-foot interval of spacing between the soldiers provided a protective buffer, both in front of and behind the poor sucker who would step on the landmine and get blasted into a bunch of blood-saturated goo.

Clint had checked his M-4, double-checking the order of movement when the ruckus started.

"What the hell?" He looked up at the front of the line. The Afghan patrol leader was screaming something, probably in Pashto, the native language, and was yelling in the direction of Sgt. Murray. Clint jogged up the front of the line near the main gate. "What's going on?" he yelled at the interpreter. Here is how Clint would later describe the event:

"Well, we got up to the gate to leave the Strong Point, and Sgt. Murray started to get everybody in position in the order of movement that we would move out under the wire. And technically, this is called the FOOM, Formation and Order of Movement. So Murray started getting everybody in position correctly. And we brought the Afghans and put them up front, the Afghan squad leader started yelling at the interpreter that he does not want to go up front.

"He wants to go behind. But, I told him that he does not have a choice. That's the way things are from here on out, and that is a decision that has been made far above my head. He argued, for a little while about that. The Afghans, there were only six of them, didn't like the new policy and were afraid to be up front. There were 16 of my men going out, and they expected us to protect them. And truthfully, they were not very good soldiers. But I held my ground, and so they moved out, but very begrudgingly. They did not like it."

With the Afghan squad now at the front of the formation, and with the American mine hound close in behind,

Clint checked his watch. *7 a.m.* The UAV flight had been completed. The dog team was in place. Helos were overhead. All checklist items complete.

"Okay, sergeant, open the gate! Time to move out!"

"Roger that, sir. Opening the gate!"

CHAPTER 22

Following Alpha Team, Clint and the other member of the headquarters element stepped out the main gate of the Strong Point, onto Old Cornerbrook Road. The bright sun, a blistering bitch, hammered them with a pulsating, radiating heat. Temperatures eclipsed 99 degrees an hour ago, and now exceeded 100 degrees. Sweat drenched his uniform, like a sponge soaking warm water, and they had not yet even started the arduous process of physically climbing over 8-foot high grape-row mounds.

This mission was scheduled to last anywhere between two and four hours, depending on what they ran into. But even if they ran into no hostile fire, the grueling heat and physical terrain challenges would make this mission harder than the hardest obstacle course that the Army had put them through during basic training.

Over to his left, one of the gun trucks, which had been permanently stationed outside the gate and armed with a 240-caliber machine gun, stood watch, as a sentinel to deter any Taliban elements from attempting to move toward the Strong Point. Across the way, Clint could see the beginning of the grape berms in the grape fields they would have to cross in order to get to the abandoned village.

Even though the dirt road outside the main gate had been swept for mines better than any other terrain in the immediate area, they nonetheless maintained their tight single file formation as they crossed the road toward the grape fields.

Across the road, maybe 30 feet away, the Army had strung c-wire all along the perimeter of the road. Clint waited as sergeant Murray unhitched the wire on the other side of the road, to give the squad room for passage into the grape fields.

Following the Afghans, Clint's men stepped across to dusty gravel road, through the opening in the c-wire, to the thickly leafed, dirt-mounded grape rows. Clint followed them across the road, ducking under the c-wire, into the edge of the southern part of the grape field.

The view of the rows from the drone's aerial footage, which resembled green horizontal lines on a yellow legal pad, seemed unrecognizable compared to standing here and staring at the long leaf-covered, mud-baked wall that they would have to climb across. From here, staring into the massive 8-foot high wall, stretching as far to the east and west as the eye could see, the long, leaf-covered walls reminded him of standing on a beach and watching a tidal wave about to roll in. The closer Clint got to it by foot, the larger the green wave appeared.

The lead elements of the patrol, with weapons strapped on their backs, began to reach up to the top of the hard, mud-baked ridge, full of grape leaves, and pull themselves up over the top.

"Move! Move!" Sgt. Murray's voice snapped from up front, as one by one, the men under his command pulled themselves up to the top of the ridge, straddled the top of it, and then dropped down to the other side. At times like this, all the physical training the paratroopers endured paid off. Clint was in excellent physical shape, as a runner, and worked out every day back at Pasab. But the physical conditioning of these men was extraordinary.

They had been repeating the same dangerous exercise, in extreme heat for the last month or more. And now, once again, they had begun to traverse a real-life obstacle course.

They moved, quickly and deliberately, each climbing over the top of the wall. A moment later, as the last man in Alpha Team reached the top of the wall, it was Clint's turn.

He looked up, strapped his rifle over his back, reached up, grabbed a hard mud clod above his head, and started to replicate a chin up maneuver. He tried putting his boot somewhere to get traction, maybe a rock or a hard dirt clod, but nothing was there, except for grapevines and leaves. He would have to do this only with upper-body strength.

Hanging onto some grape vines, he yanked himself up to the top of the ridge, then swung his feet up and pulled himself to the top of the long mound. He allowed himself a quick glance, but not too long, because up here, he could be a target for snipers. When he saw the Strong Point behind him, and the village of Sarenzai over to his left, he shifted his feet down off the other side and dropped into the opposite trench.

When he hit the bottom, what he saw reminded him of what trench warfare must have looked like in World War I. In here, he could see nothing, except a large wall of earth and vines in front of him, and a large wall of earth and vines behind him. Yes, they could walk laterally down the rows, but everyone knew that the rows had been mined with IEDs, and only the locals and the Taliban knew where the bombs were planted. The only way in and out was to climb over the walls, drop down the next wall into the trench, then do it over again.

It would be up-and-down, up-and-down, across these ridges for the next mile, all the way to the target, until they broke out into the open, a few hundred kilometers in front of the abandoned village.

As he pulled himself up over the next wall, feeling the strain of the next chin-up, he marveled at what great shape, physically, his men were in. *These men are bad asses*, he thought to himself. *The best America has to offer.*

They kept moving, single file, pulling themselves up and over baked-mud wall after baked-mud wall, dropping into the trenches, and then climbing again, moving steadily to the north. By 8 a.m., the temperature had climbed up to about 105 degrees. The men were drinking water to try and avoid dehydration.

Clint worried about the dog team. He had learned while working with the team back at Pasab that if dogs became overheated and dehydrated, it could impair their ability to sniff out explosive devices.

The German shepherd that Clint had brought from Pasab was a real trooper. He had seen the men pulling themselves over the mud walls, and tried to copy them and jump the walls himself. But an 8-foot mud-baked wall proved too much for even an athletic German shepherd. The men in the bottom of the trenches had to lift the dog up, while the men on top of the walls reached down to pick him up and pass him over to the men on the other side.

But the dog appeared to be panting too much for comfort, and Clint worried about him getting overheated. He ordered the men to get the dog a water bottle, stat. The dog responded with an energized tail wagging episode, and lapped down on the water bottle like a baby taking milk from a bottle.

They had now been in the trenches well over an hour, continuing to move north, like a long, creeping inchworm, hugging both the 8-foot dirt walls and the low crevices all at once. And after that first hour, two things became most obvious. First, it was even hotter than hell out here. And second, thank goodness he had arranged to get the helicopters up in the sky for the first part of the mission.

Having the pilots overhead gave Clint confidence that they were not blindly climbing over these grape walls and into a Taliban ambush. At least somebody in the air could see something. Clint had several soldiers around him as part of the headquarters element. This included two soldiers dedicated to radio communications, including the RTO (the old designation for Radio Telegraph Operator) and the FISTER (forward observers who are part of the Fire Support team).

They were down in the trenches, about to scale the final wall, when the first sign of trouble came over the radio.

"Sir!"

Clint turned around. The corporal who was on the radio with the airwing had a worried look on his face. Something wasn't right.

"What have you got, corporal?"

"Sir! CCA is reporting they have spotted armed insurgents. Only a few hundred meters to the east of our target area, sir." CCA was the Army's acronym for Close Combat Attack helicopters.

"How many?"

"Just a few, sir."

"That's great," Clint said. "Tell them to open fire."

"They can't open fire, sir. They lost track of the insurgents."

"Crap!" Clint thought for a second. "Okay. Tell CCA that if those insurgents come out from under their rocks and start approaching our position, I want them waxed. Is that clear, corporal?"

"Roger that, sir," the corporal said, and then proceeded to relay Clint's message back over the radio.

Great. Snipers confirmed in the area. Possibly in range. He needed the air team to keep them at bay until the squad could approach the target area.

"Okay, let's get across this wall and get this show on the road."

Clint pulled himself up, onto the final ridge, and at this point could see the target village in sight. But with snipers possibly in the area, he did not want to linger along at the top of the row and make himself an easy target.

He grabbed hold of some thick grapevines on top of the row to stabilize himself, and allowed himself to drop down the 8 feet or so to the ground. He crouched down for another visual of the village of Mullah Shin Gul, which was now a couple of hundred yards or so in front of them, across an open field to their north.

Under the hot, baking sun, which hung in the morning sky off to their right, the village resembled a Pueblo-style mud-hut village, the type that you would see in Arizona or New Mexico. In some ways, it could have been a ghost town from an old western movie, a one-street structure of continuous adobe mud that stretched from east to west.

The concern that snipers might be hiding in the village meant they could not tarry on their final approach. Although there was a direct opening across a field between the squad and the village, they moved over to their right and decided to approach the village hugging the western edge of a smaller grape field. They would not have to climb across rows, as they had before, but if they came under fire, they could duck inside the grape rows to their right for protective cover.

They inched forward, to within 20 yards of the eastern edge of the village and decided to send the Afghans in for reconnaissance. Once again, when the interpreter delivered Clint's order, the Afghan patrol leader's face reflected a look of fear, and he hesitated. The Afghan National Army was, for the most part, flat-out petrified of the Taliban.

But Clint would not take any crap off the Afghans. He ordered them to go in and do the recon to determine if anybody was in the village. After jawing for a few seconds through the interpreter, the Afghan patrol leader relented, and turned to motion his men to follow him in.

Clint and his men took a knee, just to the right of the grape rows, and waited. The Afghans were undependable. Yet, on this, his first day in command in combat in the field, he had been ordered to give them more responsibility than they wanted to accept. This presented some challenges, such as trying to turn men into soldiers who were never really soldiers to begin with, whose discipline level was low, and whose will to fight was sometimes nonexistent.

But if the U.S. Army were going to withdraw at a certain time, as President Obama had now declared, then the Afghans would have to learn to fend for themselves, or be slaughtered after the Americans left. Clint checked his watch. Five minutes had passed. Why did he have a hunch that he might have to take his patrol in there, into the village, to clean up the Afghans' mess?

About five minutes later, the Afghans emerged from a different part of the village and started walking quickly toward the Americans. They seemed excited about something, and their leader kept shouting something in an animated voice, in Pashto. "What's he yapping about?" Clint asked the interpreter.

"He says they have discovered an IED," the interpreter said.

Clint motioned the Afghan leader back over to his position, and huddled with Sgt. Murray. "Okay, gentlemen, this is my first direct encounter with an IED in the field. I'll entertain your recommendations on how to eliminate it."

As the interpreter translated Clint's words into Pashto, the Afghan platoon leader waved his arms and got more excited and more agitated.

"What's he saying?"

"He wants to destroy the IED with an RPG."

Clint looked at Sgt. Murray, who shrugged and said, "Why not?"

"Okay," Clint said. "Fine by me. But let's get our squad back far enough away from the blast zone, so that nobody gets hurt."

Clint ordered his men to pull back to the south, about 200 yards to the western edge of the smaller grape field, to give them enough of a buffer from the blast. The grape field, with its 8-foot berms, would also give them a place to duck for cover if the blast set off any sniper fire.

Motioning for the Afghan commander to lead the way, Clint walked out into the open field, to the left of the smaller grape field, to get a better angle on the site of the IED. The Afghan commander pointed to the ground under an archway at the main gate to the entrance of the village.

The Afghans' RPG launcher was a shoulder-fired, small rocket launcher, shaped like a long tube, about 5 feet long. The rocket, or the explosive "warhead" as it is sometimes called, was plugged into the front of the barrel of the tube, and shaped almost like a genie bottle.

The warhead bulged out, slightly wider than the diameter of the RPG barrel. At the back of the RPG, a hollow exhaust, almost like the tailpipe on a car, allowed the blast and smoke to shoot out behind the soldier firing it. In the bottom middle of the long, tube-like weapon, a handle grip and a trigger allowed the shooter to control and fire the launcher.

Clint watched as the Afghan commander went down on one knee, put the RPG launcher on his shoulder, gripped both handles, and stabilized the weapon by resting his elbow on his left knee, which was not on the ground. The Afghan aimed at the IED at the base of the main gate.

The commander finally seemed excited about the mission, in contrast to the cowardice he displayed earlier in the morning, when he cowered and resisted taking his troops out front. Perhaps the fact that no Taliban were in the village emboldened the Afghan commander. Regardless, Clint was pleased about the Afghan's positive attitude adjustment.

A second later, the Afghan mumbled something, and Clint put his hands over his ears to brace for the shot.

The commander pulled the trigger, igniting a sharp sound, like a loud rifle shot, then a blast and a powerful swoosh and smoke billowing out the back of the RPG launcher. The bottle-shaped warhead screeched through the air toward its target, producing the shrill sound of pressurized air, and leaving a trail of smoke behind it.

A second later, the explosion at the base of the gate shook the ground. The Afghan popped his fist in the air with excitement. Mission accomplished.

"Let's go." Clint led the Afghan back over to the edge of the grape field where his men were waiting.

As soon as he reached his men, Clint got an earful from his senior NCOs.

"Sir, please don't ever do that again!"

"What do you mean?"

"Sir, you were out in the open, totally exposed, and you could have gotten shot. That was a brave thing to do, but you were totally exposed to sniper fire if somebody had been out there. We can't afford to lose another officer."

Most of the admonition had come from Sgt. Murray. Clint had been in the Army as long as some of his senior NCOs. But he did not have the same degree of combat experience. He had been under fire many times in Iraq, but today marked the first time that he had ever taken a platoon on an offensive combat mission into enemy territory for the purpose of attacking the enemy.

His men were right. The platoon could not afford to lose another platoon leader, and not so soon after losing Lt. Latino.

But the NCOs weren't finished giving their opinions. After the RPG had blown up the IED, the NCOs were convinced that the squad was about to come under fire and urged Clint to get the heck out of Dodge.

Plus, the helicopters had just been called to another mission, and could not remain on station much longer. With the choppers leaving, the fuse had burned down closer to the dynamite.

Clint made the decision to return to base, and to take a different route back, to try and speed up the return. They would not cross back over the grape rows, but instead, would first move to the west, to a ridge of trees which ran beside Old Chilliwack Road, then turn south and head back toward the entrance of the Strong Point.

Old Chilliwack had been identified as a Taliban stronghold. Plus, there was a greater chance of IEDs planted along this route. But Clint had to speed up the return, as they were about to lose air cover. Plus, his NCOs were probably right. The armed insurgents that the helicopters had spotted an hour or so ago were still somewhere in the area, and had not been eliminated. He would have to depend on his mine hound and his dog team to ferret out any IEDs that might be up front.

"Okay, men, let's move out! Stay low and move quick. Be careful and stay tight behind the mine hound. Watch your trail."

They turned, again moving in single file behind the Afghans and headed west, over toward the tree line that ran along the north-south route of Old Chilliwack Road.

The men up near the mine hound, moving in line right behind him, had to drop baby powder along the ground, to the left and to the right, to show the borders of where the mine hound had swept the ground. The baby powder on the ground marked the outer edge of the safety lane, about three feet wide, at max.

Best to step straight down the middle of the baby-powder lane, if possible. The men farther back from the mine hound also continued to sprinkle the baby powder along the borders, to make sure that the men behind them had a clearly marked safety lane.

Often, the Taliban opened fire on an American platoon that was moving single file down a narrow baby-powder lane. Why? Because once shots were fired, a soldier's instinct was to fan out either to the left or the right and hit the ground. That's what the Taliban wanted, because bombs were planted in the ground to the left and the right.

Clint was aware of this tactic, and when the helicopters spotted armed insurgents nearby, about an hour ago, he worried that the Taliban might try something as his men moved single file toward the tree line. When they arrived at the tree line, several minutes later, fortunately, nothing had happened, perhaps because the helicopters were still overhead.

They regrouped at the road, then turned left, headed south, and walked parallel to the tree line beside Old Chilliwack Road, only a few feet to their right. From here, it was about a two-kilometer walk down (about 1.2 miles) near the intersection of Old Chilliwack Road and Old Cornerbrook Road, by the entrance of the Strong Point.

Following this route by foot, as they walked parallel to Old Chilliwack Road and the tree line to their right, they would pass the grape field on their left that they had crossed as they moved north earlier in the morning toward the village of Mullah Shin Gul.

On the return route, they would sacrifice safety for speed. The trenches protected them from sniper fire, provided that the Taliban was not also in the trenches. The problem in the trenches was that no one could see anything outside the trenches. This would leave them blinded, and without air cover up top, they could fall into a Taliban ambush, as the Taliban knew the grape fields better than the Americans. Clint would not leave his men out climbing across the grape rows, on the way back, without air cover.

They had turned south, moving down the tree line to paralleling Old Chilliwack Road, and were about halfway back, about a half-mile out, when the helicopters had to break off.

Just as soon as the helicopters left, the sound of rifle fire cracked the air.

"We're taking fire!"

The rear element of the patrol was under fire from insurgents somewhere behind the tree line along Old Chilliwack Road.

Clint recognized the sound of AK-47 rifle fire. Like the sound of a car backfiring across the street and coming down the road, the distinctive pop of the high-powered Russian bullet could not be mistaken.

He had to think fast. In most wars, American forces would turn, advance against the enemy fire, and counterattack. That was not possible in Afghanistan, because of the thick blanket of mines that had been planted in the ground. Oftentimes, the Taliban took potshots to try and bait the Americans into this tactical mistake.

If the Americans turned and charged at the shooter, the patrol would get blown up before it made it halfway across the field. The Taliban knew this all too well, which was why they were shooting. They hoped to kill an American with rifle fire, like the shot that hit Cpl. Hanes. But they really hoped to spook the patrol out of its tight single-file formation and set off a few IEDs.

Clint wasn't taking that bait.

He considered calling Sgt. Ayers, back at the Strong Point, and ordering him to launch the UAV. No. Not enough time for that.

With the lead element only about a hundred meters from the gate of the Strong Point, he had one best option. Try make it home, and take up the battle from inside.

"Okay, on the double! Stay low and get back to the Strong Point! Now!"

He turned and motioned for the men who were behind him to step up the pace. A couple of young officers had recently been disciplined for forgetting and leaving young soldiers out on the battlefield. But Clint Lorance would never leave a man behind. He would sacrifice himself before he ever left a man behind

Clint waited a second, as Bravo element and the weapons squad caught up with his position. With their heads crouched and moving at a double-time, they jogged past him, with an urgency on their faces, headed toward the open gate at the Strong Point.

Bullets whizzed by their heads, kicking up dirt all around their feet. This was the work of a Taliban sniper, coming from somewhere over along Old Chilliwack, behind the tree line. Perhaps the same sniper who shot Matthew Hanes only eight days ago.

A moment later, Sgt. Michael Herrmann, the squad leader of the weapons squad, which was catching the brunt of the fire, caught up to Clint. As he passed, he said, "Don't worry about it, sir. We will take care of it."

The sniper's shots came with a fury, echoing across the road and across the fields, so loud that the men inside the Strong Point could hear the incoming rounds. The sudden rain of bullets awakened soldiers back at the Strong Point who were trying to sleep.

Consider, for example, the testimony of Sgt. Daniel Williams, who testified at Clint's court-martial. Williams was not on the patrol, but was back at the Strong Point, trying to get some sleep after having been up all night as a sergeant of the guard.

> Civilian Defense Counsel: "And during that day, 1 July, around noon, you were back at Payenzai?"
>
> Sgt. Williams: "I was asleep, yes, sir."
>
> Civilian Defense Counsel: "And you were awakened by hearing gunfire coming from outside the wire?"
>
> Sgt. Williams: "Yes ... yes, sir."
>
> Civilian Defense Counsel: "So that was the patrol apparently was coming under fire?"
>
> Sgt. Williams: "Yes, sir."

Civilian Defense Counsel: "And you found out later that that patrol had actually been engaged as they were returning to base?"

Sgt. Williams: "Yes, sir."

As the sound of gunfire roused Sgt. Williams from his sleep, Clint arrived at the main gate with the final elements of the weapons squad. "Inside! Up on the walls. Quick. Let's give 'em hell, boys!"

CHAPTER 23

The squad had gone to the top walls of the Strong Point; their rifles came out toward the direction of the fire. "Stay low, guys. Don't give him a target." Their energy was flowing, and they wanted to take this guy out.

"Sir." Clint turned around and saw his weapons squad leader, Sgt. Herrmann. "I've got an idea that I think will take care of the problem, sir."

"Talk to me, sergeant."

"Sir, we just got in a new M-3 Goose, and I'd like to try that on these sons-of-a-bitch. I think that'll take care of the problem."

By M-3 Goose, Herrmann was referring to the M3 Multi-Role Anti-Armor Anti-Personnel Weapon System (MAAWS), a Swedish-manufactured recoilless rifle, known by the Swedes as the "Gustav Bazooka."

The powerful weapon, which the men of First Platoon called "the cannon" or the Gustav, could take out tanks, pierce armor, and eliminate enemy personnel in numbers. It fired a large, 10-inch explosive shell and had a range of 1,000 meters (1,093 yards) against stationary targets with rocket-fueled ammunition.

Like the more primitive RPG that the Afghan commander had fired at the IED at the village of Mullah Shin Gul earlier in the morning, the Gustav also featured an open propulsion system, allowing rocket blast and smoke to fire from its rear as its projectile launched toward the target.

The Gustav, a shoulder-fired missile launcher, was far more powerful than the RPG used by the Taliban commander, and far more powerful than the AK-47s used by the Taliban to ambush the American patrol.

If that 10-inch exploding shell landed anywhere near that sniper, or those snipers, that should take care of the problem. Clint had never fired the weapon, but he trusted his weapons sergeant's judgment. Plus, the men wanted to use this weapon against the Taliban sniper.

"Go for it, sergeant."

"Roger that, sir!"

Herrmann grinned and brought the weapon, which is about 3 feet in length, up to the banister, and positioned it over his shoulder. "Everybody steer clear and get out of the way!"

The men stepped aside to give Herrmann room to operate, as the sniper's bullets continued to crack the air. "Stand aside, gentlemen. We're ready to launch."

With a loud boom, the rocket shot from the Gustav leading a straight, white stream of smoke, streaking with a vengeance above the Afghan landscape, out toward the direction of the sniper's shots. A second later, a huge explosion erupted in the ground about 500 meters out, spewing smoke and flames into the air, and shaking everything all the way back to the Strong Point.

The men of the squad, still lined along the tops of the HESCO walls, broke out into cheers, igniting an electric synergy into the platoon. The shot sparked an instant morale boost that was diametrically opposite of the despondency that hallmarked their need for counseling, which had sent them back to Gariban after the Hanes shooting only a week ago.

"Okay, hold it down! Hold it down!" Clint needed to see if the strike had done its job. When the cheering subsided, so had the sniper fire. The big gun had either killed the sniper, caused him to soil his underpants, or sent him running across the field in the opposite direction.

When Sgt. Herrmann had told him, a few minutes earlier, that he would "take care of it," Clint was not sure what Herrmann meant. But now, he knew. Sgt. Herman had brought overwhelming firepower against the Taliban snipers. And frankly, after the debacle with Cpl. Hanes, Clint wanted to show the Taliban that any sniper shots, against any American, would be met with overwhelming force.

Unfortunately, as will be seen, because of the softening rules of engagement, his command would not agree.

CHAPTER 24

"THE LAW OF PROPORTIONAL FORCE"
THE EVENING OF JULY 1, 2012

Under hot, oppressive, 100-degree heat, their first mission was complete. And, thank God, no deaths or casualties. The squad dodged a bullet this morning on the final leg of its first combat foot patrol of the month. In fact, in what could only have been described as miraculous, divine protection, the men had dodged dozens of bullets fired their way on the final leg back to the Strong Point.

Taliban snipers were sometimes inaccurate from longer distances. The sniper had probably been several hundred meters away, firing at the squad in part to try and bait them into jumping outside of the mine hound's safety lane or get someone to jump out and step on an IED. That could have killed several of his men at once.

Clint's men, however, had maintained their composure under fire, kept their heads down and stayed inside the baby powder markings of safety lane. By the grace of God, they made it back to the Strong Point before a bullet struck anyone. With high-powered rounds landing in the dirt all around them, it was a miracle that nobody had been hit.

The sniper may have been outside of the AK-47's effective range of 400 meters. But although targeting became a problem beyond that distance, the AK could fire bullets up to a maximum of range of 800 meters, or about 2,600 feet.

One lucky shot fired, even from out of range, could be as deadly as a pinpoint shot fired at point-blank range. Still, although Clint's men had been lucky enough to escape the fire today, Clint kept thinking of Matthew Hanes, the young man gunned down by the Taliban sniper, only eight days ago, whom he had never met. Cpl. Hanes might have been struck by a lucky shot fired by a gunman from the rifle's effective range. And Matthew's sniper was still out there, somewhere.

Then again, after today, after that blast from the Gustav, maybe not.

That night, as Clint planned details for tomorrow's combat mission, he got a message from Gariban. Capt. Swanson, the troop commander, wanted a personal meeting, on the double. Clint did not have time for a meeting with the captain, and asked if he could send his platoon sergeant instead.

But Capt. Swanson would have none of that. He wanted Clint at Gariban, and wanted him there immediately. A little before 8 p.m., Clint dropped his crucial mission planning for the next morning and headed by armored vehicle down New Cornerbrook Road, the American-patrolled dirt road that connected Payenzai to Gariban. Note: To avoid confusion, there were two roads called "Cornerbrook" in this battlespace. "Old Cornerbrook" ran to the north of the Strong Point, and was more open to civilian traffic, while "New Cornerbrook" ran generally to the south of the Strong Point, was more heavily patrolled and controlled by the Americans, and connected Strong Point Payenzai (First Platoon encampment) to Strong Point Ghariban (Charlie Company headquarters).

Whatever Swanson had on his mind, Clint would make up the lost time by working a little longer into the early morning hours of July 2nd, after his meeting with Capt. Swanson. He had gotten no sleep for several days anyway. Why not a little bit more lack of sleep?

When Clint arrived at Gariban, a few minutes after 8 p.m., he was taken aback by the subject of the lecture. Swanson wanted a meeting to lecture Clint on the "law of proportional force."

The law of proportional force?

The platoon's use, that morning, of the Gustav cannon to wipe out the Taliban sniper on Old Chilliwack Road, who had opened fire on the American squad returning to the Strong Point, had raised concerns from up the chain of command about possible violations of then new, tightened rules of engagement.

The law of proportional force was a watered-down product of Obama's weakened rules of engagement, after unilateral announcement of the American pullout. These new rules embraced the notion that the weapons used by American forces to retaliate against the Taliban had to be just as weak as weapons that the Taliban tried to use in attacks against American forces.

Here is how Clint would later recall Swanson's lecture.

"He said, 'Clint, if they shoot you with an AK-47, you cannot fire a cannon at them.' "

Clint did not argue with Swanson. Swanson outranked him. But he later recounted to the author his opinion of the so-called law of proportional force.

"I disagreed with him," Clint said. "If you were stupid enough to fire on an American soldier, then you're stupid enough to be destroyed in any way that we can possibly destroy you.

"That's the way I looked at it," Clint continued. "It was also a psychological weapon against the enemy. And I leaned on Sgt. Herrmann, because he was our heavy-weapons guy, and he wanted to try out the new weapons system. I trusted his judgment. The whole platoon, even the Afghans, were excited about it. Because everybody loved having that kind of firepower against an enemy that would kill you as fast as they would look at you. The missile leaves a smoke trail in its wake, and it is awesome.

"But the commander did not look at it that way," he said.

In fairness to Capt. Swanson, the so-called law of proportional force wasn't his invention. It came from authorities above him in the chain of command. This suicidal rule was implemented via Defense and State Department officials in the Pentagon and at Foggy Bottom who were making efforts to appease the Taliban at this point in the war, and who were negotiating with the Taliban.

As an aside, perhaps it is a good thing that President Harry Truman was not bound by Obama's law of proportional force when he decided to end the Second World War by dropping an atomic bomb on Japan.

Moreover, this so-called law of proportional force would have violated Gen. Norman Schwarzkopf's famous use of overwhelming force in the first Iraq war that became famously known as "shock and awe."

Or can anyone tell George S. Patton, Jr. that he could only have waged war against the Nazis through the so-called law of proportional force?

Any weasel who would have dared suggest such a thing to Gen. Patton would've gotten slapped in the face, then received a steel boot up where the sun does not shine, before the great general went about his business of the destroying the enemy.

Even Gen. Colin Powell, at the time of the first Persian Gulf War, once said that "soldiers are trained to kill people and break things."

Proportional force doesn't break things or kill people. Overwhelming force does that. Proportional force, an intentional decision for the stronger combatant to fight with at least one hand tied behind his back, at best, leads to a tie amongst combatants, and even worse, leads to Americans returning home in body bags.

But there was a new sheriff in town in the White House in 2012, and his name was Barack Obama. And by the summer of 2012, the great "surge strategy" to destroy the Taliban, first suggested by Gen. McChrystal in 2009, and having at first been embraced by the president, had now been watered down into a domestic police action by U.S. soldiers on radical Islamic soil in a savage land thousands of miles from home. And the great American military doctrine known as "shock and awe," from the days of Bush and Schwarzkopf, had all but morphed, by design, into something along the lines of a pattycake game of tit-for-tat with the Taliban.

Clint kept his opinions to himself. Capt. Swanson outranked him. But Clint also knew that if his squad attempted to turn and fire in place against the sniper that afternoon, with proportional force, unable to spread out to take cover, some of his men would have been hit by bullets, probably even killed, and that the light M-4 carbines they were carrying would not have deterred a single sniper.

The sniper was likely hiding behind a tree. Or maybe a rock. The M-4 will not fire through a tree. But in Clint's own words, "that missile sure will. It will cut the tree right in half."

The bottom line is the Gustav cannon with its shoulder-launched missile had worked to stop the enemy, and to protect American lives. And no one had ever instructed Clint not to use the Gustav in response to sniper attacks. All this despite the new "law of proportional force" that Captain Swanson now advocated, as ordered by the administration.

But Clint, as a professional officer, would keep his opinions to himself, keep his mouth shut, do his job, and try not to be distracted by political bullshit, like the stuff he'd just heard from the captain, that got Americans killed.

Tomorrow, he would bring his men back into the village of Sarenzai, for the first time since Cpl. Matthew Hanes had been shot in the throat. He saluted his commander, acknowledged the lecture, and requested permission to return to his men at the Strong Point. Clint had a mission to plan.

CHAPTER 25

After his dress-down for violating the law of proportional force, the night of July 1 marked another night of restlessness. Clint could not pinpoint a single reason for his perpetual insomnia. While his mind always remained in active battle-planning mode, whatever was keeping him awake was deeper than that.

Perhaps tonight, the day's mental flashbacks about how close his men had come to death kept him churning. All throughout the night, the sound of bullets fired from somewhere off Old Chilliwack Road, rang in his ear, with sight of AK-47 rounds striking the dirt all around his men.

He took command of this platoon with a personal vow to keep all of these men safe. But in war, the margin between success and failure is often razor thin. He and his men had been on the right side of the razor today.

And then, the memory of Matthew Hanes, the young paratrooper whom Clint had never met but felt like that he had known forever, loomed large over these guys. Although nine days had passed since Matthew had been shot, the sniper barrage against the platoon on the morning of July 1 had occurred on the next day that these guys were on a combat patrol after the Hanes shooting. How close they had come to a repeat!

What a devastating blow that would have been to morale, if one of those bullets had killed one of his men. But today, they had dodged the bullet and lived to fight another day.

Only the protective hand of God had kept them from taking a bullet. It might take the hand of God sometimes, and it might take pushing from an obnoxious, hard-ass lieutenant. But whatever it took, Clint would bring these men home in one piece, come hell or high water.

Then, there was the memory of his men cheering when the Gustav cannon had done its job, and silenced the Taliban sniper in one mighty blast.

That mental image, of American soldiers, of his own men, cheering and fist-pumping, at the taste of victory, even a small victory, had brought a smile to his face more than once as he lay on his cot, replaying that scene over and over again. As close as they had come to death, how glorious it was to see his men experience the joy of victory in battle, by attacking the enemy with overwhelming force. That shot, that broadside from the cannon, had been fired for Matthew Hanes. And with all the cheering, it was like his men shook their fists at the Taliban, saying, "Take this for Matthew, you son of a bitch!"

But then came the twist that interrupted his sleep the hardest. Despite the platoon's joy over the much-deserved retaliatory strike against the Taliban, and the much-needed morale boost generated by the shot of the single cannon, the chain of command, obeying orders and policies handed down from leftwing politicians in Washington, had thrown a gallon of cold, ice water all over that victory when his company commander, Capt. Swanson, had called him back to Gariban, to ream him out, for violating the so-called law of proportionality. This bothered Clint the most, because he knew that this stupid rule, under the guise of a "law," would endanger American lives, and kill military morale.

The notion that if the Taliban fought with sticks and stones, the Americans had to retaliate with sticks and stones, was beyond comprehension. These thoughts churned together like a cold, wet load of laundry in a fast-spinning washing machine, the perfect brew for another sleepless night. Here is how Clint would later describe his inability to sleep on what would become his final night at Payenzai.

"I had stayed up until about 2 in the morning. And I remember that when I went to sleep, I told the sergeant of the guard, which would have been Sgt. Williams, that I want to be woken up at 3:30. Maybe I was trying to emulate my brigade commander, Col. Mennes, who never slept, 24/7. I remember getting only about 45 minutes of sleep that night.

"And when the sergeant woke me up, I was in one of those weird stages of sleep, and I instinctively jerked and jumped up off the cot, in an aggressive manner, for a moment not remembering where I was. I think they call it a myoclonic jerk.

"That's a psychological term where you are startled when you first wake up, you're asking, 'Where am I?' That was me. But I think I was in the wrong stage of sleep to be woken up. And when the sergeant woke me up, I kind of jumped to my feet. And he got startled by that and I felt bad about it. But I must have jumped up like a maniac, disoriented. But in reality, I was kind of in a weird sleep state and got awoken at the wrong time. I did not have enough sleep, and my body was trying to tell me to go back to sleep.

"First, I brushed my teeth, and then shaved. And then I went and got coffee to try to get more alert. I got into my uniform and headed over to the other tent, where the coffee was brewing. I needed a caffeine fix to get jump-started."

Coffee, as it turned out, was the only thing hot for the troops to consume in this hellhole. There was no hot food, and most of the troops lived and survived off MREs, which stands for Meal, Ready-to-Eat, self-contained field rations. For Clint, his go-to meal had become the Chocolate Chip CLIF Bar, which provided a nice taste and a burst of energy.

Here's how he would later describe his breakfast his final day as platoon leader of First Platoon.

> "Somebody was making coffee and it was in one of those big green— we call them green Marmite containers. They're these big thermoses, these big military containers that we store food in to keep the food warm. Except there was no warm food, except coffee. They have one that always had hot coffee in it. Other than that, we did not have hot food out there at all. We were all eating MREs, and CLIF Bars were the only thing that I ate when I was there."

Clint poured the steaming coffee into a one-liter plastic container, and took a swig. Even though the coffee was almost as hot as the air outside, or vice-versa, the results were refreshing and instantaneous. With a much-needed shot of caffeine in his system, and a spring back in his step, he headed back over to the command post tent, to begin executing the final checklist items as a run up to the beginning of this morning's mission.

Time to put on his game-day face. Today, their mission called for a dangerous foot patrol back into the village of Sarenzai. Unlike yesterday's mission to the village of Mullah Shin Gul, when they were uncertain about whether any Taliban might be present, the village of Sarenzai had a definite Taliban history. At Sarenzai, Matthew Hanes had been taken out. And on missions around this village, the platoon had lost its previous platoon leader and others.

Like yesterday's mission, today's mission would also require them to start out by climbing over steep, 8-foot dirt walls full of grape vines. They would exit their Strong Point, start crossing grape fields on a course due south, turn to the west and cross the road called New Cornerbrook Road, and then enter into another grape field. There, they would turn north and skirt along an open area beside another grape field as they approach the backside of the village.

Their route would resemble the pattern of a great fishhook—first moving out to the south, then hooking around as they crossed Old Cornerbrook, and then headed up to the north, along the grape field, to the back side of the village.

That was the plan, anyway.

John Steinbeck once warned that the best-laid plans, even of men, would sometimes go awry. Perhaps, somehow, Clint could have known that the day would bring a series of unfortunate events that would change his life forever.

With steaming coffee now in hand, Clint arrived back to the command post to receive a report from the sergeant of the guard, who at that time was Sgt. Williams, on the events of the night before.

"All clear, sir," Sgt. Williams had said, or words to that effect. For the second night in a row, the battlefields around the Strong Point had remained quiet. Good. With this pre-mission mental checklist now in full swing, time to make rounds by foot inside the compound to make sure that the guards were ready to go up in the towers.

He stepped back out into the muggy morning air, under quiet skies, and sipped more hot coffee even as perspiration began beading on his forehead. But Clint wasn't thinking about the sweat beads dripping from his nose. Even still, despite the heat, the tranquility of the early dawn painted a stark and eerie contrast to the dangerous firefight that his men had come under fewer than 20 hours before, a few hundred yards down the road, or of the bloody events that the coming day might bring.

The morning dawn screamed the question in silence. How could peace and war co-exist so closely with one another, so close in time, and so close in space?

Clint could not answer that question. And in any event, there was no time for philosophical contemplation. Not at the moment, anyway.

The mission.

His mind remained laser-focused on it—for the lives of his men would depend upon discipline, and in large part, upon his ability to focus.

Satisfied that his tower guards were in place, alert, and ready to go if needed, Clint walked back to the command post. But even before he stepped into the tent, something seemed wrong. But what?

Yes, that's it. The air was too quiet and too peaceful. He should be hearing noise by now, a buzzing noise in the sky.

Clint had issued standing orders, and had been clear on the standing orders, to put into place procedures for the protection of those men.

One hard-and-fast order—the UAV needed to be airborne at first light. That meant launching 15 to 20 minutes before sunrise, at the first sight of the gray light of dawn. But when Clint re-entered the command post, he discovered that the UAV was not in the air yet. And he was not happy about it. Here is how he later described what happened:

> "When I came back into the tent, I saw some of the NCOs moving around the command post. I ask what's going on with the UAV? They said, 'The UAV is broken.' Now it's true that the UAV is a fragile piece of equipment. The best way to describe it is that its fuselage is built out of a very hard Styrofoam. The propellers are plastic.

"But it is very expensive, and I think the price comes from the sophisticated cameras it carries. The NCOs said that the propeller was broken and the battery didn't work.

"But the UAV box that I brought from Gariban came with additional propellers. And I knew that it came with additional propellers, because when I did the inventory at the brigade, I knew about the spare parts. The reason there were so many boxes that came with the UAV was because inside one of the boxes, there is a fuselage, the next box was for all the screws. And it was very compartmentalized.

"We had the spare parts. And I knew, because I had personally done the inventory, that the soldier I'd assigned to UAV duty was full of shit, and I told him that. I told them that I did the inventory, and that I know what's in there, and I told him to go get the boxes, and find a propeller, and put it on there.

"Some of them were sort of used to giving excuses to their former platoon leader, and he would give in. And I guess they expected me to say, 'Well, I guess if it's broken, you don't have to use a UAV today.' But that wasn't going to happen.

"They also tried to bring up an issue with the batteries, saying that the UAV batteries sometimes fail. I knew that there was an issue with the batteries with the UAV. But I also knew that we brought spare batteries with us in case the battery went out. So they had no excuse for that.

"A couple of them were expecting me to say, 'Okay, we don't have to use it.' They did not want to have to piece together a new bird with all the parts. But that was the reason I told one of the soldiers (name withheld to protect the soldier's privacy) to get up early enough to get this thing ready. Because I knew there could be issues with it."

Clint would tolerate no discussions on the topic of "the UAV is broken," nor was he entertaining excuses for failure to carry out his clear order to get the UAV in the air by first light. The soldier in charge of getting the UAV in the air soon became the recipient of what is often known in the military as a good, old-fashioned "ass-chewing."

After getting in the soldier's face for failure to perform a crucial assignment on which lives depended, Clint fired the soldier from UAV duty, reassigned him to foot patrol duty, and told him to get the hell out of the tent.

He ordered Sgt. Williams, who was an E-5, to go get the platoon sergeant, Sgt. First Class Keith Ayers, who was an E-7, and the platoon's senior ranking noncommissioned officer. In many platoons, soldiers fear their platoon sergeant more than they even fear their lieutenant. One of the last things that an E-5 wants to hear is "go get the E-7," as that is the civilian equivalent of "I want to see the manager, and now!"

But Williams complied with the order, and in a few minutes, returned with Sgt. Ayers. Keith Ayers never made excuses, but only made things happen. That's why Clint had summoned him. Like Clint, Ayers had no time for bullshit, and would not tolerate bullshit, even if he had time for it.

"Sgt. Ayers," Clint said, as soon as his senior NCO stepped into the command post, "I want you to get this bird fixed, and get it in the air, now. We're not stepping off on patrol until I can get a picture of what the enemy is doing on the ground. That clear?"

"Yes, sir!"

Ayers took control of the situation, and Clint felt relieved. But he was still not happy that his immediate order had not been carried out.

Next time Clint saw Ayers, about 30 minutes later, he was standing on top of a large military convoy truck, about 20 feet in the air, holding the UAV in his hand, and barking orders to subordinates down on the ground who were holding the remote-control flight controllers. A second later, Ayers flipped a button that started the propeller on the UAV, held the buzzing bird high over his head, and tossed it into the air. The drone took to the air, as it climbed high above the grounds of the Strong Point.

Ayers was a soldier with a can-do attitude, the type of soldier who carried out his officer's orders without excuses, and who helped make the U.S. Army the best army in the history of the world. The platoon sergeant had gotten the bird into the air—albeit 30 minutes after Clint wanted it in the air—but still, with enough time to conduct aerial surveillance before the helicopters came on station.

The UAV snafu represented a minor setback, at least timewise. Now, with the need to check the live stream, conduct a pre-mission brief, and then get the platoon lined up in the proper order of movement, there was no time to spare. Clint checked his watch, then headed back toward the command post to view aerial streaming footage of the ground below, along their patrol route.

CHAPTER 26

VISITORS AT THE GATE
STRONG POINT PAYENZAI
JULY 2, 2012, 6:30 A.M.

Once again, the bird had passed close over long, stretching grape fields to the south of the strong point, then as the bird looped, it passed over more grape fields, heading back north to the village. Clint still was not happy about the delay. But no signs of enemy insurgents had been spotted in the drone footage, anywhere along the route. Even though the ground was full of land mines, hopefully, the men would be able to avoid a firefight on the first leg of the patrol.

Of course, yesterday's initial UAV footage also showed that the coast was clear, but the platoon still came under heavy sniper fire on the last leg of the mission. The drone's value was to a degree limited to the opening part of the mission. Clint would rely on the helos, once they showed up, to provide much more powerful air cover in the last part of the mission, and would pray that they were not pulled off station early again.

The UAV remained in the air, still flying circles over the proposed patrol route, to make sure that the route remained clear.

`Clint finished reviewing aerial footage, and had to move on with mission planning. He left instructions for his NCOs to alert him if anything, or anyone, popped up on the screen.

As Corporal Jared Ruhl, the assault squad leader for the day, worked to get his men in the proper order of movement prior to stepping off, Clint went over the final couple of checklist items that would need to be in place before he authorized the patrol to move out.

Victory in warfare required strategic positioning. On the high seas, that meant controlling strategic choke points, such as the Malacca Straits, the Singapore Straits, and the Bosporus, which separates the Black and Aegean seas. For victory on land, by armies moving across hostile terrain, strategic positioning was best achieved by either controlling the high ground, controlling bridges, or controlling strategic intersections that would allow for the observation of and control of traffic, particularly hostile traffic.

The threat posed by Old Chilliwack Road, the dirt road that ran north of both the Strong Point and the village, concerned Clint most. Old Chilliwack had a well-deserved reputation as a dangerous Taliban bastion. Part of the problem was that Old Chilliwack Road, at its southernmost point, made a 90-degree turn to the west and ran straight into the village, where First Platoon would be emerging from its foot patrol.

If one did not make that right turn into the village, but kept going south, Old Chilliwack bled into New Cornerbrook Road, where First Platoon would cross the road from south of Strong Point into the grape field for its approach on foot up into the village of Sarenzai. Any danger to the patrol would likely come down Old Chilliwack. So, Clint decided to position a gun truck by the intersection of Old Chilliwack and New Cornerbrook, outside the entrance to the village. This would allow the gun truck to monitor and check enemy traffic coming down Old Chilliwack from the north, which might threaten his platoon.

Consider the testimony, a year later, from Clint's court-marital, that revealed the dangerous nature of Old Chilliwack Road. Spec. Todd Fitzgerald responded to questions about the dangerous nature of the road, at page 460 of the court-martial transcript:

Civilian Defense Counsel: "And on 2 July of 2012, you knew and the members of your platoon knew that Chilliwack was a route commonly used by the Taliban."

Spec. Fitzgerald: "Yes, sir."

Civilian Defense Counsel: "It was a known enemy approach?"

Spec. Fitzgerald: "Yes, sir."

Civilian Defense Counsel: "And the day before the patrol on 1 July had received fire from Route Chilliwack?"

Spec. Fitzgerald: "Yes, sir."

Civilian Defense Counsel: (Pause) "And if you saw a motorcycle coming down Chilliwack towards friendly forces on the morning of 2 July, if it was coming quickly towards friendly forces that could look like a threat, couldn't it?"

Spec. Fitzgerald: (No response.)

Civilian Defense Counsel: "Yes or no?"

Spec. Fitzgerald: "Yes, sir."

Consider also, the sworn testimony of Pvt. First Class James Skelton, the first American to see the motorcycle speeding in, and the first American to fire on the motorcycle:

Civilian Defense Counsel: "Now, prior to engaging the motorcycle, you knew that Route Chilliwack was a common avenue of approach for the enemy, correct?"

Pvt. Skelton: "Yes."

Civilian Defense Counsel: "And you knew that the friendlies didn't use that road."

Pvt. Skelton: "They tell us they don't go up that area because it's dangerous."

Civilian Defense Counsel: "Right. So, again, you knew that the villagers didn't use Chilliwack because of the danger, correct?"

Pvt. Skelton: "That's what they've told us."

Civilian Defense Counsel: "And, sure enough, the people you've seen on Chilliwack have always been the enemy, correct?

Pvt. Skelton: "I've—from the general area of going up Chilliwack, it's usually been a hotbed for enemy activity."

Remember, the testimony we have just considered comes from soldiers who had been with First Platoon in the 30 days prior to July 2nd and who all knew the inherent danger posed by Old Chilliwack Road.

Because yesterday's near-deadly ambush had originated somewhere off of Old Chilliwack Road, Clint ordered the gun truck at the entrance of the Strong Point to move out and cover the intersection. Two soldiers manned the gun truck, which featured a 240-caliber machine gun, providing sufficient firepower to deal with anything the Taliban might try. Clint would move the gun truck a few hundred yards from the Strong Point, out to the intersection of Old Chilliwack Road, Old Cornerbrook Road, and New Cornerbrook Road.

From this position, the gun truck could see all pedestrian and vehicle traffic, if there were any, along all of the main dirt roads around the battle space where the squad would be operating this morning. By Clint's order, the gun truck would be facing to the west, generally, Old Cornerbrook

Road, meaning that it would be looking straight down the single road leading into the mud-baked village of Sarenzai.

Members of the platoon on foot patrol would first move from south to north, crossing grape fields south of the road, then would emerge from those fields, onto the middle of the village and onto Old Cornerbrook, later in the morning. Therefore, if the Taliban attempted any type of ambush against the squad as it emerged onto Old Cornerbrook Road, the gun truck could provide protective machine gun fire for the squad.

Off to its right, to the north, the gun truck could keep watch out over Old Chilliwack Road—the notorious Taliban route of choice—from which the squad had taken sniper fire just yesterday afternoon. And off to the left, or to its south, the gun truck could monitor New Cornerbrook Road, at least far enough to the bend in the road where the platoon would cross a little bit later in the morning.

Here is how Sgt. First Class Keith Ayers would later describe the decision to move the gun truck out from the gate to the position northwest of the gate at the intersection of Cornerbrook and Chilliwack. Note that he describes the danger of regular automatic weapons fire that has come against the platoon from Old Chilliwack Road.

> Sgt. Ayers: "Once we SP'd Strong Point Payenzai—no, prior to SP, we pushed the gun truck that mans the front gate out to—on Route Cornerbrook—Cornerbrook, just northwest of the Strong Point, to cover a regularly used firing point that the enemy engaged us as we were ex-filling out of our strong point. We had been—we had been engaged from that position approximately five or six times within, you know, a two- to three-week period, so—"

> Military Prosecutor: "How were you engaged there?"

Sgt. Ayers: "We would receive automatic weapons fire from that position."

Military Prosecutor: "From where, specifically?"

Sgt. Ayers: "Um (pause) uh—"

Military Prosecutor: "Just describe; was somebody dismounted ..."

Sgt. Ayers: "Dismounted, sir."

In this instance, Clint had taken Sgt. Ayers' recommendation to move the gun truck out as a protective measure, as Ayers had been present in the past for regular ambushes that had been originated from Old Chilliwack Road.

In addition to the first gun truck that Clint placed outside of the main gate, Gun Truck 1 (near the intersection of Old Chilliwack, Old Cornerbrook and New Cornerbrook), he also positioned a second gun truck, Gun Truck 2, in the far opposite corner of the battlespace from Gun Truck 1.

The positioning of the two gun trucks, in relation to the village of Sarenzai can be shown in the diagram below:

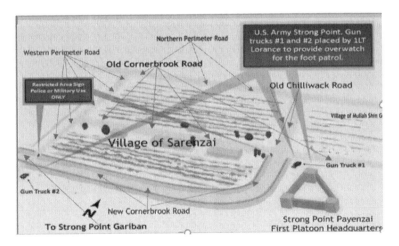

As pictured above, the village of Sarenzai had one dirt road slicing through the village, Old Cornerbrook Road, running from east to west through the one-street village.

Payenzai, home of First Platoon, was located in the space just outside the lower right of the diagram and not visible in the diagram.

Gun Truck 2 ordinarily remained on station on New Cornerbrook Road between the two Strong Points (Payenzai and Gariban). And because New Cornerbrook was the main transportation artery between Payenzai and Gariban, the second gun truck remained stationed along that road to ensure the security of the road and to try to prevent the Taliban from digging into the road and placing mines and IEDs in the road or along the road. The distance between Gariban and Payenzai was less than two miles.

To increase the security of the battle space even more, and to intercept any potential Taliban insurgents attempting to flee to the southwest, Clint moved the second gun truck closer to the battle space. He stationed it on New Cornerbrook Road, at the bottom left of this diagram.

Note, too, the Western Perimeter Road and the Northern Perimeter Road. These roads were also of great concern to Clint, because the Taliban could use them for motorcycle attacks, and as routes of escape after hitting the American platoon.

Both trucks were part of Clint's plan for reinforced security, along with a drone, and along with the helicopters, all of which would be in place before the mission even began.

*****

6:45 a.m.

Fifteen minutes until step off.

The mission was scheduled to commence at precisely 7 a.m. Part of the planned step-off time had to do with visibility. Seven a.m. came two hours after sunrise, and thus the landscape was illuminated by then. The heat was partly responsible for the start time. Afghanistan in July was hot as hell 24/7, and there was no such thing as the "coolness of the morning." The country was always an oven, and with sunrise temperatures often fluctuating between 90 and 100 degrees, combat missions always came down to pre-heat, bake, boil or fry.

With the air becoming a thermonuclear oven by mid-day, with the sun blazing down on the mud hut structures, and grape and poppy fields lining the Afghan landscape, the time difference between 7 and 8 a.m. might translate to a temperature difference of pre-heat versus bake, or perhaps bake versus broil, depending on where the temperature started to begin with. On July 2nd, the temperature at 6 a.m. hit 100 degrees, with a noontime target exceeding 110 degrees. Every extra degree above 100 felt magnified a hundredfold.

Because of rising temperatures alone, every man in the squad wanted to get the show on the road, to get the hell out there, and get the hell back, as soon as possible. Sidestepping the mines and battling the Taliban will be enough of a challenge, but battling the enemy under broiling temperatures compounded the difficulties.

Still, heat or no heat, Clint had to keep his head in the game for the safety of his men. As anxious as they all were becoming to get the mission moving, and to get it over with, there could be no distractions when it came to their safety.

With the gun truck now in place, the last element of his pre-deployment checklist was air cover from the helicopters. Clint had been assured that the birds would arrive on time. But with the air team, you never knew. There were more troops on the ground than birds in the air, and the law of supply and demand put a lot of demand on the helicopters. Depending on the situation, and on the time of day, the choppers could be called in a dozen different directions, or they could be delayed, depending on the situation on the ground elsewhere.

The last 30 minutes of yesterday's mission illustrated the helicopters' sometimes uncertain status. Clint had hoped to keep the birds overhead from the moment the squad left Strong Point until to the moment they returned. But in the mission's last 30 minutes, the choppers were pulled off station and redirected to another military emergency. It was at that point, when the choppers left early, that all hell broke loose, and the shooting broke out.

The No. 1 building block for achieving his goal, of keeping these guys alive, and bringing them home alive, was air coverage. Clint understood full well that air coverage gave American ground forces a tremendous tactical advantage. Thus, he wanted the UAV in the air prior to the mission, and the close combat attack helicopters overhead during the mission, as much as possible.

Clint believed that the Taliban understood this as well. In fact, even as they prepared for their second mission under his command, he remain convinced that had the CCA helicopters been able to remain on station for another 30 minutes the day before, that their presence would have deterred the sniper fire altogether.

Airpower provided brute force as a supplement to the ground troops. And at the end of the day, despite all their incendiary rhetoric and barbaric practices, brute force was only one thing that the Taliban understood.

Still, nothing from the air team. Clint checked his watch. As much as he wanted to pull out at 7—in large part because of the broiling called the sun—if the air team did not arrive, Clint would not allow his men to step off. Even if that meant waiting. Even if the CCA Air Team arrived a few minutes late. Given the trade-off, he would take the additional heat, if that meant waiting for air cover.

But before the call from the air team came, another problem arose.

"Sir, we've got a bunch of Afghans massing at the front gate."

"Say again?"

"There are at least four of them, sir. They are screaming and yelling about shots fired from the Strong Point yesterday."

"Get rid of 'em. Now."

"They won't leave, sir. They're demanding to talk to you."

"To me? What the hell?"

The last thing they needed was a distraction right before they stepped off onto a combat mission. These guys at the gate could be suicide bombers, with bombs strapped to their chests and under their garb, prepared to blow themselves up as soon as the squad stepped out the gate. That's how the Taliban operated. Clint smelled a rat.

"Where's the interpreter?"

"At the gate, sir."

Clint checked his watch again and walked to the entry control point, at the main gate facing north. By this time, the gun truck that would normally block the entry of the compound had been moved out to the intersection of Chilliwack and Cornerbrook, to prepare for the morning's mission. And now, they had four Afghans, screaming bloody murder. What next?

When he arrived at the entry control point, several armed soldiers stood in the area along with the interpreter and four hostile-looking Afghan men. Clint did not recognize the Afghans, who wore typical farmers garb worn by Taliban operatives.

The men yelled and shook their fists. Perhaps this was a delay tactic, to buy more time for enemy insurgents seeking to ambush the squad, or to relay information to the enemy about the U.S. troop movement.

The last thing Clint needed was a potential threat to the platoon as it stepped out of the main gate. And he could not risk intel being conveyed to the enemy. Nothing good could come of these guys at the gate.

Clint looked over at the interpreter. "What's going on?"

"They're bitching about shots fired from the Strong Point yesterday, sir."

"You mean shots that we fired back after the Taliban tried to ambush us on yesterday's patrol?" Clint would not allow his platoon to come under fire without firing back, a point he had made yesterday afternoon when he ordered snipers on the guard towers to take practice shots into the grape fields around the village. But he also had instructed his snipers to avoid hitting anyone.

Yesterday's message, with both the Gustav cannon and the fire from the towers was, "If you hit us, we'll hit back harder." Maybe the Taliban got the message, and didn't like it.

"Tell them to leave now," Clint said. "Tell them to come back later, to the shura, and we can talk about it then. But I don't need these men here when we bring the patrol out the gates. There's no telling what they're up to."

Shura was the phrase used by American forces in Afghanistan to describe occasional public meetings between U.S. military personnel and local residents of Afghan villages. The military would issue an invitation to the locals to come to the shura, usually held at the U.S. military outpost, under heavy guard and tight security. These meetings were encouraged by the U.S. military, as an attempt to improve communications and improve relations between the Army and the locals.

The translator turned and relayed Clint's instructions to the Afghans. But they were having none of it.

"They refuse to leave," the translator said. "They want to talk now."

"I don't have time to talk to them now, and we don't have time for this. We're trying to get a mission under way. Tell them to leave now or they'll wind up getting shot."

Clint was not planning on shooting the Afghans, but he needed to clear them from the area, because of the danger that they might pose his men. When the translator delivered Clint's stern message, that did the trick. The agitated Afghans turned and headed back toward the village.

"Let me know if they show up again."

Good. Now to get the helicopters on station and get this mission under way. He turned and jogged back over the staging area.

"Sir," this was the radio operator. "CCA is on the way. They'll be on station at 6:55, sir."

Great news, for a change. The choppers would be on station five minutes early. Clint had planned on rolling out at 7 a.m. However, he would take advantage of every second he had the helicopters overhead, and did not want to waste a single second of valuable air coverage.

"Cpl. Ruhl, get the men ready. We're rolling out five minutes early. At 6:55."

CHAPTER 27

SHOWTIME
STRONG POINT PAYENZAI
JULY 2, 2012, 6:55 A.M.

"Okay. Let's move out!"

At Clint's command, with the helicopter gunships now somewhere in the area and snipers positioned atop the Strong Point's northwest tower at Clint's command, the squads from First Platoon begin filing out the front of the entry control point at Payenzai. Five Afghan troops, in compliance with the Army's new "Afghan in the Lead" program, moved out first, leading the line. Right behind the Afghans came the mine hound element, led by Spec. Reyler Leon.

Spec. Leon occupied the first American position closest to the Afghan National Army. And as he went about his crucial duties of sweeping the ground in front of him for dangerous IEDs, he also occupied the most dangerous position in line of all the American paratroopers, as he would be the first American subject to get shot by sniper fire as they moved cross the hazardous landscape. As events would unfold in the day, Leon would also be the American with the best vantage point to testify about the events as they occurred.

Behind Spec. Leon, Pvt. First Class Zachary Wayne Thomas followed as the forward observer and radio telegraph operator. As a forward observer, part of Thomas's job would be to observe the situation at the front of the column, and then relay messages back to the platoon commander, Lt. Lorance, and to the company commander, Capt. Swanson. Pvt. Thomas's statements will also be crucial in understanding the Army's absurdity in later prosecuting Lt. Lorance.

Then came the lead assault squad in today's mission, headed by Cpl. Jarred Ruhl, squad leader for 3rd Squad, which followed 15 to 20 meters behind the mine hound.

Clint and other headquarters element members followed after 3rd Squad and behind Clint, came the weapons squad, bringing up the rear of the single-file line. The weapons squad was headed by Sgt. Herrmann, the NCO who had fired the Gustav cannon the day before that put a swift end to the Taliban sniper attack and also earned Clint a verbal reprimand for violating the law of proportional force.

They poured outside of the gate, in a tight, single-file line. They spaced themselves several yards apart to avoid collateral damage if someone stepped on an IED.

The men turned turn left out the gate, following the outside wall of the Strong Point, as Clint wanted them protected by machine gun fire from the northwestern tower as long as possible. With the firepower available from the gun truck and from the machine guns up top, the patrol should have had enough cover outside of the gate. But Clint remained concerned about the angry Afghans who had appeared at the entry point, and worried that they might be a scout party signaling a possible surprise attack.

Staying close to the wall cut down on possible fire angles by snipers out on the periphery, around the northwestern corner. Moving from east to west, they walked down the grape rows for several hundred feet, tight in behind the mine hound, toward New Cornerbrook Road (which ran east-west, south of the village, and then curved up from south to north just past the Strong Point's northwest tower and ended at the intersection). Clint did not want to cross New Cornerbrook at this point, too close to the intersection, for security reasons, and neither did his senior NCOs. For one thing, a crossing point this far north would be too close to

Old Chilliwack Road, the known Taliban bastion, and it will be too easy for a quick ambush attempt by the Taliban should they choose to try to rush down Old Chilliwack and get off shots.

So rather than taking the grape row all the way out to Old Cornerbrook to cross it, they decided it would be better to cross several hundred yards to the south, to give themselves a little more reaction time if the Taliban tried something from Old Chilliwack Road.

The platoon turned south again and started leapfrogging over 8-foot grape rows. In this way, they would maneuver into position to cross New Cornerbrook down at a curve in the road, where it curved from its north-south direction, over to an east-west direction. Crossing the road farther south, where the road bent back to the west, would make their position less visible from Taliban forces who were somewhere in the north, and possibly operating within the village of Sarenzai itself.

Clint moved his way down the row and waited for the men in front to climb over the 8-foot grape berms. Oppressive heat immediately drenched everyone with sweat. The overflow sweat dropped into their eyes and made visibility even tougher. But they had to live with the heat, and the sweat; they would do their jobs—and make the best of it—and carry out the mission. They were American paratroopers in the finest damn paratrooper division the world has never known, the 82nd Airborne.

Clint watched as Spec. Leon pulled himself up and over the wall. Then came Spec. Fitzgerald, Cpl. Ruhl, and Pvts. Copeland, Craig, Wingo and Thomas. After that came Pvt. Skelton, who had served as a police officer in North Carolina before joining the Army. Skelton pulled himself up onto the wall. So far, so good. They were under way, and although he was operating on no sleep, Clint prayed that today's mission would be smoother than the attempted ambush they had to fight off yesterday.

Clint reached up for the top of the berm and found a solid grip point on the ledge. As he had done in paratrooper training at Fort Benning, he executed the crude equivalent of a chin-up. Pulling himself on top of the wall, he swung his foot around, let his other foot dangle, and then let himself drop down the other side into the first trench. From down there, Clint could see nothing, except the leaf and dirt walls in front of him, and the leaf- and mud-baked walls behind him.

A call came in from the helicopter squad overhead. A group of military-age males was congregating to the northwest of the village of Sarenzai. First Platoon was at the time southeast of the center of the village, and the men reported gathering were almost on a diagonal line, straight through the village into the northwest corner near the intersection of two dirt roads, on the opposite corner of a tic-tac-toe board, for lack of a better description.

That put the Afghan men—the potential enemy—on the opposite side of the battle space, within striking distance either by foot or by motorcycle of Clint's patrol. The UAV had not picked up this earlier, in part because they were not on the projected pathway for the squad. But just because they were not on the projected pathway did not mean that they could not move into position quickly and become an immediate threat to the squad.

Capt. Catherine McNair, the lead pilot in the helicopter squadron that arrived on station, described the suspicious individuals in a sworn, written statement, given to investigators on July 19, 2012, 17 days after the shooting.

> "The Chainsaw element requested we maintain overwatch of them, and conduct recon of the area for any suspicious activity. Our team complied, and we were eventually able to identify a large group of adult males, massing and then departing the objective area, a common TTP for insurgents."

By using the phrase TTP, Capt. McNair used an acronym that stands for Tactics, Techniques and Procedures.

In other words, the air team had spotted military-aged males amassing on the ground and acting in a manner that would suggest the high probability of threat to the squad, at some point during the mission.

Because they were massing out on the village's northwest corner, Clint worried that they might try to strike from the west end of Old Cornerbrook, as the squad emerged onto the dirt street from the grape field. As a precautionary measure, in addition to the other precautionary measures that he had taken, Clint would send two of his men out ahead of the squad, to the west side of the village, to keep an eye out for potential ambush is coming in from the west side, as old Chilliwack Road ran north-south along the village's east side, with the village at the southern end of the road.

Clint ordered Sgt. Herrmann and Pvt. Carson to move out by foot to the west part of town, to get some visual identification on the potential insurgents, and to provide firepower on that side of village if the insurgents attempted a move against the squad from the west end of Old Cornerbrook.

He had a bad feeling about what was going on. But First Platoon's job was to engage and destroy the enemy, if the enemy showed up. Therefore, the squad's main element continued moving southward, away from the village, until it could reach its point to cut right across the road, then move north back up into the center of the village.

Clint reached up and climbed up onto another berm, looking over in the direction where the men were massing. But he could not see anything because the village and grape rows on the northern side blocked his view. He could not stay atop the berm for too long, because that could put him the crosshairs of a sniper scope. He swung his legs around to the other side of the berm and dropped down into the trench.

Again isolated by berms of baked mud and grape leaves, Clint could see nothing except the grape berms and sunbaked mud walls in front of him, the grape berms and sunbaked walls behind him, and the blue sky overhead. Then, he heard yelling from up front. Afghan voices.

What the hell?

Pvt. Skelton, straddling the top berm two rows over, yelled out.

"Sir, there is a motorcycle coming! It is coming right at our guys crossing the road!"

CHAPTER 28

SPLIT-SECOND DECISIONS
IN THE AFGHAN GRAPE FIELDS
JULY 2, 2012, 7:05 A.M.

The events that occurred next, as will be described in detail in this chapter, all occurred within a time span of fewer than 10 seconds of one another. Clint would have to make instant decisions, involving life-or-death consequences for his men, based on what he perceived to be an imminent threat against his platoon. The decisions were based upon information given to him from Pvt. Skelton, that a motorcycle was speeding at his men down Old Chilliwack Road, a known Taliban bastion. These decisions were made from the crevices of a grape berm, where he could see nothing but hard mud and leaves, and open sky above.

Deep within the berms, unable to see anything, Clint heard chaotic noises of the Afghans yelling. Then Pvt. Skelton began shouting, as he spotted the threat with his own eyes.

Clint knew that his platoon was in a red-hot Taliban zone, and he knew from information given by the helicopters of men massing in an aggressive manner.

In describing the events of the next few seconds, Clint answered the author's questions in this manner, word for word:

> Don: "How were you first made aware of the motorcycle approaching?"

Clint: "It was very fast. I was getting my gear situated to leap over the wall. Skelton was not on the wall right next to me, but on the next one after that. He was almost straddling it. I think I could see him from where I was. I could definitely hear him. He was almost over it when he saw it (the motorcycle coming down Old Chilliwack), and said, 'Sir, there's a motorcycle coming! It's coming right at the guys crossing the road! And it's not stopping!' He said, 'What do you want me to do?'

"I did not say anything at first. Before I could even say anything, he said, 'I'm going to shoot! Can I shoot it?'

"And I said, 'Sure.' I trusted his judgment because he had been a police officer in North Carolina, in Southern Pines, just before he joined the Army. And I had interviewed him a few days before that, and I knew that he was a Southern Pines cop. And I knew that a police officer would not ask to shoot somebody without good reason. And that gave him a lot of credibility with me.

"I knew he would not ask permission to open fire unless there were a credible threat or a reason to. So, in the millisecond I have to make a decision, in my mind I'm thinking, 'Okay, here I have a former civilian police officer asking me if he can shoot. He must have a reason.'

"So he shot, and I don't know if the round hit. If it did hit, it didn't do any damage. I knew that warning shots were not authorized, and that if we started shooting, we had to finish shooting. That was a big deal in the rules of engagement.

"There were all kinds of people yelling stuff. The ANA was up in the front, and I could hear somebody yelling that the ANA was out to shoot this guy. And this is all happening in milliseconds. And I am saying, tell the ANA to cease fire."

Meanwhile, here's how Pvt. Skelton later described his mind frame, testifying under oath, under penalty of perjury, at the court-martial of Lt. Lorance:

Defense Counsel: "And at the time that you fired, you believed that's what you were doing; you were protecting friendly forces, both American and ANA?"

Pvt. Skelton: "Based on—based on ROE and my quick threat analysis of what could happen, yes."

Defense Counsel: "Yes. So, this I'll ask you, okay. Based on what you had available to you, you saw this as a threat and you felt an obligation as an American soldier to protect friendly forces, American and ANA, correct?"

PFC Skelton: "Yes."

Clearly, Pvt. Skelton testified, under penalty of perjury, under oath, that he felt threatened by the fast-moving motorcycle coming down old Chilliiwack to the back road.

This point is crucial because the prosecution later argued that the motorcycle did not subjectively pose any threat to anyone.

In the mass confusion created first by the Afghans yelling, then by Pvt. Skelton sensing a threat and firing, and by the Afghans firing, Clint remembered that he had stationed the gun truck at the intersection of Old Chilliwack, Old Cornerbrook, and New Cornerbrook, to provide backup fire.

Clint's protective instinct for his men kicked in. With the motorcycle speeding down Old Chilliwack Road, a road only used by the Taliban, and considering the Taliban's use of motorcycles as vehicles of mass homicide, Clint made a split-second decision. He had no choice. He ordered the gun truck to open fire.

Here is how he later recounted it.

"My exact words to the gun truck, I will never forget, was, 'Fire two precision shots to eliminate the target.' The response came over the radio, 'Roger,' and then there were two shots after that. It happened really fast."

The gun truck complied, with Pvt. First Class David Shiloh firing the first shot. At that point, Clint, who was still in the irrigation ditch in the bottom of the grape row, could see nothing, except sunbaked mud walls and grape vines growing on the walls.

When questioned further by the author about the sequence of events, Clint provided this response:

> Don: "So you heard yelling coming across the radio? Or did you hear yelling coming across the field? Or what?"
>
> Clint: "I was hearing it from somewhere in front of me. I was in the bottom of the grape row and could not see. But I assumed it was from people ahead of me on the road. They are crossing the road. They were somewhere in front of me and I could not see them. But I heard the Afghans yelling and fussing about something. Then, almost immediately, as I'm hearing this yelling, my team leader gets on the radio and says these Afghans are about to shoot. He said, 'What do you want me to do?' I said, 'Tell them to cease fire.' And immediately I told the gun truck to handle it."

It is clear, however, that the Afghans did not get the message or understand Clint's order to cease fire, nor did they follow the order if they got it. Perhaps they kept firing because of the excitement and fear that they were feeling as the motorcycle approached them at high speed. Perhaps they kept firing because of the practical difficulty of translating a "ceasefire" from English to Pashto. Remember, the ANA were hyped-up foreign soldiers, in the middle of an active shooting situation, and worked up about the possibility of facing a suicide bomber on motorcycle, which was coming down a road controlled by the Taliban.

Recall that Spec. Reyler Leon, the mine hound with this mission, and as a result, was at the front of the American column and closer to the Afghans than any other soldier. Leon had the best view of the action when the shooting started at the front of the column.

Spec. Leon gave a sworn written statement (under penalty of perjury) on what he observed at the point of the shooting. He wrote his statement by hand on July 6, 2012, four days after the incident.

> "After crossing the curve on route Cornerbrook, as we were walking our approach into the east side of town, there was a small halt as (a) shot was fired toward the three individuals that were on the motorcycle. Being at the front of the moving element, I was caught by surprise when I heard the shot.... As I seen the one individual go away from the motorcycle, I heard another shot coming from my left side. *I turned towards the direction and seen it was the ANA shooting towards the motorcycles location.*" (Emphasis added.)

Thus, from Leon's sworn statement, we see that the Afghan National Army was "shooting toward the motorcycle."

As will later be seen, because of the prosecution's unrestrained zeal to attain a conviction for murder against Clint, the prosecution went to great lengths to suppress this evidence, the testimony of Spec. Leon that the Afghans were firing first.

Even worse, to try to pin a murder conviction on Clint, *the prosecution will later paint a false picture that the*

Afghans had not fired at all. But that not only contradicts Spec. Leon's sworn statement, but also cuts against the sworn statement from another paratrooper, Pvt. First Class Zachary Thomas, who gave a sworn statement that both the ANA and the Americans were firing at the motorcycle.

Pvt. Thomas in a sworn statement, written out on July 3, 2012, the day after the incident, also believed that the Afghans were firing, and wrote, under oath:

> "My best guess is around 4 to 6 people fired, but was to my knowledge, a mixed ISAF/ANA."

Thus, Pvt. Thomas, who is the forward observer, and who was almost as close to the front of the column as Spec. Leon, gave an initial sworn statement that both the ANA (Afghan National Army) and ISAF (International Security Assistance Force—in this case, meaning the Americans), were both firing at the motorcycle. This, again, cuts against the position that the prosecution later falsely proffered at trial, by claiming that the Afghans did not fire, as part of its zealous quest to try to pin a murder conviction on Clint.

The difficulty seeing from the grape rows, where Clint was located at the time of the shooting, was underscored by several witnesses. Among those testifying to the difficulty seeing out the grape rows at Clint's court-martial was Sgt. Daniel Williams:

> Sgt. Williams: "The ANA began pushing forward. I apologize—the entire element began pushing into the grape rows."
>
> Military Prosecutor: "Could you describe grape row for us?"
>
> Sgt. Williams: "The grape row can go anywhere from being two feet high or knee-high up to six-foot, seven foot, depends on the area. Ours were

generally—probably above our heads if you were down in the—

the irrigation ditch."

Military Prosecutor: "Okay, so what is the grape row?"

Sgt. Williams: "It's what—that's how they grow grapes. Basically, it's a giant mud wall that they put grape vines on, sir."

Military Prosecutor: "Okay, so the mud walls are what goes as high as your head?"

Sgt. Williams: "Yes, sir."

The platoon sergeant, Sgt. Keith Ayers, also testified at the court-marital about his own inability to see the shooting because of the grape rows:

Military Prosecutor: "Okay, so what happened next?"

Sgt. Ayers: "What happened next, I recall broken radio traffic coming across my radio and then I observed Specialist—or PFC Skelton climb on top of a mound and begin engaging shortly followed by the gun truck engaging."

Military Prosecutor: "Okay, could you see that engagement?"

Sgt. Ayers: "No, I could not, sir. I was in the grape rows still."

This difficulty in seeing anything outside the grape rows is established by the platoon sergeant's testimony, as Sgt. Ayers could not see, as Clint could not see, and in fact most of the platoon who were in the irrigation ditches between the mud walls could not see anything. Clint relied on information being fed to him, making split-second decisions from the bottom of a grape row, where he could not even see.

And the Army charges Clint with *murder*?

Once the gun truck engaged, Clint thought that the matter was over. However, in an effort to serve Clint's head to the Afghans on a silver platter, the Army would later threaten to prosecute Pvt. First Class Shiloh for murder, along with the other soldier in the gun truck, Spec. Reynoso, unless they testified against Clint. Pvt. Shiloh would be ordered to testify against Clint, under a grant of immunity.

As the UK's *Daily Mail* (a newspaper out of London) reported on Aug. 1, 2013, "The two soldiers who fired the shots have been reprimanded, but won't have to go to a full court-martial."

Pvt. Skelton also was among the soldiers threatened with prosecution and then ordered to testify against Clint, under a grant of immunity from the commanding general.

CHAPTER 29

BODIES ON THE ROAD
JULY 2, 2012, 7:35 A.M.

A few minutes before the shooting that occurred, Clint had received information from the air team that military-age males were gathering in the northwest sector of the battle space. Even after handling the emergency situation with the fast-moving motorcycle coming up on his platoon's position, Clint worried about the insurgents gathering on the west side of the village.

After shots rang out against the first motorcycle, Clint made his way across New Cornerbrook Road and directed the platoon to begin moving north toward the backside of the village of Payenzai. Preliminary reports were that two of the three riders were down. But that's all he knew at the moment. Either way, they had to keep pressing forward.

The trek back north into the village would not require the men to leapfrog over 8-foot grape rows as they had done when moving south out of the Strong Point, or like the day before, on approach to the village of Mullah Shin Gul. The northern approach into the village would take them over open land, with parallel grape rows over to their left.

Meanwhile, as the patrol approached the backside of the village, now moving to the north and paralleling New Cornerbrook Road, the choppers continued reporting on the men amassing in the northwest corner. These men were potential enemy insurgents, and the information from the choppers became even more disturbing by the minute.

Pvt. Thomas, in the same written statement of July 3rd where he swore under oath that both the Americans and the Afghan National Army were firing at the motorcycle, also described what he was hearing over the radio from the helicopters about the men massing in the northwest corner.

"Dark Horse 60 (helicopter call sign) reported a spotting of 7 to 8 packs (possible enemy insurgents) on three motorcycles located 700 meters north of the objective village. First Lieutenant Lorance instructed me to engage these individuals with something to see if they shot back or what they'll do. After talking to CCA, they said they could drop smoke on these individuals, but not engage without positive identification. After dropping smoke on the packs, they all turn around and headed west. By this time, 0730, we had made it into the village and spread out."

After the helicopters dropped smoke on the motorcycles, the motorcycles moved from a position northwest of the village to a position due west of the village. From there, the motorcycles moved to a position a few hundred yards southwest of the village. With each move, they remained within quick striking distance of First Platoon, as the squad emerged onto the main street of the village, Old Cornerbrook Road.

By 7:30 a.m., the first elements of the American squad from First Platoon emerged onto the single dusty dirt road, Old Cornerbrook Road, running straight down the middle of the village of Sarenzai. What the Americans found was jarring.

Several women, and a few children, too, converged upon the patrol, crying, some screaming. Clint moved quickly to the front of the line. Here, in his own words, is what he discovered:

"As soon as I walked into the village, there was a little small group of people. There was an Afghan woman, who looked like she was 30 or 40. And she had a couple of little kids with her. She had what looked like an 8- or 9-year-old little girl and a little boy with her. They all were crying. At that moment, the thought that the Taliban had family, too, did not cross my mind. I thought, when I saw those children, that they must be innocent, and that everybody they love must be innocent. Of course, that turns out not to be true.

"Some of them are Taliban themselves. But I did not think of that. When I saw women and children crying, I started panicking. I thought, '*Oh God, did we just shoot her husband? Or did we just shoot their whoever?*' That's why I was worried."

Clint, in retrospect, was correct. In Afghanistan, it is true that sometimes both women and children operate as Taliban terrorists.

Anyone who is seen the movie "American Sniper," directed by Clint Eastwood and released in 2014, remembers a gripping scene in which American Navy SEAL sniper Chris Kyle was placed into the most unenviable of all positions of having to shoot both a young boy, and then in the same scene, a few seconds later, shoot his mother. In the scene, based on actual events, Kyle is watching the young boy through a sniper scope, and begs the boy not to pick up the live mortar round lying on the street. When the boy picks up the mortar round and starts running toward the American troops, Kyle grimaces and pulls the trigger. The boy falls to the street. The sight tears Kyle's guts out.

Then the boy's mother, draped in black Islamic garb, who was encouraging her son to throw the mortar at the Americans, starts screaming and crying, then picks up the mortar herself and starts to charge toward the Americans. Kyle pulls the trigger again.

The gut-wrenching scene represents a microscopic crystallization of why so many American service members have suffered so much from post-traumatic stress syndrome, from their operations in both Afghanistan and Iraq. But that scene from "American Sniper," based on Chris Kyle's true story, showed both the boy and his mother operating as Taliban insurgents who were trying to throw a live mortar round at U.S. troops approaching from down the street.

As gut-wrenching as that scene is to watch, it is nonetheless a realistic portrayal of radical Islam as it has taken root in certain parts of Afghanistan through the Taliban and other radical terror organization such as ISIS, Al Qaeda, and Boko Haram, where women and children strap bombs to themselves to blow up Americans.

Now, at 7:35 a.m., only 40 minutes into their mission, and under a blazing sun with temperatures above 100 degrees, on a dusty street in a hellhole mud-baked village almost 8,000 miles from his home in Celeste, Texas, Clint Lorance is facing his own gut-wrenching experience. Unlike Chris Kyle's predicament, no women or children had been shot. But watching the human element of grief, of women and children crying, even if their loved ones had been terrorists or enemies of the United States, was hard emotionally.

Here is how Clint described what happened next, in a question-and-answer session with the author:

> Don: "Were you ever able to determine about the woman? Was she related to the people that were shot?"
>
> Clint: "I saw the woman crying with the kids, and it shocked me.
>
> I couldn't make out what she was saying. And the interpreter, he was not   doing a good job at that time, and was not doing well under pressure.

The main thing I was getting out of her, is that she wanted to take the bodies away. She kept saying, 'Want to take the bodies. Want to take bodies.' I told her yes, because they want to try to bury them as soon as possible. In the Muslim culture, they want to bury the dead as soon as humanly possible."

CHAPTER 30

STORM CLOUDS IN THE WEST
THE SECOND ENGAGEMENT
JULY 2, 2012

As the Afghan woman screamed, cried and begged to take the bodies that soaked in pools of blood on the hot dirt road, the company commander, Capt. Swanson, kept calling in on the radio and demanding a battle damage assessment. By battle damage assessment, Capt. Swanson wanted members of First Platoon to take time out from their mission and go over and examine the bodies of the Afghans who had been on the motorcycle, who had just been shot. But the helicopter spotted a potential growing threat on the west side of the village from insurgents massing along with motorcycles that remained in the area.

The insurgents gathering on the west side posed a deadly definite threat to the squadron. And Clint needed every man he could get, with a rifle in his hand, to deal with potential threats of whatever he might find out there. Stopping to conduct a battle damage assessment, with insurgency storm clouds brewing in the west end of the village, made no sense from a military standpoint.

Because of red-hot military contingencies that were still erupting in the area, and with uncertainty about what they might face at the west end of the village, from a safety standpoint, there was no time to stop and conduct a battle damage assessment. Nor was it militarily prudent at the moment. Therefore, Clint relayed the message on the radio back to Gariban, to tell Capt. Swanson that they could not do a battle damage assessment because the military situation on the ground was too dangerous.

But the captain insisted anyway.

So, Clint dispatched two paratroopers, Spec. Leon, the mine hound, along with Pvt. Wingo, who also had been working with the mine hound team, to move east down Old Cornerbrook Road to examine the bodies. Clint had to send his mine hound because the portion of the dirt road between the lead element of the squad, which had set up a perimeter on the street in the middle of the village, and the position of the bodies, several hundred yards to the east, might have IEDs planted in the road. Leon would have to sweep the dirt street with a metal detector as he and Wingo walked over toward the bodies.

This also put both men out alone in the streets and exposed to sniper fire. But the captain had ordered it.

The captain's order compromised the safety of the entire the squad, because now Clint had to give up his mine hound to conduct the battle damage assessment of the two bodies lying on the street. But Clint understood the chain of command. And if his captain insisted that he divert valuable military resources to conduct what amounted to a bureaucratic exercise in the middle of a heated Taliban war zone, Clint would do his best to carry out his orders.

As an aside, the whole battle damage assessment obsession was driven not by Capt. Swanson, but up the chain of command. This was a part of the new liberalized rules of engagement that often compromised the safety of the troops. The battle damage assessment was an attempt to ensure that those who have been shot were in fact militants, but not civilians.

While the information, on the identity of the bodies, might be helpful overall to the military's attempt to reduce civilian casualties, the need to conduct statistical record-keeping in the middle of a military hot zone had, for the most part, always taken a back seat to the immediate, operational necessity of the military mission in a war zone, and to the safety of U.S. troops.

Until now.

Having to peel off the squad's mine hound, while intelligence from multiple sources forecasted a looming danger out to the west of the village, jeopardized the safety of the entire squad. Meanwhile, as Leon and Wingo moved several hundred yards down the road to the right of headquarters element, to the east of their position, the situation got hotter in the west end of the village.

Back at Gariban, where the company headquarters were located, radio operators are now picking up handheld radio communications on ICOM radios from the Taliban, out to the west of the village, that an imminent attack against Clint's squad might soon commence. The ICOM radios were expensive hand-held two-way radios, in essence sophisticated walkie talkies, manufactured by the Icom Corp., and thus referred to as "ICOMs." The Taliban used the ICOM radios as a means of communication. Even under the liberalized rules of engagement, if an Afghan were spotted using an ICOM radio, that—in and of itself—was the functional equivalent of holding a weapon.

These handheld radios were not possessed by ordinary Afghans, as they were too expensive. But they were used by the Taliban to coordinate insurgent movements, and to detonate bombs and landmines used against American troops. The Taliban bought them with money from opium sales.

When American troops moved into an area, if the Taliban were also present, the ICOM radio traffic lit up like a Christmas tree, with the Taliban talking to each other. American intelligence monitored this traffic, trying to get an idea of the Taliban's intentions, which was happening now, even as Clint had been forced to dispatch his mine hound down to the east side of the village to conduct a battle damage assessment.

Here is how Cpl. Jarred Ruhl, in sworn testimony one year later, during Clint's court-martial, described the information that the squad received from company headquarters about intercepted radio traffic concerning the Taliban out to the west of the village.

Recall that Cpl. Ruhl was assault squad leader for 3rd Squad, responsible for getting the patrol into formation on the morning of July 2. As can be seen, he testified that ICOM messages had been intercepted by Gariban that American forces were about to be attacked. Ruhl had been promoted to sergeant by the time of Clint's trial:

> Civilian Defense Counsel: "And—under your understanding of the events of the time of the rules of engagement, having heard from Gariban, higher headquarters that they had intercepted these communications, the ICOMs were located, and the transmissions were to the effect they were about to attack American forces that would certainly be sufficient cause to engage those targets, wouldn't it?"
>
> Sgt. Ruhl: "Yes, sir."
>
> Civilian Defense Counsel: (Pause) "And the transmission that came back from Gariban was that they had intercepted these characters with an ICOM and that the I—from the communications, bad guys were getting ready to engage U.S. forces; that's what you heard?"
>
> Sgt. Ruhl: "Yes, sir."

So now, Clint is faced with a dilemma, based upon three significant factors.

1) The helicopters reported that insurgents and motorcycles were amassing out to the west of the village. 2) Balanced

against that, Clint was ordered to give up his mine hound and one other paratrooper, through this silly bureaucratic exercise known as a battle damage assessment, and to satisfy some bean-counter sitting behind a desk somewhere, all in the middle of a brewing firefight, taking away their principle mine detection capabilities. And 3) Gariban is now calling and reporting that they have intercepted ICOM radio traffic that an attack is imminent from the Taliban from the west side of the village.

The entire battlefront, from the motorcycle charge coming from the north, paralleling the east side of the village, down Old Chilliwack Road, to Old Cornerbrook Road, to the motorcycles and possible insurgents gathering on the west side of the village, and now the radio intercept that an attack may be imminent, all smelled more and more like a coordinated Taliban trap.

Most likely, the motorcycle charge down Old Chilliwack Road, bordering the eastern side of the village, which had now been eliminated, had been a coordinated distraction planned by the Taliban while its main forces congregated on the west side of the village for a surprise attack. Perhaps the Taliban plan was to distract the Americans focused in the motorcycle from the east, then attack from the west.

Now, with the updated radio intercepts from Gariban about a possible Taliban attack from the western side of the village, Clint could not wait to complete Capt. Swanson's battle damage assessment before taking action. In war, delay, paralysis, and indecision, are a recipe for death and defeat. And Clint had promised to bring all these men home—alive.

With the uncertain situation on the west side of the village worsening, Clint ordered Sgt. Herrmann to take the weapons squad and move into the western sector to conduct a threat assessment, based upon the intelligence that they were getting, first from the helicopters, and now from the intercepted the radio messages relayed by Gariban.

"Roger that, sir." Sgt. Herrmann acknowledged the order, then motioned to the men in his squad to move out.

Obeying the orders of their squad leader, the paratroopers followed Sgt. Herrmann, one by one, as they crouched low and stepped into a single-file line moving straight down the dirt road to the west. With the sun beating on the backs of the uniforms, their shadows stretched long on the road out in front of them—almost like a black, eerie arrow on the ground, pointing them in direction of the enemy.

As the four paratroopers disappeared from view, Clint's pre-mission contingency planning would give him more options. Although he was losing firepower by moving his weapons squadron out to the west side of the village, he was still covered by the gun truck sitting over to the east—the same truck, with a .240 caliber machine gun—which, along with the ANA, had opened fire on the motorcycle. And although he was forced to give up his mine hound by complying with the bureaucratic order to conduct a battle damage assessment in the midst of a brewing battle, with the brand-new dog sniffing team that he brought from Pasab, at least he had some mine-detection capabilities while the mine hound was detained on BDA duties.

Meanwhile, Sgt. Herrmann and the weapons squad, moving without the cover of the mine hound, stayed low and kept moving to the west, down the left side of Old Cornerbrook Road, the road that cut straight down the middle of the village of Sarenzai.

Their backs baking under the hot rising sun, their eyes and their guns swept in semi-circular angles, searching every alley and every crevice beside every one of the mud-baked buildings, on the lookout for anything that might pop into the street. Edging closer to the western edge of the village, the sweat dripped from their noses and foreheads, and splashed on the dirt below, marking a trail of mud droplets behind them. But in 100-plus degree temperatures, the mud drops dried up in the heat, the sweat droplets evaporating into the atmosphere.

Clint watched as the men disappeared out of view—now a few hundred yards west of the security perimeter that the squad had established in the middle of the street. Although he had taken command of the platoon only a few days ago, he knew them all by name—Pvt. Carson, Pvt. Haggard, Pvt. Rivera, and Sgt. Herrmann. He watched them all, moving toward an unknown danger, waiting somewhere beyond the end of the village. He uttered a silent prayer that they would all return, alive.

"Okay, men. Let's search these buildings and then get out of here."

With that order, members of third assault squad, led by Cpl. Ruhl, began the search of each house and building along the street, looking for Taliban operatives.

The Army called it "clearing the village," and the work was hard and dangerous. With guns up and in firing position, sweating like pigs under hundred-degree heat, members of the squad had gone to each qalat—the term used for small Afghan villages usually surrounded by mud baked walls or sometimes other fence-like structures for security—and each mud-baked home in the village, to search each crevice and each space for the Taliban.

At some houses, the men had to kick open the doors. Sometimes, when they kicked open doors, nobody was home. Sometimes, they found women and children cowering in fear. Sometimes, they were met with belligerence. Sometimes, they were met with guns.

No one liked having to do this. But the Taliban operating in such close proximity to the Strong Point was a sure recipe for disaster. Although counter-intuitive to the new, liberalized rules of engagement to go out to find and destroy the Taliban, if the paratroopers did not remain aggressive in searching for and destroying the Taliban, then the Taliban would take the battle to the Strong Point.

All this weighed on their minds, including the fact that fewer than 24 hours ago, the squadron had come under an ambush attack, by Taliban snipers. And by all accounts, the sniper who shot Matthew Hanes in the throat remained at large.

As Cpl. Ruhl and his men oversaw the Afghans as they began the buildings sweep, Clint suspected that a number of the Taliban in the village had moved out to the west side of town—as intelligence now suggested—and that the motorcycle charge from the east down Old Chilliwack Road was connected with the activity on the west. Yet, there was always a chance that Taliban remained in the village.

Nevertheless, they proceeded with their search, knowing that even as they went from hut to hut, that death could come from behind the next open door.

CHAPTER 31

The weapons squad began to take up positions along the western edge of the village. Here is how Sgt. Herrmann would describe the events, in a sworn, written statement on the evening of July 2, 2012, only hours after the patrol ended:

> "Myself and the gun team pushed past the clearing element. And begin clearing our own route to the SBF (Support by Fire) position, on the rooftop of an abandoned qalat, at the western edge of the village. We got up on the roof and set the gun in place. After five minutes up top, my gunner began ranging buildings using the LRF (Laser Rangefinder), while the AG, Carson, called out target buildings.

> "During this process, Haggard looked out at our farthest target building (338 meters) and noticed a man with an ICOM. The enemy foot mobile was speaking with a man sitting behind a wall and was roughly 120 meters from our position.

> "I gave Haggard permission to engage the far foot mobile with the H240B (machine gun). (Note:

A "foot mobile" is an enemy combatant who is moving on foot.)

"The near foot mobile, who had an ICOM as well, stood back up from behind the wall, and after reconfirming myself that he still had possession of his ICOM, I gave permission for the enemy to be engaged."

Pvt. First Class Nicholas Carson was also a part of the weapons squad with Sgt. Herrmann. Carson accompanied Herrmann in the weapons team to the western part of the village after the first shooting of the motorcycle riders, around 7:05 a.m. Like Herrmann, Carson also gave a sworn statement on the evening of the patrol, July 2, 2012, at Gariban. Carson's sworn statement also corroborates the presence of the Taliban in the area, operating with a hostile intent.

"The first engagement (referring to the motorcycle charge coming down Old Chilliwack Road) was right after we left the wire at Strong Point Payenzai.

"The second engagement was myself (meaning Pvt. Carson was personally involved in the shooting). My gunner spotted a guy almost 500 meters out. So I observed with a magnified Laser Range Finder and got PID (Note: "PID" means "positive identification.") (Note(no((on an ICOM. My squad leader (referring to Herrmann), told the 240 B Gunner to let the two riflemen engage, which I did so alone. The first round missed. But the second and third round hit. The guy went down.

"We engaged fighting age males with ICOMs, and a local national was caught in the crosshairs and shot in the arm."

Perhaps Spec. Daniel Haggard provided the most compelling statement, under oath, to Special Agent Rudy Rios of the Army Criminal Investigation Division, on July 7, 2012, five days after the event.

Haggard's sworn statement shows how tense the situation had become on the battlefront that morning of July 2nd, the morning of the incident that Lieutenant Lorance would get prosecuted for murder. The situation was tense because the area was crawling with Taliban, the enemy of the United States, with a track record of murdering Americans in mass.

Consider this brief question-and-answer exchange between Spec. Haggard and Special Agent Rios about the Taliban moving on the platoon's position in the west sector of the village. (Clint had ordered Staff Sgt. Hermann and the weapons squad to the west end of the village of Sarenzai, where they perched on top of one of the mud-baked buildings, looking out for Taliban positions, which had been reported by the helicopters and by the radio intercept.)

Rios: "Did you see a man with an ICOM radio that day?"

Spec. Haggard: "Yes. While I was on the roof, I saw a man at about 360 (degrees, meaning due north) with my naked eye, and then I verified it while looking down my optic (long-range rifle scope)."

Rios: "What did you see the man with the ICOM do?"

Spec. Haggard: "I saw him holding and talking on the ICOM, and at the same time, he would point at us and then look over to the left at his grape hut that had about six males around it."

Rios: "What do you think the man was doing during these movements?"

Spec. Haggard: "Telling his friends where we are, and how to get to us, so they can kill us."

Rios: "While you saw the man with the ICOM, were you informing others?"

Spec. Haggard: "Yes, I'm calling out what I see to the whole squad so they know what is going on and so that it can get radioed up higher (to the chain of command) and relay to Wolfhound chatter (referring to military radio network)."

Rios: "Do you believe, based on your training and experience, that the subject's movements and mannerisms formed a potential threat to you or possibly your team?"

Spec. Haggard: "Yes, because there (were) other subjects moving on our position. I believe that we were about to get shot at and I told everyone that we were about to get shot at and for everyone to get down behind cover."

Rios: "Why did you engage the male with the ICOM?"

Spec. Haggard: "SSG Herrmann told me to and also because I felt and I thought that we were fearing for our lives (because) of what the men in the field were doing."

Rios: "Did you fear for your life?"

Spec. Haggard: "Yes."

Rios: "If you did not fear for your life, would you have fired?"

Spec. Haggard: "No."

Rios: "Do you feel that you may have prevented an attack on your team?"

Spec. Haggard: "Yes."

Spec. Haggard's concerns, about the men fearing for their lives, were echoed by Spec. Cole Rivera, who was also on the rooftop with the weapons team, and who added that the men with the ICOMs were gathered in a "known firing spot." In other words, the Afghans with the ICOMs were congregated in a position from which the enemy had fired on the American platoon in the past.

Consider Spec. Rivera's responses, in this brief question-and-answer session with another criminal investigator, Special Agent Adam McIntyre of the Army Criminal Investigative Division, often referred to as CID. These responses also show the tenseness of the situation on the west side of the village.

> McIntyre: "Was Spec. Haggard looking through his optic to describe what the guy with the eye cam was doing to SSG Herrmann?"
>
> Spec. Rivera: "Yes, SPC Haggard spotted a guy without his optic first, then confirmed using his optic, an ACOG."
>
> McIntyre: "What information did SPC Haggard give to SSG Herrmann?"
>
> Spec. Rivera: "Distance and direction. Which was 200 meters away and straight ahead."
>
> McIntyre: "Did Spec. Haggard state that he feared for his safety?"
>
> Spec. Rivera: "All of us had mentioned it, because we were on a rooftop, and observing a group of guys who were observing us from a known firing spot."
>
> McIntyre: "The guy that Spec. Haggard shot at. What was he doing?"
>
> Spec. Rivera: "The guy was talking west to east on his ICOM. We were briefed when we arrived in

Afghanistan that the person must be talking on his ICOM in order to shoot because that was hostile intent. If the person only had the ICOM down by his side, that was not considered hostile."

By saying, "The guy was talking west to east," McIntyre means that the insurgent on the west side was talking to someone via radio in the east part of the village

But the criminal shakedown aside, Haggard's statement shows that First Platoon was operating in a battle zone, full of Taliban insurgents. Only nine days had passed since Spec. Hanes had been shot in the throat by a Taliban sniper a few hundred yards from this very location, as the platoon approached the village of Sarenzai. The day before, on July 1, First Platoon had been ambushed by Taliban snipers from along the same road that the motorcycle emerged.

Spec. Rivera's sworn statement verifies that the troops were concerned for their safety because all this activity on the west side originated from a "known firing spot," in other words, a place where the Taliban have been known to fire against First Platoon in the past.

The direction is significant. The east is the direction from which the motorcycle charge occurred moments earlier—the same motorcycle charge that Lieutenant Lorance had ordered his troops to fire upon. This coordination of forces in the west and then the east of the village underscores the likelihood that the platoon had stepped out into a coordinated ambush that had been planned by the Taliban, coming from both the east and west sectors of the village.

Charges were not brought against anyone except Clint, who, ironically, never fired a weapon himself. Clint, who had to rely on secondhand information although from reliable sources—his seasoned men and the helos, had to give out orders from the bottom of an irrigation ditch between 8-foot grape berms, and could not even see the insurgents speeding toward his men on a motorcycle.

Immediately after the weapons squad engaged the Taliban in the western sector, Sgt. Herrmann tried contacting Lieutenant Lorance to brief him on what had happened. But a radio malfunction had cut off communications with headquarters element.

Here's how Sgt. Herrmann described what happened next:

> "I tried to report to SFC Ayers, or LT Lorance my engaging the two enemy foot mobiles. I had an ASIP (handheld military radio) in my ready bag, but couldn't pick up anyone.

> "Around five minutes after the final burst, SFC Ayers walked down to my position to get a SITREP. I explained in detail the engagement. He then told me not to fire unless fired upon. I complied with his order."

(Editorial note: SITREP, the phrase used by Hermann in his testimony, is the military acronym for "Situational Report." Herrmann's testimony continues below.)

> "He had a look of disgust on his face (presumably from restricted rules of engagement) and let me know the clearance element was working toward my position.

> "SFC Ayers came back down, and called up to me on the roof, saying, 'We're exfilling.' The clearing element arrived minutes later."

(Editorial note: "Exfilling," the phrase used by Hermann in his testimony, is the military acronym for "exfiltrating," or moving to leave an area previously occupied by U.S. military forces. Herrmann's testimony continues below.)

"Haggard (sp) and I called to Wingo, who we passed our bags down to, and myself and the gun team got off the roof.

"But I didn't know until we returned to base that we had two detainees. One of them had been wounded. We began to RP (meaning head back to the Strong Point) after getting our bags on. We headed east through the village, then SSE through the fields, until we hit route Cornerbrook. We took Cornerbrook until we hit a break in the concertina wire, where Lt. Lorance broke away from the patrol and linked up with the truck on the route.

"We entered the Strong Point and I went to the platoon TOC (Tactical Operations Center)."

Meanwhile, Wingo and Leon had completed their battle damage assessment of the bodies that had been charging the American position on the motorcycle from down Old Chilliwack Road.

Three insurgents had been riding on the motorcycle that morning. Two had been shot, and the third escaped. Clint later learned—but did not know at the time—that the two men shot had dismounted the motorcycle, and were walking toward the ANA at the time of the shooting. The third rider was later captured.

Wingo and Leon did not find any weapons on the bodies of the two insurgents, which—unbeknownst to Clint—the government would later use as an excuse to prosecute him for murder. They could not verify either way if the motorcycle was rigged with bombs, because the villagers removed the bike from the street, and the Army never found it. But they did find identification cards.

The identity of the riders of the motorcycle, whose names are crucial to Clint's defense, are as follows:

(1)Mohammad Aslam – killed by fire either from the ANA or First Platoon on the morning of July 2, 2012.

(2)An individual identified as "Ghamai" – killed by fire either from the ANA or First Platoon on the morning of July 2, 2012.

(3)A third rider, Haji Karimullah – escaped from the motorcycle and ran and hid somewhere in the village. More information would be gathered on this person later.

The prosecution in Clint's court-martial would later hide valuable evidence from the military jury, and would try instead to paint these three Afghans motorcycle riders as if they were innocent choir boys singing the "Ave Maria" at a Catholic mass on Sunday morning.

But as would later be revealed, several months after the completion of Clint's court-martial, Clint's new lead counsel, Lt. Col. John N. Maher of Chicago, through a high-level investigative effort, discovered that these motorcycle guys were anything but choirboys. In fact, evidence would soon surface that these guys, who the prosecution portrayed as innocent grape farmers, were, in fact, Taliban insurgents, and had their fingerprints on bombs that been used to kill American paratroopers.

On the morning of July 2, the entire squad had returned back to the Strong Point by 11 a.m., about four hours after their mission had begun. When they re-entered the Strong Point, temperatures had climbed to 110 degrees. For Clint Lorance, things would soon get a lot hotter. His most unimaginable nightmare was about to unfold.

CHAPTER 32

RETURN TO GARIBAN
JULY 2, 2012, AFTERNOON

Sometime late in the afternoon, on July 2nd, Clint suspected something was odd, up above him, in the chain of command.

In an interview with the author in the fall of 2018, Clint described how the nightmare unfolded:

> Don: "When you got back to the Strong Point, the mission was over. What did you do next?"

> Clint: "We had to get the detainees out of there. I knew from working in Iraq that we have a compressed timeframe for moving detainees. I knew the longer we kept them at the point of capture, it would take away time from the intelligence interrogators."

> Don. "These were detainees that you had captured during the mission?"

> Clint. "Yes. One of them was one of the guys from the second motorcycle. On that road that goes from north to south. And the other one we found when we were searching the buildings on that road that goes from north-south." (Referring to the West Perimeter Road, bordering the west side of the village.) The second guy, we found in one of the buildings squatted down and holding his arm. He's the one who had a gunshot wound.

"These were the two detainees. They both tested positive for having homemade explosives on their hands."

Author's note: The fact that the two detainees who had been brought in off of the battlefield from that morning's action had explosive residue on their hands is significant. The presence of explosive residue on the hands of an Afghan citizen indicated in almost every instance that the Afghan had been involved making bombs to be used against American forces.

Without question, therefore, the individuals captured on the battlefield not only were Taliban, but that the intelligence from both the helicopters, and the intercept radio transmissions from Gariban, verified that the platoon had stepped into an active, hot battle zone. And as will later be seen, through a document called a SIGACT report, company headquarters knew from intelligence intercepted 40-some minutes before 7 on the morning of the mission, the Taliban planned to ambush Clint's patrol.

Again, however, when the government decided to prosecute Clint for murder, the fact that explosive residue had been found on the hands of these Taliban operatives was hidden from the military jury. The battle on the west side was kept from the jury. The helicopter reports suspecting military-aged males on the west side, about to take action against Clint's patrol, was kept from the jury. And the SIGACT showing intercepted radio messages that the Taliban planned to ambush Clint's patrol, was hidden from the jury.

The government would paint a false picture that First Platoon had been on a leisurely Sunday stroll in the park, not on active hot battlefield, and that the motorcycle riders who Clint's men shot, or who perhaps the ANA shot, were on some sort of morning joy ride. "No reason to be threatened by these leisurely motorcyclists," the prosecution would have us believe.

Had the military jury known what a hot battle space First Platoon faced that morning, then the actions that Clint and his men took in the firing on the motorcycle charge would seem reasonable to the jury. But in hiding the true conditions of the hot battle zone from the jury, the prosecution created a false impression of a "Sunday stroll in the park" approach, to argue that Clint and his men were taking potshots against poor innocent farmers on a motorcycle out for a morning joyride with no reason to be concerned about danger. As will be seen, nothing could be farther from the truth.

The Obama administration needed a conviction, and painting a false impression of the battle space as far less dangerous than it was, became one of its deceptive means to get what they wanted: Clint Lorance's scalp for *murder*.

In his own words, Clint described what happened next:

> "As soon as we got back, I told Skelton to get these guys in the computer. I told him to get them enrolled in there, meaning record their DNA in the biometrics database, and then to get them some water and ask them if they wanted anything to eat.
>
> "I told him to sit them over in a shaded area, to get to keep their blindfolds on, and make sure they were ready to move.
>
> "So, I went in and then radioed the commander, and told him that we had gotten a motorcycle. This was a second motorcycle that was actually captured. And I asked him, what do you want me to do with this motorcycle?
>
> "He says something along the lines of keep it, it is a spoil of war. He said something using the phrase 'spoils of war.' So, my plan was to paint it blue and give it to the Afghan National Police, and

turn it into a police motorcycle. Then we would hire a cop to patrol the area with the motorcycle. I instructed the men to get a convoy ready, we're going to move out and transfer these guys."

At this point, Clint still did not realize that he was in his own command's gunsights. Only after he rode back to Gariban, with the two detainees who had tested positive for explosives, that he realized there was a problem.

He went on to describe how the next events unfolded, when he realized that his world was about to change:

"I went up with the two detainees in the same vehicle to Gariban. This is a little bit after noon. Between 12 and 1.

"I'm in the Intelligence Officer's office, and I started filling out the paperwork on the detainees, while the NCOs were handling the detainees. While we were in there, the NCOs were ferrying people back and forth from the Strong Point (Payenzai to Gariban). We only have one truck, so we had to shuttle people back and forth.

"Then, as I was doing the paperwork, the commander (Capt. Swanson) came in, and said, 'Hey, Clint. Can I talk to you real quick?'

"So I got up, and walked out. And he kept walking. And he walked about halfway across the Strong Point, to the tent where we lifted weights. It was a small tent and we walked in, and I asked, 'Sir, are we going to work out?'

"And he had a real serious look on his face. And he's like, 'Clint, someone went to the district center and reported that we had CIVCAS (civilian casualties).'

"Then he said, 'So I have to undergo the normal routine of putting you on suspension. At this point, you are on suspension. I need you to stay away from anybody, and not talk to anybody while the investigation is under way.'

"He said, 'You should go get something to eat, and then try and get some sleep.'

"So I say, 'Okay.' So I return to the office, and I remember after that sitting out in the hallway, and there is another lieutenant talking to me. And he's saying, 'I am sorry you have to go through this.' Then he looks up and he says, 'There is your platoon sergeant.'

"So the platoon sergeant (Ayers) is walking through with the first sergeant, and they're walking to the command post.

"And I thought, 'Well, that's my cue.' So he said, 'Good luck.'

"So I got up to start walking over there. But the captain did not want to talk to me. He did not want to hear it from me. He wanted to hear from Sgt. Ayers.

"Capt. Swanson never asked me what happened. Ever. He never gave me an opportunity to explain anything. Capt. Swanson and I never said a word after that.

"So I sat there, and later on, it got dark outside. And I heard the convoy rolling up. And I heard the battalion commander's voice. And I'm thinking, "*Oh God!*" And this is about 10 at night. So I thought, '*Well, I better get up. He's going to want to talk to me.*'

"I got my uniform on and everything, and got my weapon, and went outside to see if the battalion commander (Lt. Col.) was here, but nobody was out there. The battalion commander went into the command post, too.

"And this was like before (meaning earlier in the afternoon when Ayers was called in). I walked over there, but the commander told me to leave the office. He said that he wanted to hear from the captain.

"I'd been sitting there with the other platoon leader early in the afternoon, and they were all going in the command post, and in retrospect, you can see the handwriting on the wall. I'm thinking, '*Why don't they want to ask me this?*' The other lieutenant said, 'I don't know.' I figured out that they did not want to hear from me.

"They never even asked me what happened. Nothing. Nothing like that. The battalion commander got his brief from the platoon sergeant, and the company commander, who obviously, is giving thirdhand knowledge. Finally, the battalion commander comes over to me, and he says 'Clint, can you tell me what you were thinking?'

"I was taken aback. I asked, 'What do you mean, sir?'

"He asked, 'What made you think you could shoot those guys?'

"I told him, straight up. I told him the whole thing.

"He said, 'So everybody saw it as a threat?'

"I said, 'Absolutely. Everybody saw the whole thing.'

"He said, 'You can't just shoot them because you think they're coming for a meeting.'

"I told him, 'Sir, that's not the way it happened.'

"But I knew then I was never going to convince him of anything. He had called his bosses, and his bosses wanted my head on a platter. I knew, by the way he was talking to me, that there was nothing I could say at that point.

"He looked at me and said, 'Okay, you're going to go with me to the squadron tonight.' He said, 'There will be an investigation, and we will see what happens from there.'

"And I am saying, 'All right, sir.'

"So I went over to the convoy, and found a vehicle to ride in. We got back to Sia Choy later that night, between 10 and 11, and the convoy pulled up. I could tell that the commander and the entire chain of command had already tried and convicted me.

"I was doomed. I could tell by the way everybody was treating me.

"The first thing that happened, as I opened the door to get out of the vehicle, the battalion commander was standing there, and he was in full gear. And he said, "Lt. Lorance ...' And that's when you know you're in real trouble when they call you by your name and rank ... He said, 'Lt. Lorance, I need you to hand me your weapon.'

"I asked, 'Am I in trouble?'

"He said, 'We have to do this. This is standard procedure.'

Don: "You had not heard from Col. Mennes?" (Brigade commander at Pasab.)

Clint: "Not one time. I have never heard from Col. Mennes throughout this entire process."

Don: "So you were dealing with Captain Swanson and Lt. Col. Howard?"

Clint: "Yes. I never heard from Col. Mennes. At Sia Choy, they assigned an intelligence officer to accompany me. Lt. Franks, I think, his name was, and he looked like he was about 20 years old.

"He comes over to me, and looked nervous, and he says, 'Hey, man, the colonel wants me to show you all around, and to show you where the officers tent is, and make sure you are all right, and everything.'

"I said, 'Okay.'

"Then, he took me all around and showed me everything, and finally we went and got chow, and I asked him, 'So what kind of stuff are you hearing? What's going on?'

"And he said, 'I don't know. They don't tell me anything. They told me not to talk about it.'

"I could tell they thought I was some sort of unhinged murderer, or something like that. So I went back to the tent and just slept for a long time.

"I had had a bunch of allergies, so I took a whole bunch of Benadryl. I slept at least 16 hours a day for the next three or four days that I was there."

Don: "Did you ever see members of your whole platoon?"

Clint: "Some of them had come up, but they were staying in the separate tent, and I was told not to talk to them."

CHAPTER 33

In a fog of disbelief, Clint sat between his two lawyers, Mr. Guy Womack, the retired Marine JAG officer whose fees had been paid for by borrowed money, and his appointed U.S. Army JAG defense counsel, Capt. William Grady. The military judge, after having announced that he was guilty of murder, now gave instructions to the military jury on their duty to sentence him.

Murder?

Could this be happening? Murder? For ordering his men to fire on a charging motorcycle in a Taliban hot zone? That was speeding down a road used almost exclusively by the Taliban? When the Taliban had been killing Americans with suicide motorcycle attacks?

What was he supposed to do? Just wait until some Taliban rushes his men and blows themselves up, and kill his men? And do nothing? Doing nothing against these motorcycle attacks had gotten Americans killed. Those National Guardsmen from Ohio—three of them killed in a Taliban motorcycle charge in Faryab Province. And three weeks before Clint's last day as platoon leader, the motorcycle charge at the main gate at Kandahar, killed 22 pro-American Afghans and wounded another 50.

Even since Clint had returned to Fort Bragg, in 2013, the Taliban had continued to kill by motorcycle bombs. As recently as June of that year, about 60 days before his trial began, two American soldiers, an Afghan policeman, and 10 children had been killed by a motorcycle suicide bomber. Before that, across the Afghan border in Pakistan, the Talban had killed 84 people in a powerful motorcycle bombing attack in January.

He had been given a split-second that day to make a decision, deep in between a grape berm where he could see nothing. What was he supposed to do? Pray that the motorcycle was not going to blow the hell up and take out his men with it? Or do the responsible thing and try to stop what was a clear threat?

What kind of an officer would he be if he had done nothing, and four or five of his men had been transformed to goo by bombs strapped under some Taliban members robe, then sent home in body bags to their wives, children and mothers?

Okay, so the men at the time weren't armed when they checked the bodies. And they never knew if the motorcycle was armed with bombs, because the locals came and took it before it could be checked.

And for this, for trying his best to protect American soldiers, he was guilty of murder?

Didn't the government care about American soldiers in deadly battle zones?

Or did they care more about the Taliban? It sure as hell sounded like somebody, somewhere, up the chain of command cared more about the Taliban, than about American lives. Which is why morale was sagging in the military.

Maybe none of this was real. Maybe a long nightmare. Maybe he would wake up and none of this ever happened.

But then, as Judge Brunson continued to instruct the jury about his sentence, these words sent cold shivers down his spine:

> "The maximum punishment that may be adjudged in this case is forfeiture of all pay and allowances, confinement for life without eligibility for parole, and dismissal from the service. The maximum punishment is a ceiling on your discretion."

Dear Jesus. What did she say? Did she say I could get a life sentence without any parole?

Members of the military jury, who had just convicted him of murder, leaned forward, staring at the judge with wide eyes, and hanging on her every word, as if taking some kind of cue from her on what should happen to him for the rest of his life.

> "You then vote on the proposed sentences by secret, written ballot. All must vote; you may not abstain. Vote on each proposed sentence in its entirety, beginning with the lightest until you've arrive at the required concurrence, which is two-thirds of seven members.

> "A sentence which includes confinement for life without eligibility for parole or confinement for life or confinement in excess of 10 years requires the concurrence of three-fourths or eight members.

She said it again! *Confinement for life without eligibility for parole or confinement for life or confinement in excess of 10 years.* The military judge was suggesting that they put him away for the rest of his life. Or if not that, for many, many years. All for a split-second decision to try and protect his men's lives in a battle zone.

How could this happen? Clint had been willing to die for his country. Why would the Army turn on its own? Clint looked at his lawyer, who stared stoically at the military judge. Couldn't they do something? Couldn't they say something?

He had tried to stand up for his men. Now, the battle was all but lost.

The judge continued, laying the groundwork for what seemed like an unsaid, but understood pact with the military jury, to arrange for the end of his life.

"As I have already said, this court may sentence the accused to confinement for life without eligibility for parole ..."

There she goes again. *Life without eligibility of parole.* She still wasn't finished.

"... unless confinement for life without eligibility for parole or confinement for life is adjudged, a sentence to confinement should be adjudged in either full days or full months or full years; fractions such as one-half or one-third should not be employed to confinement for life without eligibility for parole."

That marked the fourth time the judge had used that phrase. *Life without eligibility of parole.* And if not that, she repeatedly suggested a sentence "in excess of 10 years." They had branded him as a murderer. Now, they were locked in on one another, the judge and the members, preparing for the coup-de-grâce. There was no question that the hammer was about to fall and life, as he knew it, would come to an end.

All he ever wanted to do was serve his country and protect his men. How could this happen to an American soldier?

American lives matter.

CHAPTER 34

The jury had been out forever, or so it seemed.

Every *tick-tock* of the clock became a torturous reminder that his life was one tick closer to ending. The time had passed without much conversation with anyone. Never had he felt lonelier.

Then, just before 10 p.m. local time, a knock at the door from inside the deliberation room.

The military jury had reached a verdict.

The bailiff alerted the judge, who returned to the bench and ordered the bailiff to bring the members back into the jury box.

Clint took his place at the defense table, between his lawyers, and watched as they entered the jury box, one by one, in Army dress blue uniforms. As they had a couple of hours earlier, when they pronounced him guilty of murder, each man avoided eye contact. Their faces were stoic, some stone-cold hard.

"I understand the members have agreed on a sentence," the judge said.

"We have, your honor." This was the full-bird colonel, who served as president of the jury.

"The bailiff will retrieve the sentencing worksheet and bring it to the court, for the court's review."

"Yes, your honor."

Clint watched, through a visual blur, as the events now unfolded in slow motion. The bailiff took the worksheet from the president, walked to the military judge, and handed the worksheet to the judge. Judge Brunson unfolded the paper, studied it and gave no indication at all, from the look on her face, as to what it might say.

"The court has reviewed the sentencing worksheet, and it appears to be in order. The bailiff will return the sentencing worksheet to the president of the court-martial, who, upon the court's instruction, shall pronounce the sentence of the court." She looked over at the defense table.

"The accused and counsel please rise, and face the members."

Flanked by his lawyers, Guy Womack and Capt. William Grady, Clint rose. He turned at an angle, and faced the men who would pronounce his final fate.

"The president will announce the sentence of the court."

The colonel who was the president and senior member of the military jury rose, and held the paper out in front of him. He began to read.

"Lt. Clint Lorance, United States Army, this court sentences as follows—"

The colonel paused for a moment, as Clint's heart pounded like a jackhammer inside his chest.

"—to a dishonorable discharge from the United States Army. To forfeiture of all pay and allowance. And to confinement, for a period of 20 years."

"Very well," the judge said. "The military policemen will take custody of the prisoner. This court is adjourned."

The hammer had fallen, and it had fallen hard. And as mumbling arose from the back of the courtroom, Clint knew that he had not awoken from the nightmare.

Clint's civilian defense counsel, Guy Womack, looked at Clint. "Well, I hear it's not so bad out there in Leavenworth. I hear that they have cottages for the officers." Womack opened his briefcase, stuffed papers in it, closed his briefcase, and walked out.

These were the last words that Clint would hear from Womack. The man came highly recommended as an ex-Marine, and Clint had borrowed $40,000 to hire him.

Clint wondered how Womack could have prepared for a murder trial, with the two having spent so little time together. But he had trusted him nonetheless.

Now, Womack was gone.

The MPs who had been assigned to Clint's prison detail offered to take him out the backside of the courthouse. "That way, you can avoid the cameras, if you want, lieutenant," one of them said.

Clint knew he had nothing to hide, and nothing to be ashamed for. He would prefer to hold his head high, and face the cameras head on, one last time. And while he appreciated the offers that the MPs had made, and even after all he had been through, he still took pride in the U.S. Army, and wasn't going to send any signals that he had run out the back, like a coward.

Clint appreciated the offer, but declined. "If it's okay, I'd rather go out the front of the courthouse, in full dress uniform."

"If that's what you'd prefer sir."

"That's what I would prefer."

"Very well, sir. Are you ready?"

"I'm ready."

Clint's desire to leave the courthouse in his service dress uniform would not be granted. The lead military prosecutor, Capt. Kirk Otto, fresh off a conviction for murder, and in a petty move with no apparent motive other than heaping on more humiliation, ordered him out of his service dress blue uniform as a means of humiliating him as he was brought out before the cameras.

Clint had hoped to wear his uniform out of the courthouse, to keep some sense of dignity while still in the public eye, until he arrived at the MPs station after court. But Otto would have none of it, and dispatched his NCOs to order him to disrobe and change into a set of Army PTs. In other words, the prosecution—only minutes after his sentencing—would parade him out in public, at 10 p.m., in a gray T-shirt and a pair of black shorts, even before he left the courthouse, when the MP station was a mere five minutes away by van ride.

The decision to parade Clint in front of television cameras in a gray T-shirt and black shorts was emblematic of the pettiness and vindictiveness of the Army prosecutors, who, as will be shown, were so zealous to frame Clint and gain a conviction that they hid exonerating evidence from the jury.

As an aside, even Sgt. Bo Bergdahl, a traitor to his country who pleaded guilty to desertion, and whose actions cost the lives of six Americans who went searching for him, got to leave the courthouse with his uniform on. But not Clint. The prosecution has a special hatred for him.

Clint's friend, First Lt. Ross Creech, who had been in the courtroom to support him at trial, accompanied him into the dressing room and took Clint's uniform after he obeyed Otto's order to change into the gray shirt and black shorts.

"Let's go."

Fine.

They could take his uniform, they could take his freedom, they could try and brand him for murder, and they could try and take his dignity. But at the end of the day, they could never take the truth. Clint knew the truth, and somehow, some way, the truth would emerge.

Now surrounded by MPs, they led him out the main entrance to the courtroom and a few minutes later, stepped onto the front portico of the courthouse. The bright lights from the television cameras were blinding, as he stepped into the warm Carolina night.

The Cumberland County temperatures by 10 p.m. were in the mid-70s, much milder than the scorching days and baking nights of Afghanistan. But in other ways, the temperature was just as hot as the moment of the motorcycle charge.

The MPs led him in a swift walk down the front steps of the courthouse. Reporters with cameras and flashing strobe lights pushed in, as close as possible. They shouted questions at him, but he had nothing to say.

His time as an active-duty Army officer would soon come to end. He never dreamed it would end this way.

The MPs opened the door of the van, and he stepped in. One of the MPs closed the door behind him.

A moment later, the driver hit the accelerator, and the van sped away into the dark night.

CHAPTER 35

Earlier in the evening, about the time they pronounced him guilty of murder, a waning crescent moon—the symbol of the Islamic world that had now changed his own world—had been hanging in the Carolina skies. In some strange twist, the lit crescent had appeared over most of his court-martial. But by the time his sentence had been rendered, closer to 10 p.m. on the night of the 1st, the crescent moon had dipped below the horizon, leaving a deep darkness overhead.

There was something ironic about it all, perhaps. The crescent moon, now gone, yielding to darkness. And now, as the MPs brought him to the temporary brig facility, he took his first step in a long journey that would rob him of the next 20 years of his life. The deep dark of the moonless Carolina sky had now flooded into his soul.

No, he had not been given life in prison. But with 20 years of confinement, he may as well have been. He was only 28 years old on the night that his sentence was handed down, and only 27 the day he ordered his soldiers to fire. The heavy-handed sentence of 20 years was almost as long as the life he had already lived.

Now, scorned, betrayed by his country, and branded a murderer, all for making a snap decision in a war zone, as the MPs opened the van doors to begin his long life of confinement, Clint's mind raced about all the thing he would miss out on. On getting married. On having children. On furthering his education. On the career in the Army he so desperately wanted.

Clint did the math, over and over in his head. If he served the entire sentence, he would be 47 years old when he was out of prison. That's almost 50 years old. Most of his life would probably be behind him when he saw freedom again—his best years spent in prison. Dear Jesus, what had he done to deserve this?

His lawyer had dismissed him, with a patronizing comment about cottages at Leavenworth, and now, here he was alone, in the dark of the Carolina night, with his own country and military family—he had considered the military his family— making him a prisoner, in the hands of U.S. Army military policemen.

Where was his hope? Gone. Dissipated. Ripped away.

Hope had vanished as quickly as the dew under the hot Afghan sunshine. Only a quiet despair remained, a deep helplessness that twisted his soul in knots.

They brought him into the MP station, now stripped out of his uniform wearing the U.S. Army PT clothing, gray workout gear. This, in and of itself, had been a calculated slap of dishonor, deliberately planned by the military prosecutor, to try and strip him of every bit of dignity.

It wasn't going to work.

Clint's long journey to Leavenworth was about to begin, and here is how he described the beginning of the journey:

> Don: "Once they announced the sentence, how many days passed before they started the movement to take you to Fort Leavenworth?"
>
> Clint: "Two days. I spent that Friday night of the conviction in the military police station at Fort Bragg. I got there about 2200 hours after having been sentenced to 20 years. The MP station has a

very small jail. It's so small that it's ridiculous. It's pretty much like a storage closet turned into a cell for people who have been convicted. I think it has four cells and one shower.

"The next day, for lunch on Saturday, one of the lieutenants brought me a hamburger and some other things to eat. Then on Saturday afternoon, Capt. William Grady, my military defense counsel, working alongside Guy Womack, came up to talk to me in the cell. We had a good conversation, and he was gracious. He and I lived in the same neighborhood on Fort Bragg."

Don: "What do you recall Capt. Grady talking to you about? I mean, obviously Womack had said that there are cottages for the officers at Fort Leavenworth and then left you. Was Capt. Grady that insensitive, also?"

Clint: "No. Capt. Grady was completely the opposite. I think Capt. Grady, when he gets out of the Army, is going to be a very good attorney in the civilian world. I think if he did not have so many people on his caseload, it would help him. He is a sensitive guy. He was a Southern guy, I think, from Tennessee.

"But that afternoon, Capt. Grady came in and said something to me that changed my life. I'd felt no hope at all. I felt despair, and I didn't know anything about military justice system at all. I thought that 20 years meant 20 years.

"But the captain said, 'In six years, you will be up for parole.'

"And I said, 'Huh?' I said, 'What did you say?'

"And he told me again that I'll be eligible for parole in six years. And I was asking, 'There is parole?' I had no idea. I was overwhelmed by that, that I think I started crying at that point. I thought, *'Thank God, there is still a chance I can salvage part of my life.'*

"Capt. Grady apologized to me, and said, 'I apologize for the way everything turned out.' At a certain point during the course of the trial, I had begun to ask myself if I would have been better off to have gone with Capt. Grady by himself."

Perhaps Clint was right, that he may have done better with the captain in charge of his defense. Womack had arrived late at night, the night before a contested, double murder and attempted murder trial, in which his client faced life imprisonment, and did not meet Clint for trial preparation until the morning of trial.

Most prominent criminal defense lawyers would spend more time, one on one with the client, attempting not only to ascertain the facts of the case, but exploring every possible avenue of defense. Perhaps there was some method to Womack's approach, that is, waiting until the morning of a trial when he is about to defend the client facing life in prison, that he believes makes it more effective.

We will never know.

But one thing Clint knew is that now, Capt. Grady had brought him a sliver of hope, something that he did not have only 12 hours before.

The news about the possibility of parole, delivered by the captain, had brought a ray of sunlight to Clint's living nightmare. At least there was hope, if nothing else, that he might be out before 20 years had passed.

Even still, eligibility for parole and being granted parole are two different animals, especially in high-profile cases where political stakes are involved. Many high-profile inmates, and especially those convicted for murder, had been turned down repeatedly, every year, that their cases come up for review.

But still, hope was alive—even if that hope was as dim as the thin edge of the setting crescent moon.

CHAPTER 36

THE LONG ROAD TO LEAVENWORTH
AUG. 2-3, 2013

A little over 13 months before, Clint had been moving in quick order from one military post to the next—first from Pasab to Shia Choy, then from Shia Choy to Gariban, and then from Gariban to Payenzai. The movement, and the logistics involved, as he moved from one ultimate duty station to the other, was almost dizzying, as he was responsible for movement of equipment, for execution of paperwork, and for preparation in taking command of his platoon.

Now, he prepared for another type of movement—this time from a military courthouse to a military brig. They would transfer him in a drab military van in chains, surrounded by a small military security detail. The trip would last two to three days. And during that time, he would get to spend the night in at least two separate civilian jails, mixed not with a military population, but a civilian population. At each of the stops at the civilian jails, he would have to get in-processed.

In other words, on at least two separate occasions, between Bragg and Leavenworth, he would get to have his mug shot taken and be forced to submit to fingerprints and give information so that local jail officials could fill out paperwork. And after all that, they mixed him in with the general civilian jail population, many of whom had committed violent crimes, some who were hopeless drunks or drug attics, and many who were still waiting to go on trial themselves.

Think about that for a moment. Clint Lorance had on many occasions risked his life in service to this country. Now, they were going to transport him halfway across the country, from North Carolina to Kansas, and they would spend the night not in even a motel room, but in civilian jails, where he would be fingerprinted like a common criminal.

Perhaps for some people, especially a decorated army officer who up until the point he had gotten railroaded by the system, was considered to be at rising star in the military, having to mix with civilian jail populations might feel like a punch in the gut, or a cool slap in the face. But Clint was different. Just as he had a big heart for the men with whom he served, the two nights that he would spend in civilian jails would leave an indelible impression upon him.

His first stop along the way would be at the Lee County Jail, at the Lee County courthouse, in Sanford, N.C.

Sanford, a small town 35 miles northwest of Fort Bragg, with a population of 28,000 people, is 42 miles southwest of the state capital in Raleigh. Known as the brick capital of the world—because at one time it supposedly produced more red brick than any place on the planet—the laid-back little Southern town lived up to its reputation. Almost everything was brick—red brick everywhere.

The red-brick theme included the old Lee County Courthouse, which could pass for any old, early-20th century vintage, middle-of-the town square courthouse—with one notable exception. The Lee County Courthouse, built in 1908, was redder than the reddest firetruck. Even the six stately round columns that towered high to the top of the front portico were red as a cherry, filled with thousands of Lee County bricks, no doubt made from red clay scooped out of the quarries around the county seat.

In the bottom of the red monstrosity of a courthouse, there was the Lee County Jail. The Army had an agreement with Lee County that soldiers convicted of crimes at Fort Bragg, and destined for Fort Leavenworth, spend their first night of their journey in the jail cell in the basement of the courthouse.

The afternoon and evening that he would spend in Lee County would leave an impression that he would never forget.

Don: "So night number one is at the MP station on Fort Bragg. What about the second night?"

Clint: "The next day, Sunday, the soldiers who eventually would transport me all the way to Kansas came by and picked me up, and transported me to the Lee County Jail in Sanford, N.C., about 30 miles northwest of Fort Bragg. I was there one night."

Don: "What were your impressions of the Lee County Jail versus the jail at the MP station on Fort Bragg?"

Clint: "Lee County Jail was all black people and all drugs. I got the impression that the jail would be empty if drugs are legalized."

Don: "How did it make you feel, being in there? You are a highly decorated officer in the Army, and suddenly you're in the Lee County Jail. Tell us about that."

Clint: "When I was in college, I was a lot more idealistic that I am now. I was a lot less realistic and perhaps a lot more liberal. To me, I feel frustrated that the Lee County Jail was just about all black people who are inmates. I thought, to me, there is an issue in this country with that, and I am seeing it firsthand right now. But the thing is, they were all respectful of me, because they had all seen me on TV before I got there. And my nickname was 'My

Man the LT.' This was a term of endearment for them. Anyway, they wanted to know all about my case, and I shared my story with them.

"There had been a TV on the wall, and they had seen my trial on TV, and they said, 'You are that dude from Fort Bragg.'

"Some of them were talking about their cases and I'm thinking, *"My God. One guy had been there for five years and he was still pretrial."*

"This frustrated me that he had been there for five years and had not had a trial.

"What's funny is that he had a little tattoo on his face, a little tear, which I think meant that he killed somebody at one point. Apparently, soldiers convicted at Fort Bragg spend some time in Lee County Jail before they get transferred.

"When I finally arrived at Leavenworth, another soldier-inmate who had been in the Lee County Jail told me he had talked to the same guy. He asked, 'Did you see that dude in Lee County with the tears tattooed on his face?' I said yes. He said, 'I remember him. He still there?'

"It's absurd how long they're in pretrial confinement. Literally, we are in the basement of the Lee County Courthouse. They had remodeled the basement and made it into a cellblock. So, we had to go downstairs below the courthouse. But to me, it felt like, these are the people that they want to hide from everybody. Because you had to walk a long way to get down there, through a lot of corridors, and it wasn't the general population. They put us all in a very small space. There may have been 20 cells in the area. It reminded me of a dungeon."

Clint would never forget that night. None of the inmates were like him, in that they were all from different races and socio-economic backgrounds. Many came from impoverished backgrounds where they never had much of a chance from the beginning. Perhaps some of them deserved to be there. But it appeared that many did not. But the differences did not block the compassion that he felt in his heart for them.

But Clint would leave with a deep appreciation for the kindness so many of them had shown him, when they did not have to show him kindness, and he would leave concerned that many would never receive a fair shake in the justice system.

Next morning, one of the deputies came to unlock his cell and transport him back up to the main level of the courthouse. "It's time to roll, LT," the staff sergeant on the security detail announced.

The next leg of their journey would take them about 45 miles up U.S. Highway 421, where they would hit Interstate 40 west near Greensboro. The journey down Interstate 40 would take them into the Blue Ridge Mountains of North Carolina. Not long after they passed by Asheville, the interstate followed a number of loops and curves and hills as they made their way through the Pisgah National Forest, on their way to the Tennessee border.

The Blue Ridge Mountains are not as rocky, as jagged, or as snow-covered as the Rocky Mountains out west, or the Chilzina Mountains that overlooked Kandahar from a distance. But the Appalachians were full of evergreen trees, green leaves and blooming flowers. On the curving, twisting roads of the interstate through the forest, lush green and white and pink flowers rose all around him. In some ways, the sight proved to be a tonic, a temporary respite from the nightmare that had unfolded in his life.

They crossed west into Tennessee, moving west toward Knoxville, and after they passed the Pigeon Forge exit, the mountainous terrain yielded to rolling, stretching fields, as the landscaped flattened beyond the eastern border of the Volunteer State. Four hundred miles after leaving Fort Bragg, they arrived in the town of Kingston, Tenn.

Kingston is the county seat of Roane County. It is much smaller, even, than Sanford. And unlike Lee County, there would be no stately, multi-columned, early 20th-century vintage courthouse, complete with a jail in the basement, anywhere to be found. In Roane County, the Sheriff's Department and jailhouse shared the same building with a Dollar General store.

Here is how Clint would describe his second night on the road, to the author, as he arrived at the Roane County jail:

> Don: "So on the second night, do they drop you off at a local jail to spend the night while you're on the way in transition?"
>
> Clint: "Yes. I spent the night in the local jail in Roane County, Tenn. It was interesting, because the jail, in the sheriff's department, shared a building with the Dollar General store. I thought that was interesting, and I remember thinking, 'My gosh. Where are we? We are in the middle of nowhere.'"
>
> Don: "Was anybody else in the prison with you that night?"
>
> Clint: "A woman was in the prison cell next to me, who appeared to be a crackhead. And at some point, after that, they brought a drunk in. The drunk started talking to me, and asking, 'What are you doing here?' I told him who I was, and found out that he had been a Vietnam veteran."

They would leave early the next morning, hoping to drive straight through from Roane County to Fort Leavenworth, a distance of 730 miles, and a 10-hour drive, depending on traffic. Their route would take them west through Nashville, then cutting up through the western edge of Kentucky, through Illinois, and then through St. Louis for the final jaunt across Missouri to Kansas City and then the final 22 miles across the Missouri River into Kansas for the final leg to Fort Leavenworth.

CHAPTER 37

THE LITTLE GIRL WITH THE PIGTAILS
SOMEWHERE OFF INTERSTATE 24
SOUTHERN ILLINOIS
AUG. 3, 2012

Southern Illinois marked the halfway mark between Kingston and Fort Leavenworth. They pulled over at a truck stop somewhere along Interstate 24 to stretch their legs and to give the soldiers transporting Clint an opportunity for a smoking break.

August 3rd marked their third day together, since they took him into custody. By now, Clint had developed a trusting relationship with the Army security team on transport detail, and they weren't worried about him running anywhere. Not that he could get far, even if he tried.

They let him get out to stretch his legs, with leg irons and handcuffs on.

Clint shuffled over toward the backside of the van, as the sound of chain irons connecting his ankles clanked against the asphalt. The guard detail wasn't paying much attention to him and the guys were standing up toward the front of the van, lighting up their cigarettes and engaging in mundane chatter.

The fresh air felt good to his lungs, and he was grateful that they let him out of the van for a few minutes

A moment later, he looked over beside the van. And there, beside them, was a family who had just parked in their car. A little girl stood outside the family's car, as her mom was getting something out of the backseat. A moment later, the girl looked over toward Clint.

When she saw Clint in chains, a petrified look came over her face. The girl stared for a second, then turned, ran to her mother and grabbed her tightly around the legs. Clint heard everything she said. "Mommy, who's that bad man over there?"

Here's how Clint would describe the experience, in a question-and-answer session with the author:

Don: "Tell me about seeing the little girl at the truck stop in Southern Illinois."

Clint: "That was the first time I interacted with anyone in the public as a prisoner."

Don: "What do you remember about the little girl? Can you give me a description?"

Clint: "Oh, yes. I remember her. She looked like she could have been one of my nieces. She was a blonde-haired, blue-eyed little thing. And yay tall. And she looked like she had some sort of candy in her hand. The family reminded me a lot of my sister and her kids."

Don: "How old did she appear to be?"

Clint: "I'd say maybe 5. She was very small, and still at that age where she was trying to figure everything out about our relationship with the world. She saw me, and she thought I was bad, or evil, because they had me in chains. The mom grabbed the little girl and went quickly around to the other side of their car to shield her from me. I got back in the van."

And Clint sat down in the van, alone. In some ways, it was nice to get out of the van and stretch, even with the leg shackles on. The busy activity of cars and trucks stopping in from the off-ramp from the Interstate created a vibrancy and displayed the energy of a free America, the country that he would have given his life for.

By the time they had pulled over a few moments earlier, the soldiers who were guarding him were at least treating him with respect, and as if he were one of the guys. They were certainly not treating him like a mass murderer or like he was some kind of criminal.

But the little girl? The little cute girl who reminded him so much of his nieces? The girl's reaction made him feel like someone had punched him in the stomach.

Clint felt sick that he frightened such a sweet, innocent little child. Perhaps it was the chains around his feet, or the sounds of chains clanking on the asphalt parking lot that scared her. Or maybe she saw with his wrists chained together. Whatever it was, he was the closest thing to a living monster that the girl had ever witnessed.

He hoped she would not have nightmares about him tonight, or that her mother would not have to rock her to sleep on account of him. From this point on, he had seen in the little girl's face that he would be viewed as a bad man, as a murderer, as someone who mothers would want to protect their children from, and as a criminal pariah to society.

All because he had given a simple order, in a split-second, to try and protect his men from Taliban suicide bombers on a motorcycle, in the most dangerous, anti-American country in the world.

They would not arrive at Fort Leavenworth for at least another six hours. But the little girl's reaction reminded him of a cold, harsh reality. He may have been sitting in the back of a military van, in a trucking stop parking lot, somewhere off Interstate 24 in southern Illinois. But in reality, despite all his years in service to the Army, despite all the medals and awards that had been bestowed upon him as an enlisted man and an officer, despite all the bullets and mortars that had been fired his way in service to his country, he had already arrived at Leavenworth.

His country had made him a branded man.

CHAPTER 38

For more than 150 years, this small, tough little town on the Kansas side of the Missouri River had enjoyed the rough-and-tumble reputation as the gateway to the Old West. Home to the gunfighter and lawman Wild Bill Hickok to "Buffalo Bill" Cody who won the Medal of Honor in the Indian Wars in 1872, and to William Tecumseh Sherman, the ruthless Union general who scorched a large swath of the American South from Atlanta to the sea, who first established his law office in Leavenworth in 1858, three years before the Civil War, the gunslinging and sometimes ruthless characters who settled in Leavenworth only fueled its reputation as a home to tough guys.

From Leavenworth, much of the Old West was settled. As the origination point for the Oregon and Santa Fe trails, many easterners flooded into Kansas City, by train, then crossed the Missouri River to hitch wagon trains and ride horses to the prospect of a new life along the American western frontier. Many headed to the northwest. Others went southwest. But from Leavenworth, it was westward, always.

But the one thing that Leavenworth was known for the most, and feared for the most, was its reputation as the prison capital of the United States. In the late 1800s, in towns sprouting up all over the West, the threat of sending someone to Leavenworth could spark cold sweats and chills, enough to deter anyone thinking about messing around with the law.

Even today, a large civilian federal penitentiary sits in Leavenworth, not far from the banks of the Missouri River. But Leavenworth was first known, and is still primarily known, for the military prison that is located there, the U.S. Disciplinary Barracks, on the grounds of the U.S. Army Installation at Fort Leavenworth.

From the time that Col. Henry Leavenworth chose the site for the original fort in 1827, until Congress appropriated money for the construction of the original U.S. Disciplinary Barracks in 1874, overlooking the banks of the Missouri River, until today, Fort Leavenworth has enjoyed the reputation for housing the highest-profile, and in some cases the most notorious inmates in the U.S. military.

The current U.S. Disciplinary Barracks, or USDB, which sits in an obscure location on post about four miles north of the main gate to the post, is relatively new, and has more of a modern feel, having first opened its doors in September of 2002. Ironically perhaps, like the old Lee County Courthouse, the main entrance of the facility is also a red brick facade, with the white letters "USDB" drilled into the brick over the main entrance.

But unlike the Lee County Courthouse, which is red brick from head to toe, and all the way around, the red brick facade is only found at the entrance of the USDB. Everything else is large gray cinder block and concertina wire.

In fact, miles of concertina wire are strung all around the perimeter, just like the concertina wire strung around Strong Point Payenzai, Forward Operating Base Pasab, and the other military outposts in Iraq and Afghanistan where Clint Lorance had served.

In another twist of irony, the prison has three pods, where the prisoners live. And the pods, like the shape of Payenzai, which Clint often described as a "Dorito" from the air, are all triangular. He had gone from one "Dorito" to another. And the red brick, the miles of razor-sharp concertina wire, and the triangular shaped fortresses—Clint had all seen before.

The older USDB facility, a large portion of which has now been torn down, was at the center of the base, and was known as the "Castle," or in some corners as the "Hot House." The rumors about it are legion. When German spies who infiltrated the United States on a U-boat in World War II were captured on Long Island, rumor has it that every one of them was strung up by the neck and hung by piano wire in the elevator shaft of the "Hot House," on direct order of President Roosevelt. The author to date has been unable to fully verify, or to fully discount that particular rumor.

The author has confirmed as an eyewitness, however, that two rows of German prisoners, about 14 Germans altogether, are buried in a small, well-kept and manicured cemetery, known as the Fort Leavenworth Military Prison Cemetery, not far from the new USDB. These 14 Germans were executed by American military prison officials, ostensibly, for their role in murdering a fellow inmate. Their bodies remain buried on American soil, never returned to their Fatherland. Altogether, the cemetery contains the bodies of 298 soldiers who died in the USDB. A total of 58 of those graves remain unmarked, a mystery that continues to plague both the cemetery and Disciplinary Barracks.

In recent years, the Army has adopted a new policy that encourages family members to reclaim the bodies of soldiers who die in prison here. All this underscores a point.

Leavenworth is a place where prisoners in many cases come to die. Or, in cases such as Clint Lorance, to give up the best years of their lives.

Notable inmates at the USDB have included Capt. William Calley, who was convicted in 1971 as part of the My Lai massacre in Vietnam, and been given a life sentence for the alleged murder of 21 Vietnamese civilians in 1968. In more recent years, there was the notorious Fort Hood murderer, the Muslim Army psychiatrist- turned-terrorist, Maj. Nidal Hasan, who had pulled a pistol and shouted "Allah Akbar" as he went on a shooting rampage at Fort Hood, murdering 13 people and injuring 31 others.

Then there was Hasan Akbar, another soldier-turned-Islamic-terrorist, convicted for killing two fellow soldiers, including an Army captain and an Army major, and injuring 14 others in an attack in Kuwait in 2003. Akbar tossed a grenade into his fellow soldiers' tent. Akbar also received the death penalty, and like Nidal Hasan, remains on death row at the U.S. Disciplinary Barracks at Fort Leavenworth, even today.

Having said that, in some ways, the overall atmosphere amongst inmates at Fort Leavenworth is more controlled than the typical long-term civilian federal or state penitentiary in the United States. For one thing, all of the inmates had at least one thing in common. They all had served in the military, which means that they all had been through either boot camp, basic training, officer candidate school, or one of the service academies.

That cannot be said for civilian penitentiaries, as most of the inmate population has had no military training. Therefore, whatever crime the inmates were incarcerated for at Fort Leavenworth, and all have been convicted of serious felonies under the Uniform Code of Military Justice, there was a higher degree of discipline amongst the prison population in a military prison.

The prisoners who are on death row, such as the aforementioned Hasan Akbar and Maj. Nidal Hasan, are kept segregated, for security and other reasons, from the general population. Prisoners with life sentences, and with major long-term sentences like Clint, are a part of the general population and are all mixed together, from time to time, on a strictly controlled basis.

Virtually all of the prisoners who are housed at Fort Leavenworth, or who have ever been housed there, have physically done something to commit a crime. Perhaps they pulled the trigger on a pistol to shoot someone else, such as Maj. Hasan. In some cases, they raped someone. In other cases, they picked up a knife and stabbed someone. Or maybe they uploaded classified documents to WikiLeaks, such as Chelsea Manning, who used to be called a man (Bradley Manning), but then decided to call himself or herself a woman.

Clint did not pick up a gun, did not pull the trigger, did not pick up a knife, did not physically rape anyone, and did not physically upload classified materials to WikiLeaks. He had never seen the alleged victims for whom he was convicted of murder, did not know their names beforehand, and acted on information, to the best of his ability, in a split-second, believing that his men were in danger in a red-hot war zone.

And for that, his name would be added to the roles of the notorious. All because of a split-second decision to try and save his men.

American lives matter.

CHAPTER 39

U.S. DISCIPLINARY BARRACKS
"A SOLDIER'S DISGRACE"
SPRING 2014

By the spring of 2014, Clint entered his sixth month as a convicted murderer. He had now lost six months of his life. Six months down, 19 years and six months to go, unless he got lucky and got parole. And he now knew enough to know that parole was no guarantee, especially for someone with his multiple convictions. Besides, he was not eligible for consideration until he served at least one-third of his sentence.

He had enjoyed little contact with the outside world, with the exception of his mother, Anna; his dad, Tracy; his two older sisters, Deanna and Jeni; and his kid brother, Cody. His Aunt Jean had also been there for him. But other than that, he had been cut off from the world, constantly battling against feelings of isolation. Without some means of self-discipline, long-term imprisonment could drive a man mad.

Clint had always been a voracious reader and a physical fitness nut. And facing a mammoth prison term, he determined that his only means of survival was to try and strengthen both mind and body, to the best of his ability. All this meant that as much as prison regulations would allow, he would maximize his time, and maximize his opportunities at two internal destinations within the USDB: the prison gymnasium and prison library.

Discipline of body, and discipline of mind. This was part of his hope for survival. The other part of his hope was to somehow, some way, clear his name.

Though he did not make an entry in his diary to reflect the exact date, sometime in late March or early April of 2014, Clint saw a book in the library that grabbed him by the throat. Even though he had not yet read the book, the title screamed out about the injustice that he was now living, subjugated to a long-term military prison based on cooked-up charges.

A SOLDIER'S DISGRACE,
by Don Snyder

A Soldier's Disgrace. Clint now knew all about that. *A Soldier's Disgrace.* And in some ways, the disgrace, and the false accusations, hurt more than even the unjust incarceration.

Clint's heart skipped a beat. A hope, even a dim hope, that someone else out there might understand his own personal hell. A hope that someone might believe him. He ripped the book off the library shelf and read the tagline on the front cover.

> *"Ronald Alley died trying to clear his name. His widow continued the battle. Finally, a writer uncovered the truth."*

Clint gripped the book, gripped it hard, sat down, and started reading. Soon, he lost track of time.

"A Soldier's Disgrace" by Don Snyder describes the plight of an American POW from the Korean War, Maj. Ronald Alley, who spent three years in a North Korean prison camp. But when Maj. Alley was released from the North Korean POW Camp, the Army arrested him and falsely charged him with collaborating with the enemy. Like Clint, with the overwhelming force of the government positioned against him, an Army court-martial convicted Maj. Alley for a crime he did not commit.

"A Soldier's Disgrace" was a powerful story of injustice and false accusations by the government against an innocent officer, and the story of how, even after he passed away, the major's widow spent the rest of her life seeking his exoneration.

It was like someone had placed this book, right there, in the right place, and at the right time. Clint would spend the next couple of days immersed in Mr. Snyder's book, absorbing every detail of the injustice that had been inflicted upon the major. As he kept reading, not only did Clint see that Mr. Snyder was a great author, but everything about the book showed Don Snyder to be a passionate warrior for justice. Clint, somehow, had to meet the man.

Here's how Clint would describe what happened when he found Mr. Snyder's book.

> "In March or April (of 2014), I read Don Snyder's book, 'A Soldier's Disgrace.' We (my family) had set up a website to show that this is kind of the thing that happens in our military. But before it happened to me, I would never have believed that it happened in my military, until it happened to me.

> "I literally slept on the floor after I started reading it. I could not put it down. I finished it within 24 hours and called Mom and said, 'I don't know if this guy is still alive or not, but if he is, can you contact him and ask if we could put the book on the website?' I wanted people to see that it wasn't just me that it happened to.

> "My mom said okay. So, she contacted the publisher, to ask about linking 'A Soldier's Disgrace' on our website. And the publisher said we had to contact the author directly. And my mom did that. She reached Mr. Snyder on the phone and

had a great conversation with him. Then he took the train from his home in Maine, and came out here to see me the next week. And after a day or two, he says something about a young lawyer that he recently met at a wedding he attended, who was an expert in military law, and that he was very impressive."

That lawyer's name is Lt. Col. John N. Maher of Chicago, who had served on active duty in Afghanistan, the Balkans, Germany, and at the Defense Intelligence Agency. Still in the Army Reserve, he was a lieutenant colonel and a recent U.S. Army War College graduate. After Lt. Col. Maher left active duty on Sept. 6, 2001, to become a civilian Justice Department lawyer, 9/11 five days later compelled him to stay in the Reserve. As a civilian and drilling Reservist, he had worked as a litigation counsel for Mayer Brown, one of the largest law firms in the United States, with offices all over the world, including Chicago, Washington, New York, Hong Kong and London. After that, Maher became a partner in another international super firm, the law firm of Duane Morris, headquartered in Philadelphia, but also with offices all over the world, including London, Singapore, Vietnam, Oman, Myanmar, Shanghai and Taiwan.

Maher went on to become general counsel to the U.S. Office of Personnel Management, becoming chief legal counsel to a presidential cabinet-level appointment, toward the end of the George W. Bush Administration.

Translated, that meant that Lt. Col. Maher provided legal advice to the Director of OPM for personnel legal matters dealing with every civilian employee of the federal government, across every agency of the government, except direct presidential appointees. It was a mammoth job, and in many ways, perhaps the most significant general counsel position in the entire U.S. government. Even after he left his job with in the Bush administration, the colonel had been mobilized back to active duty, to Afghanistan, where he had spent over a year as counsel to U.S. forces in Kabul.

Col. Maher maintained his status in the Individual Ready Reserves, and was one of the foremost experts on military law in the world.

Clint listened to Snyder talk about the need for new legal counsel. It had not dawned upon him, until later in the process, that his prosecution had in effect been a political prosecution, in part as an example-maker for Obama's ridiculously tightened rules of engagement, which threatened American lives. And his prosecution was also carried out to serve an American soldier's head on a silver platter to President Hamid Karzai, and to angry Afghan Muslims, as recompense for the Kandahar massacre.

Maybe Don Snyder was right. Clint had been railroaded by a political-legal machine, something larger than life, and something too big for most ordinary lawyers to handle.

Mr. Snyder's recommendation of Lt. Col. Maher might prove to be a game-changer. If there were ever any chance to exonerate his name, he would need a super-lawyer, someone with the chops, the stature, the experience, and the expertise to push back harder than the government pushed.

But would a man like Maher take his case?

And even if he did, how could Clint afford him?

Clint had been forced to borrow money for Womack's $40,000 fee, and then, his family back in Celeste, Texas, had been forced to scrape all their pennies together to raise money from the community for Clint's appeal after his conviction. And Clint had seen Womack only twice. Once, briefly at the Article 32 investigation, several months ago. And he never saw him again until the day of his trial for murder. Now, he was serving a 20-year sentence on the backside of Mr. Womack's $40,000 fee.

With respect to Guy Womack, he may have tried lots of courts-martial, and like many lawyers, some things he did well, and some he did not. But either way, Womack was no John N. Maher. But in fairness to Mr. Womack, only a small handful of lawyers had ever accomplished what Lt. Col. Maher had accomplished during the course of his professional career.

But would the former general counsel for the OPM have an interest in helping an Army lieutenant whose family's means was middle class at best?

Maybe Maher would be a game-changer, if Clint could retain him.

Then again, maybe this was pie in the sky.

"Let me see what I can do," Snyder said. "Maybe John would be interested."

CHAPTER 40

John N. Maher stood in his father's living room behind the ironing board holding a hot steam iron in his hand, in the Irish-Catholic southside of Chicago. The Mahers of Chicago were a close-knit family, and they took care of each other, sometimes down to the smallest of details, such as ironing each other's garments.

In this instance, John, or as his dad called him, Johnny, was the best of the Maher men in the crucial task of operating a steam iron to eliminate wrinkles, and apply a crispness to the men's dress shirts. This skill had been acquired, in part, because of John's squared-away military lifestyle, where he had served as a lieutenant colonel in the U.S. Army.

The Army taught its officers discipline in the finest of details, including spit-polish and shine, the elimination of wrinkles from all garments of clothing, closely cropped haircuts and gentlemanly manners, 24 hours a day, seven days a week. In all of these disciplines, John had learned well. He made consistent discipline and hard work a part of his being.

Applying one of the disciplines he had perfected in the military, John had volunteered for ironing duty this morning. He had just finished ironing his own shirt, was in the midst of ironing his brother's shirt, and was thinking about his father's shirt, when his cellphone rang.

John looked up. His cellphone was lying on a footstool at the end of the living room sofa. He checked his watch. He was in a tight time squeeze, about to head out to a funeral.

Forget it.

Then, instinct took over. He put down the iron and walked over and picked up the phone, to see who was calling. It might have something to do with the funeral.

John Carr.

John Maher had first met John Carr in August of 2004 when Maher returned from Army reserve duty in Washington, D.C., to the Maher family home in Chicago. Maher became Team 5 leader with the 91st Legal Support Organization on Fort Sheridan, Ill., that month, and Carr was a member of the team.

Maher and Carr also served together when Maher served as deputy staff judge advocate for the 416th Theater Engineer Command in Darien, Ill. They had also served together at Fort Campbell, Ky.; in Manheim, Germany; and at Walter Reed Army Medical Center in Washington, D.C.

John Carr was good people. Almost like family.

This one, he would take, if only for a few seconds. He swiped the answer screen on the cellphone.

"How's it going, John?"

"Johnny," Carr said, "a lieutenant in the 82nd Airborne is in legal trouble. Will you help?"

"I'm in," Maher said, without hesitating, as he trusted Carr's instincts. If John Carr had picked up the phone to ask for help for a young officer, that's all he needed to know. "However, I'm on my way out the door to my cousin's funeral. Can I call you afterwards?"

"Sure."

Maher hung up the phone. His cousin, Joseph Maher, at the young age of 30, had taken his own life. Maher was in a rush. It would be a hard day for the family.

Two hours later, the funeral was over. The afternoon had been difficult, as John had been close to his cousin, who died in the prime of his life. He served as a pallbearer at the graveside on that cold, dreary Chicago morning.

The familial bonds of Irish-American blood ran deep. Still, even at the funeral, on the cold, windswept lawn of Oak Hill Cemetery on the far southwest side of Chicago, Maher could not shake John Carr's call from the back of his mind.

With a loving affection for his cousin, John helped carry the casket from the hearse to the graveside, then stepped back, in a line with the other pallbearers, as the priest administered his last rites.

Carr, an Army JAG reservist, and a damn fine lawyer in his own right, had been buddies with Maher for a number of years. Carr had served in a JAG reserve unit over which Maher had been deputy commander.

John lingered a few minutes with the family, said his final graveside goodbyes to his departed cousin, Joe, then got into his car to head back to his home in Roscoe Village, across town on the northside.

During the drive, his mind returned to his friend, John Carr, and the call that came before he left for the funeral. John Carr head recently gotten married in Pennsylvania, and John Maher had flown out for the ceremony. The wedding had been a formal military affair, with all of the officers and military guests in uniform. Maher had pulled out his dress blues for the occasion, and was happy not only to be there to support his good friend Carr, but also to reconnect and fellowship with a number of other fellow officers and friends from his active duty days in the U.S. Army.

All this was on his mind as he drove home that afternoon, picked up his phone, and returned Carr's call.

"Johnny!" Maher greeted his friend with an enthusiasm in his voice. "How is the newlywed?"

"Doing great, John. Things are great here. How about you? How's the Windy City? How is Kathryn?"

"Couldn't be better! She sends her love." They engaged in a few minutes of jovial banter, swapping a few war stories and memories, as they always did, and trading barbs peppered with a mutual fraternal ribbing that could only be understood or appreciated within the ranks of the Army officer corps.

Then, Maher cut to the chase.

"So, what's up with this 82nd Airborne lieutenant you called about earlier."

"John," Carr said, "do you remember the author who was the best man in my wedding, Don Snyder?"

"Sure, I remember Snyder. From Maine, as I recall. Great guy. Authored some fine books, and a lot of fun to be around. How's he doing?"

"He's doing well. But he's met a young officer in the 82nd Airborne who read one of his books and reached out to him. That officer is in trouble. A lot of trouble. Would you be willing to help?"

"Like I said this morning, I'm in. What's the problem?"

"Murder, John. They've charged the kid with murder."

"Murder?" Had he heard that right? "An 82nd Airborne officer?"

"Yes. On the battlefield. In Afghanistan. In Kandahar Province. The lieutenant ordered a couple of his men to fire on three Afghans for rushing their platoon's position with a motorcycle. And for that, they charged with him with murder. And convicted him. The kid never picked up a weapon, Johnny. He never fired at these guys, and had a couple of seconds to make a split-second decision."

A pause followed. Something did not compute. "And they prosecuted him for murder? Did I get that right? For shots ordered in a hot battle zone?"

"Roger that," Carr said. "They claimed he violated the rules of engagement. Charged him, convicted him, and gave him 20 years. Kid got railroaded. Now, he's at Leavenworth. Sounds like a railroad job to me. Would you talk to him?"

"You bet, I'll talk to him. What's his name?"

"Lorance. First Lt. Clint Lorance. Spelled L-O-R-A-N-C-E. Infantry paratrooper. Platoon leader. First Platoon, Charlie Company, 4/73 Cav. 82nd Airborne Division."

"Roger that." Maher wrote down the officer's name and unit number on a legal pad. "I'll take it from here. Let me reach out and try to make contact."

And with that conversation, Lt. Col. John N. Maher, former general counsel for OPM, first became involved in the case of the United States vs First Lt. Clint Lorance. It was a call that would change Maher's life.

And it was a case, although he did not know it at the time, that would be more important than anything he had ever handled in his illustrious legal career, including the presidential cabinet-level legal advice that he had dispensed as general counsel for OPM.

A young officer's freedom was on the line, because of a prosecution that, at first whiff, smelled like a rotten perch lying in the hot sunshine on the deck at the end of Navy Pier in the middle of July. Based on what John Carr had described, there was putrid smell about this case. And Maher felt that trial lawyer's check in his gut.

Why would the 82nd Airborne prosecute one of its own officers for ordering his men to fire on a motorcycle, in Afghanistan, that was threatening the platoon's position, when the Taliban had been using motorcycles with increasing regularity as instruments of suicide and martyrdom? They had been blowing up Americans, and blowing up Afghans, too, with these fast motorcycle charges.

Something didn't add up.

Even before he ever met Clint Lorance, John Maher had some homework to do. If he dug into the case and discovered that Lorance was really guilty, fine. He'd leave it at that. But the basic facts, if John Carr was right, did not point to guilt Those facts pointed to a prosecutor sniffing a controlled substance. After all, ordinarily, when civilians are killed during combat, they are not murdered, but by international law, are considered "collateral damage" in the fog of war.

John needed to get to the bottom of it, and he would get to the bottom of it.

He would order the record of trial through his contacts in the Army, and then, he would contact the U.S. Disciplinary Barracks at Fort Leavenworth to try and arrange for a personal meeting with Lt. Clint Lorance.

This case, he already knew, would prove to be larger than life.

CHAPTER 41

THE DEFENSE GAINS A STAR
LIEUTENANT COLONEL JOHN
N. MAHER OF CHICAGO
JUDGE ADVOCATE GENERAL CORPS
U.S. ARMY

John N. Maher had been off full-time active duty now for several years, although he had been called back several times for extended periods, to serve his country during the war on terror. A former prosecutor with the First Infantry Division, he deployed to the Balkans during a United Nations peacekeeping mission to prevent the spread of ethnic cleansing, then served as a defense counsel before leaving active duty to become a civilian Justice Department attorney. As a reservist, he had mobilized to Afghanistan for 13 months, and to the Defense Intelligence Agency.

At 45 years old, with sparkling blue eyes and a trim physique that could have rivaled a professional soccer player, Maher still worked out, ran a couple of races each year, and could still fit into his military service dress-blue uniform like the first day he was commissioned.

His résumé sported the academic and professional pedigree of someone who might one day vie for a spot on the U.S. Supreme Court. As general counsel to the OPM director, a presidential cabinet-level position, with DOJ and big firm experience, Maher could open about any legal door that he desired. He had recently graduated from the U.S. Army War College, earned an MBA, already had a master's in law, or an "LLM," in addition to his juris doctorate, and was teaching as an adjunct professor of law while managing his practice and small business.

Still, with all he had accomplished professionally, and having been a partner with one of the top law firms in the world, John was not above taking the time to iron his daddy's shirt, to iron his brother's shirt, or to do whatever else his dad or his brother needed him to do. The principles of love, duty, honor, family and country drove him far more than any money he had made, the high places he had been, or the powerful shoulders of people whose elbows he had rubbed.

With a humble, personable and unassuming demeanor, one would never know that John Maher was a legal machine unless one had reason to know. All the legal accolades aside, Maher remained a soldier at heart—a soldier always—and an officer and a gentleman who sincerely cared about the other guy.

While he had dealt with some of the highest officials in the American government, Lt. Col. Maher's heart burned with compassion for the combat soldier on the ground. His love and concern was for the GI who would never be a part of high-level Pentagon strategy, or of esoteric policymaking, but who were ready to put their hearts, their souls, their minds and their lives on the line for their country and for one another.

Maher had a heart for men like Clint Lorance. He had worked with men like Clint and knew that warfare was hell. He also knew that no American soldier, who will give more than most Americans will ever dream of giving, should ever be crushed in the steel vice of a policy issue, to satisfy some colonel seeking a star, or some brigadier general seeking a third or fourth star.

Of course, Clint had no idea whether Maher would give him the time of day. Why would he?

After Snyder mentioned Maher's name, and after Snyder left from his visit at the USDB, Clint had done his homework on Maher. One of the many traits that Clint had employed as an officer was preparation and homework. It was the extra work that helped him find the UAV for First Platoon, the dog team, and the Cerberus camera. And that same penchant for research, Clint had applied to learning everything he could about Maher.

Here is part of what Clint learned about Lt. Col. Maher.

The Senior Executive Service in Washington, D.C., of which Lt. Col. Maher had joined of when he became general counsel for OPM, has a pay grade and a civilian rank structure that is analogous to the military rank structure in the Army. Within the Senior Executive Service, the highest ranking possible was designated as SES III, a designation assigned to the general counsel of OPM.

By federal-designated analogy, the position of SES III is the civilian equivalent of a three-star general, also known as a lieutenant general, in the U.S. Army.

In other words, it dawned upon Clint, that Lt. Col. Maher's position within the federal government in Washington, D.C., as the equivalent of a three-star general, outranked even the commander of the 82nd Airborne Division, who was a two-star general.

If Maher somehow joined his defense team, aside from the fact that he was one of the foremost experts in the world on military law, the gravitas alone that Maher would bring would pack a powerful punch and, hopefully, bring a renewed sense of credibility to Clint's cause.

But how could his family afford a lawyer like that?

Aside from the personal discipline that he employed in the weight room and in the library, Clint's quest to find a reason to hope had been one of the keys to survival and this hellhole of a place called Leavenworth.

It wasn't the staff or the soldiers working at Leavenworth who served as his captors that made it a hellhole. In fact, the military prison staff had been cordial for the most part, had treated him professionally.

Clint himself had once been an MP in Iraq and appreciated that his captors had a hard, and sometimes thankless, job.

Rather, the thing that made Leavenworth a hellhole was knowing that he would be confined here for up to 20 years, and that his presence here reminded him that he had lost his name, had lost his reputation, and had been falsely branded as a murderer.

As far as Lt. Col. Maher was concerned, Clint decided to take it all in stride. The more he learned about this guy, Maher, the more he was impressed, and the more he wondered, "Can I get this guy to believe in me?" and, "Would he consider ever taking my case?"

He would not get his hopes up, because at the end of the day, getting a lawyer of that magnitude, having someone like a John N. Maher take over his case, was probably a pipe dream.

But then, one day, it happened. Word came to Clint that Lt. Col. John Maher, the former general counsel of the Office of Personnel Management, was coming to Leavenworth, and he was coming to meet with him.

A surge of hope flooded his soul. And at a place like Leavenworth, there was little to hang on to, except hope.

CHAPTER 42

It had been about 60 days since John Maher had taken the call from his friend John Carr, and about 60 days since he had first heard the name of Clint Lorance. The basic facts of the case, or what he knew of the facts, had eaten at him, and bothered him from the time he took the first call from John Carr on the morning of his cousin's funeral.

The process of ordering the record of trial, receiving it, and reviewing it, had been a time-consuming ordeal, and had taken 60 days. Maher had dived into all the press accounts of the prosecution, trying to wrap his arms around what had happened.

But having not yet met Clint, and having studied the record in detail before the first client meeting, he continued to be nagged by the Army's decision to bring a murder prosecution in this situation. First Platoon had been on an enemy battlefield, where American soldiers had been shot and blown up, in the most dangerous, Taliban-infested section of the world.

Why?

Why under these circumstances would the Army even think about prosecution? This was one of the craziest decisions—the decision to prosecute— that Maher had ever witnessed in his legal career.

Maybe if he got to meet Clint today, maybe Clint could shed some sort of light on what really happened.

The flight from Chicago to Kansas City took about 90 minutes. After grabbing a rental car at Kansas City International, John had now made his way along the easy 20-mile drive thorough the western Missouri countryside, across the old steel bridge spanning the Missouri River and into the town of Leavenworth. From the bridge, to the old clock tower of the base, Fort Leavenworth's most recognizable landmark could be seen over to the right.

Off to the left, the sleepy downtown of Leavenworth, with two-story buildings, and 1940s-vintage homes along the riverfront, presented an image of small-town Americana, perhaps like a landscape in an old, idyllic Norman Rockwell painting.

Maher crossed the bridge, and two blocks later, turned right, and drove a couple of hundred yards to the main gate of the base.

As a senior Army officer, Fort Leavenworth wasn't new to John Maher. Known as the Intellectual Center of the Army, many of the Army's mid-level officers cycled through the base, as new majors, to learn how to serve on the staffs of senior officers, prior to becoming battalion commanders. Maher had also graduated from Leavenworth, and spent a full two weeks on the post prior to his graduation.

But never had he come to the post for anything like this … to possibly take up the case of an officer convicted of double murder. He stopped at the main gate, pulled out his reservist ID and handed it to the security guard, who scanned it in, and waved him through.

The main drag from the front gate, cutting through the heart of the post, Grant Avenue, runs from south to north, and parallels the river off to the right. The road snakes by George S. Patton, Jr., Junior High School, passes the post Holiday Inn on the left and the post exchange and a statue of Gen. Grant himself on the left, before circling around the old clock tower and the location of the old USDB.

The new USDB, where Clint Lorance was housed, was located along the road past the main attractions on base, past the post airstrip and past the post shooting range. About 10 minutes after clearing the main gate, John pulled into the parking lot in front of the huge military prison, got his briefcase, got out of the car, and made his way into the front entrance.

Maher passed the prison commandant and command sergeant majors' offices on the right, climbed two flights of stairs, and immediately came to a guard station with metal detectors manned by two MPs.

"May I help you, sir?"

"Lt. Col. John Maher to see Lt. Clint Lorance."

The MP, a sergeant in charge of manning the front desk, pulled out a note book and looked through loose leaf paper in a three-ring binder. "Command Judge Advocate's Office?" The sergeant looked up, after searching for several minutes for the right paperwork.

"That's right," John said. "I'm here for an attorney visit with Lt. Lorance."

"One moment, sir. I'll have to get you an escort."

A few minutes later, a young army private, wearing drab-green the Army camouflage uniform, walked into the waiting area. "Col. Maher. I'm a paralegal specialist with the Command Judge Advocate's Office. I'm here to escort you back to see the inmate."

"You can walk through the metal detector now, sir,"

"Roger that."

John walked through the metal detector, but the guards weren't finished.

"Sir, would you hold your arms out and let me check you with the wand?"

"Not a problem."

John stood in a spread-eagle position as the sergeant did a quick scan of his wrists, arms, and legs with a wand, the long, handheld metal detector that looks like a curling iron.

"You're good to go, sir," the sergeant said.

"Right this way, sir," the private said.

There was a loud *click,* the sound of cold steel unlocking, as the private led John into a small holding area. Then more loud steel clicks, then the sound of steel locks bolting behind them. Then came the sound of an electronic buzz, and more clicks. Another steel door opened, and the private let John into a long, antiseptic-looking hallway, to the loud sound of steel bolts slamming shut behind him and the smell of industrial cleaning fluid filled the air.

This was what Clint Lorance's life had become, after risking his life for his country in the U.S. Army. Incarcerated for 20 years behind the clanging sound of steel locks and buzzing electronic doors, walking down hallways that smelled like Lysol whenever they let him out of his cell for chow, to go to the prison library, or for an attorney visit. John followed the private, maybe 30 yards down the hallway, where the private opened a door over to the right, leading to a suite of offices occupied by the command judge advocate, who was the military legal counsel for the prison commandant.

"The lieutenant is in the conference room at the end of the hallway, sir. I'll take you to him."

"Roger that."

They stepped down another hallway, down the middle of the CJA offices, this one much smaller and more intimate than the larger hallway outside. Just past the lieutenant colonel's office who served as command judge advocate, at the end of the hallway, they came to a door, with a sign that said, "Trial Defense Services."

The private opened the door, and said, "Lieutenant, you have a visitor."

John stepped into the office, as a young man wearing a brown prison jumpsuit rose to his feet from the other side of a small desk in the small room.

John extended his hand and said, "I'm John Maher."

"Clint Lorance," the young officer said, greeting John with a firm handshake, looking him right in the eye. His voice exuded confidence, and his eyes sparkled with hope. "Thank you for coming, sir."

By this time, John had not only read the record of trial, but had mastered it. He knew all the government witnesses, what they said, and what they had not said. He had read all the questions that had been asked at trial by Clint's civilian defense counsel, Guy Womack, and the questions and points not raised by the defense. John's review of the record had left him with the same conclusion that his gut instinct has told him the day he got John Carr's call: that Clint Lorance had been railroaded.

But a main piece of the puzzle still remained. Meeting the man himself. Maybe Clint was a horse's ass or something, who had hacked off the chain of command. Maybe he had done something that was not reflected in the record.

You don't prosecute one of your own for shots fired in the battlefield, even if civilians had been mistakenly shot in the fog of war. Civilian casualties, unfortunately, had been a part of every war in history since the beginning of time.

Maybe meeting Clint would provide some sort of clue to explain what the Army had done, or why they had done it. One of the first things John wanted to do was to make Clint comfortable with the relationship. John wanted peer-to-peer, not colonel to lieutenant. "Please don't call me colonel or sir. I'm not on active duty anymore. Just call me John."

Clint obliged, and then after they exchanged a few more pleasantries, John got down to business.

"Tell me what was going through your mind, Clint."

John took copious notes of Clint's answers. Here's what Clint told him, verbatim:

"John, I take full responsibility for my men. And if I did not give that order, and the motorcycle detonated and killed or wounded my men, I would be in a different kind of prison for the rest of my life. My only intent was to protect my men and bring them back safely."

In a question-and-answer session with the author, John Maher shared some of his detailed impressions of that first meeting:

> Don: "You had an initial gut feeling about this case based on what your friend, John Carr, called and briefed you on it. But you wanted to do some homework by ordering the record and reading it, and doing some additional investigation beforehand. When you met Clint for the first time, was there any initial change in your initial gut feel about the case?"

> John: "Meeting Clint in person reinforced my gut feeling that something went terribly wrong with the investigation and prosecution of this case. This was the first time in 20 years of doing this work that my head and my heart tell me the client is not only not guilty, but truly innocent of double murder and attempted murder."

> Don: "What was he like, personally? Or a better way to ask is, what was his personality like?"

> John: "Lorance broke every stereotype of what most people might think of a convicted double murderer and attempted murderer. He is self-effacing, intelligent, deferential, mannered, and without an ounce of guile or meanness or temper or anger. He might even be an empath."

> Don: "I know you had lots of questions before you met Clint. Questions about why the Army would prosecute one of its own officers for ordering fire

in a spit-second decision on the battlefield. And I know you wanted to interview Clint to get a feel for his demeanor, etc. Did you ever have any doubts, before you met him, about whether he broke the law?"

John: "If I had any doubts about whether Clint was hell bent on indiscriminately killing any motorcycle riders as the prosecution told the jury, they evaporated forever after having met Clint. He doesn't fit the bill of a bad-person killer or murderer."

Two hours later, John Maher left his first meeting with Clint more convinced that the Army made up its mind within hours of the July 2, 2012, shooting that Lorance was a murderer, and from that point on, the die was cast. Clint Lorance had been railroaded by the U.S. Army, sacrificed on the altar of a political prosecution.

And from that, both a friendship, and an attorney-client relationship, was born. John had already prepared, even before he arrived to meet Clint, a petition for a new trial with the Army Court of Criminal Appeals, which sits in Fort Belvoir, Va. That's how skeptical he had been about the Army's decision to prosecute, even before he met Clint, that he went ahead to the next step, procedurally in the process, and prepared the motion.

As his plane took off that afternoon from Kansas City International Airport, en route back to Chicago, John could not shake from his mind the impressive young officer he had just met. This much he knew, beyond any question, and beyond any doubt: Clint Lorance is an innocent man.

John had to find a way to get Clint Lorance out of that place called Leavenworth, and rightfully, to clear his name from the stench of a false accusation and from any ill-gotten convictions that were the product of a rotting, stinking political prosecution.

But how?

At the moment, he wasn't yet sure. But this he knew:

He would help Clint Lorance clear his name, come hell or high water.

CHAPTER 43

John Maher stood in his study in his home in Chicago's Northside and, crossing his arms, looked out the spacious second-floor window of his modern, airy home in Roscoe Village, next to Lincoln Park and Lakeview. Behind him, the floor-to-ceiling bookshelves reflected interests in law, government, history, philosophy, Second World War, Civil War, and biographies.

Thanksgiving week had descended upon Chicago, and with it, so had the freezing Chicago weather that epitomized the Windy City this time of year.

Outside the large bay windows of the three-story walk-up, and beyond the dark green walls and white window trim of his study, bare tree limbs pointed to the cloudy skies, and leaves swirled in the wind on the frozen ground. Indeed, the gray signs of winter had descended over the neighborhood, a reminder that Chicago was on the doorsteps of another change of season, this time from the breezy autumn on the Great Lakes, to the freeze of the holiday winter.

About a mile east, by the flight of the crow from John's home office, Wrigley Field stood in cold silence. On summer evenings with the windows open, one could hear the crowd cheering during night games at the "friendly confines" from Maher's home. But now, two months after another losing season by his beloved Cubbies—whose losing performance in the 2014 season had been about as chilly as the 28-degree noontime temperatures in Chicago on Tuesday, the 25th of November—the old ballpark had gone stone-cold silent again.

Chicagoans had entered the holiday season. The traffic in his neighborhood had died down, as many had started their Thanksgiving vacation. A few pedestrians, wearing overcoats and gloves, were out on the streets. But for the most part, Thanksgiving was in the air.

It was a stark contrast to the infernal hellhole of 110 degrees that Clint Lorance and First Platoon had endured some two years and four months ago, in a place called Payenzai in the deadliest country in all the world.

On the shiny hardwood floors of John's study, all around him, 12 reams of paper, each one thicker than the Chicago phone book, sat on floor in an organized fashion. These reams of paper represented Clint Lorance's record of trial. They included exhibits that had been offered by the prosecution, maps of the battlespace, photos of the Afghans shot in the exchange, and written statements of the soldiers called to testify against Clint.

The more John had studied the record, the more obvious it had become that the Army had set out with a purposeful intent of railroading Clint Lorance. In order to get several of his men to testify against him, they had informed nine of the soldiers in Clint's platoon that they were themselves suspected of murder and could be prosecuted.

Then they were given immunity and ordered to cooperate against Lorance. To strong-arm them into cooperating, the commanding general had issued a written order for them to testify and had granted immunity, which meant that if they cooperated, they would not be prosecuted for murder.

To make matters worse, the military jury had never been made aware of this fact, that the nine soldiers testifying against Clint had been threatened with prosecution themselves if they did not cooperate. Nor was the jury informed that the soldiers were testifying under an order and grant of immunity.

Based upon on the record, the prosecution's conduct had been questionable on several points. For one thing, prosecutors deliberately avoided showing any evidence to the jury that a firefight had occurred on the west side of the village, moments after the shooting of the three Afghans in the motorcycle.

The prosecutor did everything in his power to hide from the military jury that this was a dangerous battlefield, and that the whole platoon was operating in a hot situation. Obviously, the prosecution wanted to portray First Platoon's mission as a "Sunday stroll in the park," where there was no reason to be concerned about three Afghans charging the platoon's position on a motorcycle. That was a deceitful approach by the prosecution, to hide evidence, as the military jury never got the rest of the story, by prosecutorial design. And the defense counsel did not push very hard against the prosecutor in carrying out the government's railroad job against Clint.

And even though two paratroopers from First Platoon—including Spec. Reyler Leon, who was physically closest to the shooting, *had given sworn statements that the Afghan National Army had fired first at the three motorcycle riders*—the prosecutor worked hard to deliberately keep this information away from the jury.

When the defense counsel tried to enter this information at trial, that the Afghan National Army had fired first, the prosecutor objected based upon hearsay, and the judge sustained that objection. The defense counsel, Mr. Womack, could have cited several exceptions to the hearsay rule to get the evidence before the jury, but for whatever reason, elected not to try.

What was the significance of this evidence? That the Afghans fired first? To Maher, the significance was clear.

First off, bullets from the Afghan National Army might have killed the two Afghan motorcycle riders, and not bullets from Clint's platoon. No autopsies were done, so we don't know what bullets killed the riders. But the prosecutor decided to hide this information from the jury, in his unbridled zeal to convict Clint Lorance.

Second, it shows that the Afghan National Army also viewed the motorcycle to be a mortal threat, so much so that they, too, opened fire. The Afghans also knew that Old Chilliwack Road, the motorcycle's route of approach, was a Taliban-controlled road.

And, of course, had the firefight on the west side of the village been revealed to the jury, would have given the jury at least some idea of how hot and dangerous the situation was faced by First Platoon on the morning of July 2.

But the jury was not able to judge Clint's mind frame in light of all the factual circumstances surrounding his order to open fire, because the prosecutor deliberately worked to conceal evidence that flat-out would have led to an acquittal. The prosecution's concerted attempt to hide the sworn statements of witnesses that the Afghans fired first, and its attempt to hide from the jury the firefight on the west side of the small village, minutes after the firing on the motorcycle, marked at least two deliberate "hide-the-ball" tactics employed by the prosecution that John had discovered so far, all to ensure that Clint's head got delivered on a silver platter.

Surely, either the command, or the Army Court of Criminal Appeals, when this hide-the-ball tactic was brought to light, would correct this travesty, disallow the conviction, and set Clint free. So far, the Army Court of Criminal Appeals had been silent on his petition for a new trial. But even so, John felt something in his gut. Something was missing.

What had he missed?

Then, like a flash of hot lightning bolting through the cold Chicago skies, it hit him.

The prosecutor had crossed out the names of the Afghans on the charge sheet. So just who were the two Afghans that were killed and the third who escaped?

Biometrics!

Of course! Where was the biometrics evidence on these motorcycle riders? Why wasn't this evidence part of the record? What would the biometrics evidence show about the three riders on the motorcycle?

John sat in front of his computer and sent an email to Afghanistan. "Bill, please call me."

Several hours passed. The hours felt like days. Maybe Bill Carney wouldn't call or return his email. And even if he did call, there was no guarantee that he could help.

But John had to have an answer to this question. After all, Clint had been charged with the murder of Afghan civilians. If anybody could run a search and get him an answer to his questions, as quickly as possible, without having to serve additional discovery or a Freedom of Information Act request on the government, Bill Carney was the man. The retired New York City police detective still worked in Afghanistan on the U.S. government's national biometric enrollment program.

John and Bill knew each other from their service together in Afghanistan. Carney had worked under John's direction in supervision on a special project in Parwan, Afghanistan, two years ago. John hoped and prayed that based upon their previous relationship, Carney would be willing to help out.

Hopefully, Bill Carney would respond.

In an interview with the author, Maher described what happened next.

"I sent Bill Carney an email asking for a call. We spoke the next day, he in Afghanistan and I was at my home office one mile west of Wrigley Field in Chicago. I explained the case, and that we had names of Afghan victims crossed out on the charge sheet and in the CID agent activity summaries."

Here, John Maher is referring to the fact that the military prosecutor had physically crossed out the names of the Afghan "victims," who were on the motorcycle, from the charge sheet. The charge sheet is the equivalent of the military's version of a criminal indictment, officially telling an accused what crime he is being charged with. In this case, they charged Clint with murder of the unnamed Afghans. However, Maher found the names of the "victims" in other parts of the record of trial, which were not crossed out, but which the jury never saw.

John finished drafting his email to Carney, addressing him casually as "Coach," as Carney had been a young women's basketball coach for many years for his two daughters while he was on the NYPD:

"Coach, I have a favor—will you try and pull the biometric enrollment records and see if there are any 'hits'?"

Carney responded immediately. "I'll see what I can do. Email me the specifics."

John followed up and emailed Carney the names of the three Afghans on the motorcycle—allegedly civilians, two of whom had been killed—which triggered the murder prosecution against Clint. He also emailed the name of a fourth Afghan, who had been captured in the firefight on the west side of the village, moments after the motorcycle shooting.

If the biometrics data tied any of these four Afghans to bombmaking, particularly any of the three who are on that motorcycle, then this could be a game-changer for Clint.

For now, he could only wait.

American lives matter.

CHAPTER 44

THE AMERICAN BIOMETRICS PROGRAM
AFGHANISTAN
2009-ONGOING

As John paced back and forth on the third floor of his Chicago home, he knew, in his gut, that missing pieces of the puzzle were still out there, somewhere, the pieces that would tell the rest of the story of Clint's case. These undiscovered links to the truth had not been revealed at the court-martial or in the record of trial, and John suspected that was by prosecutorial design.

After all, within days of July 2, 2012, the Army had made special condolence payments, called "solatia" payments, to local Afghans claiming to have lost loved ones in the shooting. The Army had also refused to let CID continue to interview witnesses, per Capt. Patten, the command legal advisor. The CID agent activity reports note that Capt. Patten would not authorize, nor would the command authorize, the CID to finish its interviews. That meant that witnesses who would exonerate Clint would not be interviewed.

When the notion finally struck him that the trial records showed nothing whatsoever about biometrics data at all concerning any of the alleged victims or anyone captured on the battlefield on July 2, 2012, the only thing that had surprised John Maher was how long it had taken for the light bulb to go on. That was because only a year before, John had held one of the most important legal jobs in the world involving the prosecution of cases using biometrics evidence.

It was a top-secret position, at the time, in Parwan, Afghanistan, and the position had come about because of the rapid United States drawdown and pullout of military and other resources from Afghanistan. And in many ways, the top-secret prosecution program harkened back to President Obama's walk in Arlington National Cemetery on Veterans Day of 2009.

When President Barack Obama had announced United States' withdrawal from Afghanistan, on June 22, 2011, in the midst of the American surge that was crippling the Taliban's warfighting capabilities, a trickle-down effect cascaded across the U.S. military.

But it was not just the U.S. military that was affected by Obama's sudden, unilateral withdrawal announcement. Two of the non-military federal agencies, the Department of State and the FBI, were heavily involved in logistics of the American draw-down as well.

To understand all of this, let's dig a little deeper on what was formerly a secret military program in Afghanistan that most Americans still don't know about.

In September of 2010, the Army revealed publicly a secret program that had been ongoing for a number of months—a program to take biometric data on every man, woman and child in Afghanistan. That was the goal, anyway, and that program was aggressively implemented starting in 2009.

That year, 2009, U.S. soldiers were issued biometrics collections kits, and began collecting biometrics data from thousands and thousands of Afghan citizens. The data collected by the American soldiers was fed into central computer systems, largely to identify insurgents and Taliban suspected of bombmaking and anti-American activities.

Biometrics, in this case, meant collecting identifying data on every Afghan, including iris scans, face scans and other means of identification. But the two main components of biometric evidence came down to 1) fingerprints collections and 2) DNA collections.

Because Afghanistan was a giant field of bombs dug into the ground, and because so many Americans were getting killed by hidden IEDs, the U.S. needed a way to track the bombmakers. The U.S. planned to collect all shrapnel of bombs that blew up and maimed or killed Americans, and then to study every piece of shrapnel, every piece of metal, every piece of the detonation cord, or anything else that could be found connected to a bomb—no matter how small—to search for biometrics evidence on that bomb residue.

If American forensics teams could even find a partial fingerprint, partial smudge, drop of perspiration—even if it had evaporated, blood particle, fingernails or hair, they could instantly identify the bombmaker. Or if the bombmaker were not yet in the database, investigators could later get a match if the bombmaker were later biometrically enrolled in the database and his prints or DNA matched those already uploaded.

Although the program started out slowly, as the military-generated biometrics database grew, the program began to work. The American Army became increasingly efficient at collecting bomb shrapnel parts, collecting biometrics data from Afghan nationals, and tying fingerprint and DNA matches to bombs that killed Americans. This allowed the Army to go out, find, capture, and before the rules of engagement became so Taliban-friendly, punish insurgent bombmakers who had killed Americans. It also prevented terrorists from gaining access to U.S. installations.

The Army's initial collection program demonstrated phenomenal success, so much that the federal government decided to bring in biometrics reinforcements. The Obama administration dispatched the FBI to Afghanistan also, to set up its own biometrics laboratories and databases, relying on data collected from the Army, and work in conjunction with the Army not only to identify terrorists operating within

Afghanistan, but track terrorists who might also be operating in the United States and elsewhere worldwide.

They called the program AABIS, which was the acronym for Afghan Automated Biometrics Information System.

The AABIS program continued to grow, and became increasingly successful. In April of 2011, the Army published, for dissemination to all U.S. Army commanders in Afghanistan, a publication known as "U.S. Army Commander's Guide to Biometrics in Afghanistan." By that time, every American combat unit on the ground was now assigned with the task of having soldiers collect biometrics data from Afghan nationals. The military also paid Afghan locals, like American census takers, to go from house to house to collect biometrics data.

Here is language that the Army put out to its commanders to explain that part (Afghan biometrics collectors) of the program, in the "Commander's Guide to Biometrics":

"Throughout the Afghan government, Afghan leaders are embracing biometrics not only to defeat insurgents and identify criminals, but also to verify its lawful citizens. In partnership with the Afghan Ministry of Interior, the coalition is employing 1,000 Afghan citizens to conduct biometric enrollments of the Afghan population in a program that will support the Afghan national identification card. Over the next two years, these enrollers will operate in every province, district, border port of entry, and major airport in Afghanistan."

By April of 2014, about the same time that Clint Lorance would first meet Don Snyder at the Fort Leavenworth prison, the respected intelligence website Public Intelligence published an article titled "Identity Dominance: The U.S. Military's Biometric War in Afghanistan." In other words, the U.S. had used biometrics as a powerful tool in identifying bombmakers bent on killing Americans.

To illustrate the power of biometrics in identifying bombmakers, in October of 2018, shortly before the United States congressional mid-term elections, several prominent Democrat lawmakers and journalists received packages in the mail that were subsequently identified as pipe bombs. It was unclear as to whether any of the packages contained real bombs, as none of the devices, fortunately, ever exploded or even demonstrated much of a capacity to explode.

Nevertheless, once the FBI examined the packages for biometrics, an arrest was made, almost instantaneously, of a suspect in South Florida identified as Cesar Sayoc, known in some quarters as the "MAGA bomber." The description came from the mainstream press, because Mr. Sayoc was supposedly a fan of President Trump and his "Make America Great Again" campaign.

But the speed and effectiveness of arresting the so-called MAGA Bomber, Cesar Sayoc, demonstrates the swiftness and the power of using biometrics as a tool for identifying bombmakers. But in fact, though not known to most of the American public, this process of identifying and arresting bombmakers had been under way in Afghanistan for a period of at least nine years before anyone ever heard of Mr. Sayoc.

In the fall of 2012, the U.S. State Department, in an attempt to help the Afghan government function on its own after the announced United States withdrawal, took on the issue of prosecuting terrorists and bombmakers after the American pullout. In the minds of State Department policymakers, Afghanistan needed a criminal prosecutions system, to mirror United States law, to help the Afghan government identify these bombmakers, prosecute them, and then help them eventually re-integrate into Afghan society through the Afghan criminal justice system.

And it was a result of this proposed State Department prosecution program, which had initially been classified as top secret, that John N. Maher would be called back for one final assignment in Afghanistan.

CHAPTER 45

In January of 2013, when John stepped off the plane in Kabul, Afghanistan, the cold wind and 35-degree temperatures reminded him more of his hometown of Chicago than the blistering heat First Platoon had endured seven months in Kandahar Province. In fact, the high in Parwan, for the entire month of January of 2013, did not rise above 37 degrees. A Chicago native could easily adapt to cold weather, although John's new assignment that he was about to commence was anything but cold. By contrast, his work would become an internationally sensitive hot potato.

The call that started this journey had come in November of 2012, almost two years to the day before the cold Thanksgiving week of 2014 in Chicago.

"John," said the caller, whose name is withheld to protect his identity, "the State Department would like to interview you for a position in Afghanistan to manage a top-secret program involving a large team of American and Afghan lawyers, investigators, and legal support personnel. You interested in talking to them?"

"I'm interested," John said.

A few days later, John arrived in Washington for a series of interviews. The offer followed shortly thereafter. A few weeks after that, after a medical examination and two weeks of training in northern Virginia in January of 2013, he was on a plane to Afghanistan.

Technically, the State Department had contracted with a private company, called Pacific Architects and Engineers, a name chosen in part to hide the top-secret work that was about to be implemented in Parwan. But the State Department wanted John to run the program.

And now, John had returned to the backwards country that time had forgotten, that had claimed more than 2,000 American lives over the past 10 years. His job, now, was to help wind things down, through the top-secret program, by overseeing the prosecution of Taliban terrorists held at the Detention Facility in Parwan or DFIP.

The DFIP sits near the mammoth Bagram Air Base, the largest American military base in Afghanistan, located north of the capital city of Kabul in Parwan Province. The Detention Facility remains the largest military prison in Afghanistan. Originally built by the administration of president George W. Bush, it housed prisoners captured on the battlefield, including foreign and local combatants, including Taliban terrorists. Many were members of widespread IED bombmaking cells.

In early 2012, as Clint and members of First Platoon were arriving in Afghanistan, control of the American-built facility was handed back over to Afghanistan. This transfer occurred pursuant to a memorandum of understanding signed between the two countries on March 9, 2012. The turnover was part of Obama's plan, announced June 22, 2011, to pull out all Americans from Afghanistan by 2014.

However, under the agreement regarding the prison facility, the United States would continue to provide logistical support for at least a year, as a joint U.S.-Afghan commission would decide on any detainee releases until a more permanent pact was adopted.

On Sept. 10, 2012, the day before Islamist militants in Benghazi ransacked a U.S. special missions compound and killed the U.S. ambassador, American military authorities in Parwan turned over some 3,000 terrorists, including Taliban fighters, to the Afghan authorities.

These Taliban fighters would remain in Afghan custody, at the detention center in Parwan, until the governments of the United States and of the Islamic Republic of Afghanistan could figure out what to do with them. Within a few short weeks, John N. Maher would become part of the international solution in disposing of these terrorists.

Meanwhile, 7,000 miles away, back home at Fort Bragg, the Army commenced its Article 32 preliminary hearing against Clint. An Article 32 is a preliminary hearing under military law, under which the prosecutor presents evidence to an investigating officer, and the investigating officer then makes a formal recommendation to the commander to convene a court-martial against a member of the military.

In theory, the investigating officer could recommend against a court martial. But that would not happen here.

Lt. Col. Douglas C. VanWeeldeen had been selected as the investigating officer for the Article 32, and the first hearing commenced against Clint on Tuesday, Jan. 15, 2013. The die had been cast. VanWeeldeen would recommend a court-martial for murder, alleging that Clint changed the rules of engagement so his soldiers could indiscriminately kill any riders of motorcycles on sight.

Everybody knew it. The fix was in.

As Clint's Article 32 hearing was getting under way, John had begun his assignment in Parwan. Little did he realize at the time that his top-secret assignment in early 2013 would eventually lead to the smoking-gun evidence of the prosecution's inexcusable cover-up in hiding exonerating evidence in its case against Clint Lorance. That revelation would come later.

But for now, John N. Maher had a job to do.

CHAPTER 46

THE JUSTICE CENTER IN PARWAN (JCIP)
THE TOP-SECRET BIOMETRICS
PROSECUTION PROGRAM
JANUARY 2013

The Justice Center in Parwan, or JCIP, as it was referred to in the military vernacular, which became John Maher's principal duty station for the entire calendar year of 2013, was unique among criminal courts in the world. American-built, but controlled and operated by the Afghans in early 2013, the top-secret court dealt with terrorism and national security cases.

The JCIP and the Detention Facility in Parwan (DFIP) were located close to one another, but not within the protective confines of the large Bagram Air Base. They were located four miles away from the air base, at Camp Sabalu-Harrison, which was a housing area for troops near the prison, and whose purpose, largely, was to service the prison and the Justice Center.

With dozens of Alaska tents erected on post to house the troops, rocky ground spread everywhere, wide open spaces, and the snow-capped peaks of the Hindu Kush Mountains off in the background, the camp was protected by miles of coiled concertina wire and a light security force to deal with any threats that might originate from the outside.

Camp Sabalu-Harrison was named for two American soldiers killed in 2007. Col. James Harrison, who was from Missouri, and Master Sgt. Roberto Sabalu, who, like John

Maher was from Chicago, were working to revamp the Afghan prison system at the time they were shot to death in their vehicle, when exiting a prison gate, by an Afghan soldier who had been portrayed as an American ally. In fact, both soldiers were shot dead while working at a prison facility, at the Pul-e-Charkhi prison near Kabul. Thus, the mission of the camp, named in their honor, was focused on housing war prisoners, and later, on the prosecution of Taliban insurgents and other radical Islamic terrorists.

Such was the danger to Americans in Afghanistan. You could get killed in an instant, even if you were not on the battlefield. They called it "green-on-blue" violence, meaning that even "friendly" allies within the Afghan National Army could turn on a dime and murder an American serviceman. It happened with increasing frequency, and the names Sabalu and Harrison were a constant reminder to every American at the camp of that looming danger.

This same danger threatened John Maher when he reported for duty in January of 2013. Like Sabalu and Harrison before him, Maher could have been gunned down in an incident in a green-on-blue Afghan shooter who only wanted to kill the first American who crossed his gunsights. But like any good American soldier, he did not approach his new assignment in Parwan with fear in his mind. John N. Maher had a job to do. All of his focus was on that job.

The State Department selected John as the principal counsel and program manager in charge at the JCIP. Each and every day, under John's supervision of Afghan prosecutors, judges, and defense counsel, prosecutions of dozens of terrorists and insurgents would take place at the JCIP facility.

As the judicial center and detention facility were located close to one another, U.S. military personnel (Army, Air Force, Navy, and Marine Corps) would put the insurgents in orange jumpsuits, blindfold them, put wrist and leg irons on them, and use small buses with armed guards to transport them from the DFIP to the JCIP holding cell, where they would then appear before the Afghan judges for trial, after having an opportunity to meet and consult with Afghan defense counsel, who had fingerprint and DNA evidence disclosed to them by the prosecution.

Most of the successful prosecutions under the program involved biometrics data, often fingerprints and DNA, often lifted off bomb parts, which had been blown to smithereens. The Army had such a massive database of fingerprints and DNA that it was able to, in many of these cases, share this information with the Afghan prosecutors, working under U.S. supervision, to obtain convictions.

At times, the information was initially classified, but for use in the prosecutions, the information was declassified and released to the government of the Islamic Republic of Afghanistan, that is, the information entered the public domain.

CHAPTER 47

A COP CALLED "COACH"
PARWAN, AFGHANISTAN
JANUARY 2013

Maher led a team of more than 100 U.S. and Afghan employees implementing the U.S. Department of State, Bureau of International Narcotics and Law Enforcement's "Rule of Law" program at the Justice Center in Parwan. John's team included the attorneys, paralegals, and investigators who trained, mentored, and advised Afghan judges, prosecutors, and investigators to prosecute former Law of Armed Conflict (LOAC) detainees referred for trial under Afghan domestic law. These defendants were often Taliban members and insurgents who used bombs and IEDs against coalition forces (primarily American, British, Canadian, Italian and Afghan National Army).

Of the more than 100 professionals that John managed and evaluated, no one was more crucial to the nuts-and-bolts operation of the mission than a retired New York City cop named William Carney. One of the principal investigators working in the program at the time at Parwan, Bill Carney had retired as a New York City police officer, then became a preeminent expert on the Army's biometrics program, which collected data from Afghan citizens and used that data to prosecute radical terrorists and Taliban operatives.

Now in his early 60s, Carney was trim and remarkably fit, wore a closely cropped haircut, had an affinity for short-sleeve, dark-blue pullover shirts and khaki slacks. The dark blue shirt caused his gray hair to stand out, and his well-toned biceps reflected a consistent regimen of workouts and calisthenics. In some ways, he looked more the part of retired Marine general than a retired New York City cop. Carney bore a slight resemblance to the four-star Marine Gen. James "Mad Dog" Mattis, except he had a younger-looking face than the "Mad Dog."

Although in civilian clothing, many times junior active duty personnel would salute Carney, thinking he was a general or a senior officer. Carney looked the part based on his bearing. The man had an aura that oozed respect and commanded it, and could easily play the part of the tough guy in a Hollywood action-thriller.

Despite his tough-guy image and his thick New York accent, Carney also had a softer side about him. In what little spare time he had gotten in the long hours that he had spent as a New York City cop, Carney spent his off-hours in New York City coaching girls' basketball teams and was head coach of his daughters' team. In all the hours he spent diagramming plays, teaching zone and man-to-man defenses, teaching shooting techniques and working on fast break and secondary breaks, the girls who played for him over the years affectionately began to call him "Coach."

The name stuck, even in professional settings.

And as Coach Carney became the go-to guy for the girls who surrounded him in huddles on the court in late-game situations, in many ways, he also became the go-to guy for the team of prosecutors seeking to match prints and DNA evidence with bombmakers on trial at the Parwan Justice Center.

With unmatched expertise, Bill Carney helped collect, process and analyze biometrics matches. He provided instruction on tactical sight exploitation and evidence-gathering to military personnel. When U.S. or coalition forces diffused an IED or after a bomb exploded, standard operating procedure is to pick up the pieces, literally, and send them to the lab for fingerprint and DNA testing. This IED event is given a number, the date is recorded, and the GRID coordinate is entered, as well as any personnel hurt or killed by the bomb. The prints and DNA are then run against the ABIS data to determine if there are any matches or hits, just like U.S. law enforcement in the states. If there are no matches, the information remains in the database, and, later, when an Afghan is biometrically enrolled, a match can occur that way.

And when prosecutors found a suspect's prints or DNA on bomb parts that killed Americans, in the overwhelming majority of cases, that meant a conviction. No one was more important to the top-secret prosecution program than Bill Carney, who may have been the foremost expert in the world on the American biometrics database in Afghanistan.

While Clint Lorance was going through hell on Earth back at Fort Bragg, facing investigations, the Article 32 hearing, and ultimately a court-martial where the Army would rob him of his reputation and 20 years of his life, John Maher would spend nearly a whole year managing the biometrics prosecutions in Parwan. His trusted colleague in Afghanistan, a retired NYC police detective and girls' basketball coach, understood the American-built, Afghan biometrics database, probably better than anyone in the world.

At the end of the day, that retired NYC cop who they called Coach might be the key to exposing the real truth, and the rest of the story behind the Army's bulldoze prosecution job to crush one of its finest young officers.

CHAPTER 48

All around the nation, and in the great city of Chicago, "Black Friday" had finally arrived. For many Americans, the day after Thanksgiving meant a rush to the malls to get a jump on Christmas shopping. For others, it marked the beginning of the Christmas season.

In the Maher household, for John and his fiancée, Kathryn, Black Friday meant a continuation of Thanksgiving week, of snacking on turkey sandwiches with stuffing and cranberry on the side, of sipping red wine and decorating the Christmas tree, with Christmas carols playing softly in the background.

It had been a long, cold Thanksgiving week, with the highs since Tuesday only reaching 32 degrees. Yesterday, Thanksgiving Day had brought dusting of light snow, the perfect ambiance for a Hallmark holiday movie, with the high temperatures barely reaching 28 degrees. Kathryn and John had the fireplace going.

Today would bring more of the same, and it had been snowing off and on in the wee hours or the morning, enough to cast a skiff of white on the ground and sidewalks. The cold, gray snow-tinged landscape outside the windows presented a stark contrast with the warm festive red-and-green colors of the holiday season within.

It was 10 o'clock in the morning and the snow had stopped falling.

As Kathryn gave meticulous attention to the Christmas tree, hanging shiny ornaments—one from each Christmas since her childhood—and adjusting the positions of miniature white lights, John sat on the floor, still in his white terrycloth robe, in front of the roaring fire in the brick fireplace. Bankers boxes full of papers, containing the record of trial, surrounded him, all of the evidence that the prosecution had selectively presented in the case of the United States v. First Lieutenant Clint Lorance.

Thanksgiving with Kathryn had been delightful, and the holiday spirit permeated the air. The holidays ushered in a wonderful time of year for reflection and new beginnings. But even still, John's mind remained on Clint Lorance.

Yesterday marked John's first Thanksgiving since meeting Clint. And on the holiday, especially, he worried about the young lieutenant, sequestered away at a military prison 525 miles to the southwest of Chicago, unable to spend Thanksgiving with his family and friends. Unless the Army somehow came to its senses, Clint faced the next 18 Thanksgivings locked up, away from his loved ones. But getting the Army to do the right thing, even to correct a miscarriage of justice, was like trying to push a glacier with a garden hoe.

Nonetheless, John had to find a way to get the chain of command to see the light. Never had he seen such a grave injustice, in all his career, as the error-ridden investigation and faulty prosecution of Clint Lorance.

Three days had passed since he communicated with his friend, Bill Carney in Afghanistan. So far, no response to his email, requesting identifying biometrics data on the names of the four Afghans in question. No telephone calls. No emails. No nothing in response.

Despite their friendship, and despite the fact that Bill worked under John in Parwan, perhaps Bill decided that it would be too much of a personal risk to stick his neck out and provide any information to help out someone who had been convicted of double murder.

Maybe Carney had run the search and found nothing at all. Maybe that's why he had gone silent. After all, if Carney had placed any of the names in the database and hit the search button, the results would have popped up, almost instantaneously. Either there was a match, or there wasn't.

It was Thanksgiving week, which might account for the delay. But John's request to Bill had gone out the Tuesday before Thanksgiving. If Bill had run the request on that day, on Tuesday, or on the following day, Wednesday, the result should have been back by now.

Should he call Bill? Should he send him another email to check on things? Or should he leave it as is? If Bill Carney responded to John's request, under the current circumstances, that would be going above and beyond the call of duty. If the answers went against the government's version of this case, that Clint was a murderer, that might rock the boat for Bill.

Maher decided to sit tight, confident that his friend would let him know either way the evidence shook out.

Still, why had the prosecution remained silent on biometrics matches? John had replayed this question in his mind a dozen times.

As sophisticated as the biometrics database was, and John knew that for a fact from his work in Parwan, checking for a possible match would be as simple as running a simple Google search online. If the motorcycle riders had been in the database, or the material witnesses had been enrolled, their names would pop up. And, if they left their prints or DNA on bombs, as hits.

Most likely, a search had been run, and their names had not popped up as biometric links to any bombmaking.

Of course.

What else could explain having no information at all about possible biometrics match anywhere in the file? Or about running a search and determining that there was no match? After all, the military had called these Afghans civilian casualties. How would they know they are civilians unless they had run a biometrics search?

Unlike Carney's lack of response, surely the prosecution would have included that information there had there been a match. Or would have included a "no" if there had been no biometric match. The office of the lead prosecutor, Capt. Kirk Otto, was right across the hallway from the intelligence officer's office at Fort Bragg.

In fact, the Brigade Staff Judge Advocate's Office was located within Building C-1140 on Fort Bragg. That building is U-shaped, and the reception area is the horizontal bridge of the "U." The command hallway is to the left vertical extension and the staff shops are all on the right. The military prosecutor's office is located directly across a 6-foot wide hallway from the Brigade Intelligence offices, the "S2" shop. Capt. Otto or any of his assistant prosecutors could have walked 20 steps from his desk to the desk of the intelligence analysts and asked for an intel officer to dig into the "victims" identities.

All Otto would've had to do would have been to walk across the hallway and say, "Hey, I need a favor. I need you to run these guys in our biometrics database and see what we have."

That had to be it. Even Afghan defense counsel was provided with biometrics matches to defend their clients. And the United States was the world's standard-bearer for full disclosure by the prosecution of all material evidence that might benefit a defendant at trial.

Surely, that had been done, and nothing had come of it. Why else would the record be silent on the issue of biometric identification?

But, then again, Capt. Otto had lined out the Afghan names on the charge sheet. He did that for a reason not explained in the record. Had he run the biometrics and determined they were terrorists, and decided to conceal their identities?

Maybe John was reading too much into this. Probably so.

And the military defense counsel served a discovery request on the prosecution asking for any and all evidence of criminal activity of any one in the battle zone, to include the deceased motorcycle riders. Complying with that request would have necessitated a biometrics search. The prosecution had not responded to that request, as it should have done, even if nothing had been found.

The lack of a response had to mean that nothing had been found. Yes. That had to be it.

With all these thoughts swirling in his mind, John needed a break to clear his head. He thought about going upstairs, putting on his clothes, grabbing his leather jacket and stepping outside for some fresh air. Or maybe throwing on his running gear and doing a 5K.

He'd learned, over the years, that some of the greatest thinking befell him in one of two places, either 1) in the shower, or 2) while on a long run. Not only that, but those runs had helped him keep in shape to get in his officer's uniform, even still. Yes, that's what he'd do, he decided. He'd go get his gear on and do a quick 5K run.

But before he could make a move to go upstairs, the doorbell rang. He checked his watch. 10 a.m. on the money.

"I'll get it." John walked down the three flights of stairs to the front door, as Kathryn hung shiny tinsel on the Christmas tree. When he opened the front door, a cold blast of air greeted him, which helped clear his head. The 40-something-looking burly man smiled and extended his arm, holding a yellow envelope package with the acronym "DHL" written in large red letters across the bottom of the envelope.

"Are you Mr. Maher?"

"I am."

"I have a DHL package for you, sir. If you would sign here, please."

"Of course."

John signed for the package, thanked the delivery man, stepped back in the house and closed the door.

He stopped in the foyer and looked at the return address.

Parwan, Afghanistan.

"Carney! You son of a …"

Of course! The wily old cop had used personal delivery because he did not want sensitive but unclassified information to be intercepted via less-than-secure servers in the commercial email system. And, of course, all calls coming in from overseas, and especially from Afghanistan, were subject to monitoring. Whatever information was in the package, Bill Carney wanted to keep relatively secure.

John jogged upstairs, sat down, ripped open the package, and started to read.

It took him a few minutes to begin to absorb the magnitude of the information before him.

"Kathryn!"

CHAPTER 49

THE SMOKING GUN IN THE DHL PACKAGE
CHICAGO
NOV. 28, 2014

Sitting in his living room, with "Silver Bells" playing softly in the background and the papers in his hand that had just arrived from Afghanistan, John studied the reports, and then re-read them again. No wonder Bill Carney had opted against telephone or email or text in relaying the information, but had instead relied on DHL.

As far as John was concerned, this report was a smoking-gun hot potato, both politically and legally, that cast inexcusable shame and wrongdoing at the feet of the prosecution. Either the prosecution had deliberately withheld exonerating evidence, or had been criminally negligent in failing to turn over exonerating evidence that should have been made available to the defense—and the military jury— from the beginning. Carney must have discovered this, too, as soon as he ran the search.

As he read the reports again, for a third time, John felt himself flush in the face at what the prosecution had done to Clint Lorance. How could men, let alone officers sworn to defend the U.S. Constitution, do this to another man, let alone one of their own?

In his email request, John had asked Bill Carney to run a database search for possible matches on four Afghans citizens who were involved in the military actions by First

Platoon on the morning of July 2, 2012, in the village of Sarenzai, Afghanistan. Three of the four had been riding on the single motorcycle that Clint's men and the Afghan National Army opened fire on. The fourth had been picked up on the west side of the village, right after the firefight involving the weapons team, led by Sgt. Herrmann.

The three motorcycle riders were identified as 1) Aslam, 2) Ghamai (first name not known) and 3) Haji Karimullah. The CID interviewed a man named Ahad who knew the riders and provided this information.

Of these three riders, Aslam and Ghamai were killed from shots on the battlefield, fired on either by Clint's men, or the Afghan National Army. Haji Karimullah, the third rider, had dismounted from the motorcycle and ran across the dirt road, where he escaped into the village and avoided getting shot that morning. This was the basis for the prosecution's attempted murder and double murder charges.

Clint was convicted of murdering of Aslam and Ghamai, and the attempted murder of Karimullah. He was given 20 years imprisonment for these crimes, with that sentence later reduced to 19 years by the Commander of the 82nd Airborne Division. Their names, Aslam, Ghamai and Karimullah, had been lined out from the charge sheet, perhaps to avoid triggering the notion of an easy database sort of the biometrics system. But their names were all over the Army's CID reports, where John had gotten their names and asked Carney to run the search.

Of the men riding on the motorcycle, two of the three left their prints and DNA on IEDs at GRID coordinates where American soldiers were killed or wounded. In other words, at least two of the three motorcycle riders that Clint's men opened fire on were enemy combatants.

This fact, that at least two of the motorcycle riders were enemy combatants, was withheld from the defense and the jury. And the third rider left his prints and DNA on IEDs.

The prosecution led the military jury to believe that the men were merely civilian casualties, with no interest in the war effort, completely innocent and shot by the order of an overzealous lieutenant.

The fourth name was of an Afghan identified as Mohammad Rahim. Rahim had been picked up by American troops after the firefight on the west side of the village. Rahim had been shot in the arm by Sgt. Herrmann's forces from the weapon squad. The bullet that struck Rahim had probably been fired by Pvt. First Class Carson.

Rahim, also, had a biometric linkage to bombmaking, and his prints and DNA were found on bombs that killed American soldiers. Clint wasn't prosecuted for Carson having shot Rahim. Neither was Carson. The prosecution carefully hid from the jury all evidence of shootings on the west side of the village, obviously to fool the jury into thinking this was not a war zone, when, at all times, an Army report concluded that Lorance's platoon was being scouted for an impending attack or ambush, and that at least one insurgent was confirmed killed in action.

John was astounded. How could the prosecution have not revealed any of this, in good faith? After all, the prosecutors were soldiers and officers and veterans of the wars in Iraq and Afghanistan. They had to know to look for this information to identify who the Afghans were on the field that day as part of a professional and thorough investigation, before bringing charges that carry life in prison. The information in the reports constituted almost prosecutorial misconduct in the extreme.

Of the five Afghans whose identities had been run in the American-built biometrics database, four of the five had clear biometrics bombmaking activity, where their fingerprints or DNA was found on bombs killing American servicemen. All were biometrically enrolled and had matches showing their fingerprints and DNA on IED components.

The so-called village elder had ties to bombmakers. Two of his sons were among the biggest bombmakers in the village. And of the two bombmakers on the motorcycle with the village elder at the time of the shooting, one was the village elder's bombmaker son.

In other words, four of the five were Taliban bombmakers, and would most likely would have been convicted had they been prosecuted in the top-secret court in Parwan where John served as supervising attorney.

Of the four whose biometrics data proved them to be makers of bombs that killed Americans, two had been riding on the motorcycle that Clint ordered his men to fire upon. In other words, two of the three so-called civilians on the motorcycle were in reality, American-killing bombmakers, as was the insurgent captured in the firefight on the west side. Even if all three had been civilians, under these circumstances, on this hot battle zone with the motorcycle charging at the position of first platoon, the shooting would have been justified. But now, to make matters worse, Clint was sitting in prison, wrongly convicted in a kangaroo prosecution, because his men had shot at the enemy.

Every bit of this evidence had been hidden from the defense counsel, and even more seriously, had been hidden from the military jury.

The Army's railroad job against Lt. Clint Lorance had been borderline criminal. No prosecutor should ever, under any circumstances, hide and or conceal exonerating evidence from a jury in order to gain at conviction for the sake of political expediency. But John Maher knew at this point that this is exactly what had happened in the prosecution of Clint Lorance. The prosecution did not seek justice in Clint's case, but only a symbolic head on a silver platter, the full facts and the truth be damned.

He had to alert the powers that be, and try to persuade someone to right the injustice that had been forced upon Clint.

CHAPTER 50

THE AMERICANS KILLED BY THE MOTORCYCLE RIDERS

The first Taliban bombmaker who was shot and killed on the motorcycle the morning of July 2nd was identified as Ghamai. Based on biometrics data in the Amy's Afghan database, Ghamai's DNA was found on a bomb that exploded on May 12, 2009, in the Zhari District of Kandahar Province, killing an American soldier.

In the biometrics database, the explosion that killed the American soldier has an event number. In Clint's case, IED Event # 12/1229 designates the bomb explosion tied to the motorcycle rider Ghamai.

Staff Sgt. Israel P. Nuanes
Killed by the Motorcycle Rider Ghamai

But in the eyes of his family, the American soldier killed by the motorcycle rider Ghamai was not just a number. He had a name: Staff Sgt. Israel P. Nuanes of Las Cruces, N.M. Staff Sgt. Nuanes, whose nickname was "Iz," first joined the Army in 1992, and was in his 20th year of service to his country at the time he lost his life. Israel is survived by his wife, Rosina; his son, Israel Javier; and his daughter, Laurissa Marie. Because of this motorcycle rider, Ghamai, Rosina Nuanes lost her husband and Israel and Laurissa lost their father.

And Clint Lorance is in prison for killing this criminal thug?

Here's the bottom line. Ghamai killed Staff Sgt. Nuanes. Clint's men, in a split-second, life-or-death decision on the battlefield, shot at, and possibly killed Ghamai. Now Clint is in prison, branded as a murderer, for having his men in a battle zone shoot at and kill an enemy insurgent, Ghamai, who killed an American soldier, Israel Nuanes.

That is beyond twisted.

Six Paratroopers Who Died Where the Motorcycle-Riding Haji Karimullah Planted Bombs

Now we come to the second motorcycle rider, Haji Karimullah. This is the guy (one of the three) who was riding the motorcycle toward the American platoon, but was not killed by Clint's men (or by the Afghan National Army). Rather, Karimullah got off the motorcycle and ran. For his split-second decision to order his men to fire at this clown, Clint got convicted of "attempted murder."

In retrospect, Clint's men should have shot this guy through the head and killed him on the spot. Why is this?

Because on Aug. 31, 2012, fewer than 60 days after July 2nd, one of the bombs handled by the motorcycle-riding Karimullah exploded on an American soldier in Kandahar Province. Fortunately, that attack was not fatal. But nonetheless, it marked an act of war against U.S. forces, showing that Karimullah, who was not even struck by a bullet, was anything but a civilian, as the prosecution claimed.

The motorcycle-riding Karimullah's activities as an anti-American bombmaker go even beyond the Aug. 31, 2012, incident. The motorcycle-riding Karimullah's fingerprints were found on bombs planted at Military Grid Coordinates 41RQQ3810598507, in the Panjwai District in Kandahar Province. Those military grid coordinates are located at a specific latitude and longitudinal point, and to be precise, at 31°35'49.4" north latitude, and 65°30'34.4" east longitude.

At that specific location, where Karimullah's prints were found on bombs, six American soldiers were killed by bombs planted by the Taliban.

In other words, the Taliban targeted American soldiers in the area where Karimullah's IEDs were found, because the U.S. Army operated in the area, which is why Karimullah and other insurgents planted bombs there.

The Americans killed at this location include 1) Spec. Brendan Neenan, an American 82nd Airborne paratrooper, of Enterprise, Ala.; 2) Spec. Christian San Nicholas, a second 82nd Airborne paratrooper of Anaheim, Calif.; 3) U.S. Army Staff Sgt. Alexander G. Povilaitis of Atlanta; 4) Pvt. First Class Cody Towse of Pasadena, Calif., who was a Bronze Star recipient; 5) Spec. William Gilbert of Hacienda Heights, Calif.; and 6) Spec. Mitchell Daehling of Pittsfield, Mass.

So, the second motorcycle rider, Karimullah, clearly targeted Americans, and had his fingerprints all over bombs, which had been planted near American military operations. And while we do not know whether any of these bombs actually killed an American, we know that Americans were killed in the same place where Karimullah's bombs were found. And we know that Karimullah made every effort to kill Americans.

Karimullah was no civilian casualty, as the Army claimed. He was an enemy combatant and an enemy of the United States. So was Ghamai. Yet, Clint received a 20-year prison sentence for having his men fire against enemy combatants who kill Americans or have tried to kill Americans.

Remember that Ghamai (whose bomb killed Sgt. Nuanes) and Karimullah (whose bombs were found on a grid point that killed six Americans) were riding the motorcycle that charged the platoon on the east side of the village. The third rider, even if he were not a bombmaker, was collateral damage under international law, not a murder victim. Even in Afghanistan, three men on a single motorcycle is odd, especially in a rural area where U.S. forces engage the enemy daily, and the riders did not need a minesweeper to safely ride through the area.

But remember also, that the firefight on the west side of the village, led by Staff Sgt. Herrmann, commenced only moments after the motorcycle shooting on the east side of the village.

Recall, also, that the prosecution went to great lengths to hide from the jury firefight on the west side of the village away. This firefight would have proven that the platoon was in an active battle zone, and would have destroyed the prosecution's attempt to portray the platoon's patrol as taking a Sunday walk in the peaceful park.

But on the west side, American paratroopers fired on at least two insurgents. Insurgents on the west side were using ICOM radios—a known Taliban tool. One was killed. The other was captured. Both of these insurgents also had biometric links to bombsites that killed Americans. Their names were Jam Mohammad and Mohammad Rahim.

We have already mentioned Rahim. He was picked up and brought back to Payenzai, where he tested positive for explosive residue on his hands.

Haji Karimullah, the insurgent riding the motorcycle whose fingerprints were found on multiple bombs, admitted in an interview with Army CID agents right after the incident that he is good friends with Mohammed Rahim.

So Karimullah, attacking by motorcycle from the east side, with fingerprints on bombs planning to kill Americans, is good friends with Rahim, on the west side, who was found with explosive residue on his hands.

And Karimullah is riding the same motorcycle as the insurgent identified as Ghamai, whose bomb killed Staff Sgt. Nuanes.

All these Afghans, the motorcycle riders on the east side who Clint's men shot at, and the insurgents on the west side, are all tied together, either by family ties or by admitted close associations and friendships with each other. They all were either directly or indirectly linked with bombmaking. This shows evidence of coordination between activities on the west side of the village, with the firefight involving Sgt. Herrmann's men, and the motorcycle charge on the east side of the village, which involved two Taliban insurgents and a third with Taliban ties. Rahim (west side attacker) and Karimullah (east side attacker) were good friends. And this entire operation was not coordinated by the Taliban?

Mohammad Rahim (west side attacker) was not only friends with Haji Karimullah (the motorcycle rider who ran), but was also biometrically connected to an IED event that occurred in the Zhari District on June 12, 2012, at one of the most IED-prone locations in Kandahar. So, Mohammad Rahim, who had explosive residue on his hands and who was friends with the motorcycle rider Haji Karimullah, also planted bombs designed to kill Americans.

This American platoon was on patrol in the hot fire zone, facing enemy insurgents hell bent on killing them, and not on a Sunday walk in the park.

Here's the bombshell.

All this biometric evidence, linking these motorcycle-riding Afghans to bombs designed to kill Americans, was deliberately hidden from the defense, and from the military jury. The jury had no clue that the motorcycle-rider Ghamai's bomb had killed Staff Sgt. Nuanes. The jury had no clue that the motorcycle-rider Karimullah had planted multiple bombs, targeting Americans. The jury had no clue that Mohamad Rahim, who was captured on the west side of the village and was good friends with the motorcycle-rider Haji Karimullah, had explosive bomb residue on his hands.

The prosecution's deliberate decision to hide biometric evidence of bombmaking by the motorcycle riders from the defense, and to hide that evidence from the military jury, all was part of an out-of-control and zealous determination to convict an American officer in order to satisfy a political debt to the Afghans, and is borderline criminal.

Now if the military jury had known that two of the three Afghans on the motorcycle had been involved in bombmaking that ether killed Americans or attempted to kill Americans, and that insurgents on the west side of the village also were found with explosive bomb residue, designed to kill Americans, there is no way in hell that Clint Lorance ever would have been convicted.

Abdul Ahad
The Bomb Maker and American Killer
Related to the Three Motorcycle Riders

But the government coverup of evidence that would have exonerated Clint only gets worse. On the date of the shooting, July 2, 2012, the Army picked up another Afghan in the village, identified as Abdul Ahad. Now this Abdul Ahad was interviewed by U.S. Army CID agents and provided invaluable information concerning the three motorcycle riders, who are the subject of Clint's conviction for murder, and the shameful 20-year prison sentence that followed.

Mr. Abdul Ahad, as it turns out, is related to all three motorcycle riders who were fired on by Clint's men.

Here's how.

Abdul Ahad is the brother to Ghamai, the motorcycle rider whose bomb killed Staff Sgt. Israel Nuanes. So Ahad's motorcycle-riding brother is an American-killer.

Abdul Ahad is the nephew of the motorcycle riding Haji Karimullah (whose fingerprints were found all over bombs designed to kill Americans). Ahad's father, Mohammad Aslam, was also one of the three motorcycle riders.

So, Abdul Ahad's brother Ghamai (who killed an American soldier); his uncle, Haji Karimullah (who planted many bombs designed to kill American soldiers); and his father, Mohammad Aslam (the so-called "village elder"), were all motorcycle riders charging the American platoon.

But not only do Ahad's relatives on the motorcycle have ties to bombmaking American killing, so does Mr. Ahad himself. On four separate occasions, Ahad's DNA was found on bombs aimed at killing Americans. These IED events are as follows: 1) Nov. 26, 2010, Abdul's DNA was found on bomb components in the Zhari District of Kandahar Province; 2) March 11, 2011, Abdul's DNA and fingerprints were found on IED components in the Zhari District of Kandahar Province; 3) March 16, 2011, Abdul's DNA and fingerprints were found on IED components in the Zhari District of Kandahar Province; 4) March 18, 2013, Abdul's DNA and fingerprints were found on IED components in the Zhari District of Kandahar Province.

Abdul himself, brother of American-killer and motorcycle rider Ghamai, nephew of Taliban bomb-maker and motorcycle rider Haji Karimullah, and son of the third motorcycle rider, Mohammad Aslam, the so-called village elder, was himself an accomplished Taliban bomb-maker who had placed IEDs to kill Americans.

And speaking of the third motorcycle rider, Mohammad Aslam, consider this: the Army, in its kangaroo-court prosecution against Clint, spun poor, old Mohammad Aslam, the third motorcycle, as an innocent village elder.

Well, consider this about the poor, ole village elder Mohammad Aslam, who was shot and killed that morning. First off, his son, Ghamai, a Taliban bombmaker whose IED by all accounts killed Staff Sgt. Nuanes, was riding on the motorcycle with him. His brother-in-law, Haji Karimullah—whose fingerprints were found on at least six IEDs strategically planted to kill American forces, the same bombmaker who was good friends with the bomb-maker Mohammad Rahim, shot by Sgt. Herrmann's men on the west side of the village—was on the motorcycle with him. And his other son, Abdul Ahad, had his DNA and fingerprints on at least four IEDs strategically placed to kill Americans.

Now is it possible that the poor old village elder, with his two sons as accomplished American-killing bombmakers and killers, and with his own brother-in-law on the motorcycle with him an accomplished American-killing bombmaker, was unaware of their sinister activities, and this relatively small village of maybe a few hundred people at most? Anything is possible—including, perhaps, the possibility of warm, sandy, palm tree-lined, beach-front property in Adak, Alaska, on the sunny waters of the Bearing Sea. There are remote possibilities, and then there is common sense.

There is no way in hell that the so-called village elder was not in the thick of it all, with total knowledge of his sons and his brother-in-law are up to, all the while portraying himself as a peaceful village elder so that he could get information from the American platoon.

Bombmaking and American-killing was a family sport for these Taliban operatives. And, in fact, there are numerous other biometrics links that this family had to other major IED bombmakers that killed many American soldiers. If we were to spell out the entire sinister bombmaking network uncovered by Carney's research, we would see dozens upon dozens of IED associates maintained by this family, that the names and numbers of American-killing Taliban members would be too mind-boggling to comprehend for purposes of this book.

Nonetheless, this was the deadly atmosphere faced by First Platoon and its leader, Lt. Lorance, during foot patrols on July 1 and July 2, 2012. And these are the people that his men shot at. These men were not innocent farmers who had no dog in the fight. They were American killers.

And not one word of this was ever disclosed the military jury. Not one word. Why? Because the prosecution knew that it would be a cold day in hell before the military jury would ever convict Clint Lorance if they knew that Clint's men shot at bombmakers, and were in a firefight with bombmakers all over the village that morning. That's why.

Therefore, the biometrics evidence had to be hidden. And it was hidden.

When John Maher learned of this travesty, he first alerted both the command at Fort Bragg and the Army Court of Criminal Appeals by email, the judge advocate general of the Army, Lt. Gen. Flora Darpino, and provided the newly discovered evidence that proved so-called civilian motorcycle riders to be bombmakers who killed Americans.

A lieutenant colonel in the JAG Corps reserve at the time, Maher knew of Army Regulation 27-26, Rules of Professional Conduct for Lawyers, June 28, 2018, ¶ 3.8(g) (1)(2) and (3) and ¶ 3.8(h) (e.g., when an Army lawyer learns of new, credible, and material evidence or information creating a reasonable likelihood that a convicted accused did not commit an offense of which the accused was convicted at court-martial, the Army lawyer shall disclose that evidence to the accused, make reasonable efforts to cause an investigation, and seek to remedy the conviction.) Surely, the senior-most uniformed legal officer charged with overseeing the Army Court and ensuring the integrity of the military justice system would right this wrong, vacate Clint's conviction, and release him from his imprisonment at Leavenworth.

But to John Maher's surprise and disappointment, the Army's high brass dug in their heels and defended the flawed result of the trial rather than make it right. They didn't want to face facts that exonerated Clint, as the facts would interfere with an agenda.

The Army was so intent on sacrificing Clint, for political reasons, to appease the Afghans after the Kandahar massacre, which Clint had nothing to do with, that it turned a deaf ear to the exonerating biometrics evidence uncovered by John Maher and Bill Carney. It is important to note that the Army Court of Criminal Appeals did not ever deny the authenticity of the biometrics evidence. Nor did the attorneys representing the prosecution on appeal.

Rather, they responded that Clint would have had no way of knowing that these men were enemy combatants ahead of time and therefore, the evidence was "irrelevant." The Army Court agreed with the government.

What?

Given that demented response from the Army Court of Criminal Appeals, no soldier who ever shot at a Taliban insurgent in Afghanistan would ever know ahead of time, because they all dress in the same garb as local farmers. They wear that garb when they plant bombs and kill Americans. They all look the same, and they all dress the same, which is by design.

But here's the difference. No innocent Afghans would ever charge at U.S. Army patrol, in a known battle zone, much less three men on a single motorcycle, from what the Army called "historical avenues of approach," with signs in the area warning that the roads were open only to police and military traffic. Only Taliban insurgents display that sort of all audacity, especially the ability to ride through the area without a minesweeper. Put another way, the motorcycle riders knew where the bombs were planted.

Recall also that Clint's platoon was targeted for an impending ambush, and that at least one enemy insurgent was reported as "killed in action," in a report that was neither disclosed to the defense nor the military jury.

But that's what happened in the village of Sarenzai on the morning of July 2, 2012.

The fact remains that enemy combatants, not innocent civilian or elders, were shot and killed that morning, and that information was hidden from the military jury. Remember, the Zhari District of Afghanistan was in the most Taliban-infested area of the world and the ancestral home of the Taliban.

And now, Lt. Lorance had lost his as freedom and had been branded as a murderer, because his men shot at the enemy in a known battle zone in the most dangerous country in the world for Americans. On this same battlefield, the platoon had recently lost four paratroopers to enemy fires and bombs, to include the platoon leader who Clint replaced, who had suffered peppering shrapnel wounds to the face, eyes, and abdomen and was medically evacuated from the field when a hidden IED exploded into his body.

But even if the motorcycle riders were really innocent civilians, and not the American-killing bombmakers that they turned out to be, this case still should have never been brought to trial. Under the circumstances, Clint had no choice. In that split-second on that Monday morning in early July, he had to order fire to protect his men from the potential of having their legs and arms blown off, or from having their lives ended in an instant by what appeared to be suicide riders, taking aggressive action toward the American patrol.

One of his experienced paratroopers, a former civilian police officer from North Carolina, recognized the threat, and believed the motorcycle and its three riders could have hidden explosives under their clothing, do drive-by grenade tosses or drive-by AK-47 fire. He was so convinced they were a threat that he fired his rifle, but missed. At that time, Clint radioed a gun truck he had placed in an overwatch position to protect the platoon to open fire. Clint's intent was not to murder anybody, but instead, to protect his platoon, which is after all, his sacred duty as an airborne officer.

Pvt. Skelton's threat assessment, when he initially asked for permission to fire after seeing the motorcycle approaching from the top of the grape berm, justified Lorance's order to fire that ultimately killed bombmakers. Even if the Afghans were civilians, they were collateral damage in the fog of war and not murder victims. On this point alone, the convictions and sentence are constitutionally insufficient.

The Army did not prosecute the soldier who fired at the riders but missed for three counts of attempted murder.

Instead, the Army targeted Clint, the officer, and a more significant scalp. Had the biometric information that the riders left their fingerprints or DNA on bombs been disclosed to him, Clint could have made the following strong defense: the paratrooper who fired at the riders complied with the rules of engagement and the shots from the gun truck were fired based on that ROE-compliant threat assessment. In other words, they were shooting at the enemy.

On that point alone, Clint is not guilty of murder or attempted murder. Now, add in that the rounds hit insurgent bombmakers, and it is not possible that a jury would convict. After all, rules of engagement compliance that results in the death of the enemy is precisely what we ask our paratroopers to do—it is their duty. Had Clint not ordered the fire—and the motorcycle detonated as one did in Faryab Province, killing members of the Buckeye Brigade—Clint would have been court-martialed for willful dereliction of duty. Leavenworth casts a long shadow.

The time has come to right this wrong.

CHAPTER 51

LENIENCY FOR THE TRAITORS, BUT PRISON FOR CLINT

Sgt. Bowe Bergdahl is a traitor to his country. On May 17, 2009, Bergdahl walked away from his platoon and eastern Afghanistan. He deserted his position and walked straight into the hands of the Taliban.

His disappearance set off a massive manhunt by the U.S. Army, which sent numerous patrols out to search for him. These patrols had to cover some of the most dangerous enemy terrain in the world, which included navigating through landmines and IEDs so thick that stepping a half-inch off course could mean losing a leg, losing a limb, or losing a life. In fact, Americans died searching for this yellowbelly.

On June 2, 2014, after Bergdahl was freed by the Taliban in exchange for the Obama administration turning over five Taliban prisoners who had been detained at Guantanamo Bay, Mark Thompson of *Time* magazine wrote an article titled, "The Six U.S. Soldiers Who Died Searching for Bowe Bergdahl."

The article reveals the soldiers who gave their lives for this traitor:

Staff Sgt. Clayton Bowen of San Antonio, Texas, and Pvt. First Class Morris Walker of Chapel Hill, N.C., who died together when they were killed by a roadside bomb on Aug. 18, 2009, looking for Bergdahl.

Staff Sgt. Kurt Curtis of Murray Utah, was shot to death on Aug. 26, 2009, also searching for Bergdahl.

Second Lt. Darryn Andrews of Dallas Texas, died on Sept. 4, 2009, when his vehicle hit an IED implanted in the road. This was the same type of IED that motorcycle riders Haji Karimullah, Ghamai, and others (fired upon by Clint's men) had planted in the ground to try and kill Americans. Lieutenant Andrews died searching for Bergdahl.

Staff Sgt. Michael Murphrey of Snyder Texas, died on Sept. 6, 2009, from an IED blast while searching for Bergdahl. This was the same type of deadly IED planted by two of the three motorcycle riders who Clint's men fired upon.

Pvt. First Class Matthew Martinek of DeKalb, Ill., died looking for Bergdahl on Sept. 4, 2009, killed by an IED explosion. And again, from the same type of IED built and/or handled by the motorcycle riders Ghamai and Karimullah, who Clint's men fired on in the village of Sarenzai.

These men—Bowen, Walker, Curtis, Andrews, Murphrey and Martinek—all died to bring this coward home. Adding insult to injury, Barack Obama turned over five Taliban terrorists held in Guantanamo Bay to secure Bergdahl's release. Then, the Obama White House brought Bergdahl's parents to the White House for a celebratory press conference in the Rose Garden. There, Bergdahl's father took the podium and gave praises to Allah, beginning his remarks by saying, "in the name of Allah, the merciful, the compassionate." Obama looked on and smiled as Bergdahl praised Allah.

Bergdahl, the traitor who threw off his gear and walked off in the middle of the night, straight into the arms of his willing Taliban captors, later pleaded guilty to desertion, which carries a maximum punishment of the death penalty in time of war. In fact, Article 85 of the Uniform Code of Military Justice mandates the death penalty for deserters in time of war. Here is that language:

c) Any person found guilty of desertion or attempt to desert shall be punished, if the offense is committed in time of war, by death or such other punishment as a court-martial made direct ..."

Although the United States Congress had never issued a formal declaration of war on Afghanistan, or against the Taliban, nonetheless, the Congress had authorized the Bush Administration to deploy forces to Afghanistan for military action, in what later became known as the United States' "War on Terror." Clearly, American military actions in Afghanistan occurred during a "time of war," which means that Article 85 could have justifiably served as a basis for seeking the death penalty against Bergdahl. The last notable deserter from the U.S. Army, Pvt. Eddie Slovik, was shot and executed by the Army on Jan. 31, 1945, for desertion from the Army in World War II. Sixty-nine years later, the parents of deserters are brought to the White House, where they declare praises to Allah to the smiling, approving nod of the commander in chief.

How things have changed.

After Bergdahl pleaded guilty to desertion, and after six American soldiers lost their lives trying to save the scumbag, a military judge at Fort Bragg let Bergdahl walk away with no punishment at all, other than the removal of his military rank and a dishonorable discharge from the Army. Yet Clint Lorance, who did not cause the deaths of any of his men, but brought them all home alive, and who performed brilliantly in a battle zone full of Taliban insurgents who were making bombs on the side to kill Americans, is branded as a murderer, and given 20 years in prison at the U.S. Disciplinary Barracks at Fort Leavenworth. This is one of the greatest miscarriages of justice in the history of the United States military.

Then there is the infamous espionage case of Pvt. First Class Bradley Manning, who later changed his name to

Chelsea and decided that he wanted to be known as a female, then tried to get the military to pay for a sex change operation. Manning, who downloaded thousands of pages of classified information with hundreds of national secrets, then gave that information to Wikileaks, got 35 years in prison at Fort Leavenworth for espionage.

But on Jan. 17, 2017, three days before the end of his administration, President Obama commuted Manning's sentence to a mere seven years, which meant that he or she walked out of Fort Leavenworth within weeks after the president's commutation.

It is a despicable notion to think that Manning and Bergdahl, both of whom betrayed their country and committed serious offenses against the nation, such as desertion and espionage, and both of whom pleaded guilty to those despicable crimes, received enormous leniency by the Obama administration. Yet Clint Lorance, who committed no crime, but whose head was served on a silver platter as an appeasement to the Afghan government as quid pro quo for the Kandahar massacre, was dubbed a murderer and given 20 years imprisonment, where he remains today.

So, the government grants leniency to traitors, but bulldozes a decorated officer for the sake of political correctness and to pay a political get to a foreign country.

Perhaps Clint would have been better off if his daddy had gone to the White House and sung praises to Allah, like Bergdahl's daddy did, and then Clint had declared himself to be a woman and requested a government-funded sex change operation, like Bradley Manning. How sick have we become as a nation, that we would glorify that sort of conduct to push certain political agendas, as in the case of Manning and Bergdahl, but crush and destroy a hero like Clint Lorance who would readily give his life for this country?

The time has come to right this wrong.

CHAPTER 52

THE SIGNIFICANT ACTIVITY REPORT
THE PROSECUTOR'S GAME OF "HIDE THE BALL"
REPREHENSIBLE PROSECUTORIAL
MISCONDUCT

Throughout the entire handling of Clint's matter, the prosecutor's conduct, and the conduct of certain members of the Army judiciary, have been so outrageous, and appalling, in demonstrating a coordinated effort to railroad Clint Lorance above all considerations of justice, that their actions have brought a stain upon the military justice system.

Prosecutors have a legal and ethical duty to turn over all exonerating evidence to a defense attorney, and to allow the defense counsel to attempt to introduce evidence in defense of his or her client. It is not the job of the prosecutor, whether in the military or the civilian world, to secure a conviction at all costs. Justice must always be the goal of any prosecutor. And if there is a reasonable doubt as to guilt, the prosecutor should never bring the case to begin with.

When a prosecutor becomes so zealous that the goal is to secure a conviction, come hell or high water, even if that means hiding crucial evidence from the defense, there is a stain on the entire criminal justice system, and more importantly, a stain on the U.S. Constitution.

In Clint's case, perhaps the biggest, criminal, hide-the-ball of all involves the prosecution's refusal to reveal a Significant Activities Report, or SIGACT report, showing the true danger and the true threat assessment of the village of Payenzai at the time Clint's platoon stepped off on their patrol on the morning of July 2, 2012.

To understand the significance of this grave omission by the prosecution, think back to the early morning hours of July 2, 2012, in the Zhari District of Kandahar Province. Even though Lt. Lorance and the patrol from First Platoon were scheduled to step off at 7 a.m. from Payenzai, at company headquarters at Gariban, intelligence officers had been monitoring local radio traffic from Taliban ICOM radios for several hours before 7 a.m., to try and gauge the level of threat that the platoon would face when it moved out.

Beginning at around 5:30 a.m., intelligence officers at Gariban started intercepting radio messages from the Taliban in and around the village of Sarenzai. The radio traffic indicated that Clint's platoon at Payenzai was about to be ambushed. In other words, the Taliban had targeted Clint's patrol for an ambush from the moment they stepped off on their mission that morning. The radio traffic from Taliban sources about the ambush to Clint's platoon, started at 6:19 a.m.

So, Clint's company, that is Charlie Company, back at Gariban, knew at least 41 minutes before Clint's patrol stepped off that morning that they were likely to be ambushed. Clint had also heard radio reports from the air cover above about military-aged males gathering in the northwest corner of the village.

There was no question—based on intelligence ahead of time as gathered by the company and also based dip on intelligence after the fact, based upon biometrics matches— that First Platoon was in a hot zone and being targeted for ambush by the Taliban that morning.

The Army knew that an ambush was planned against Clint's platoon that morning, but prosecuted Clint anyway for murder. This despite the fact that unidentified Afghans charged their position on a motorcycle coming from a road,

Old Chilliwack Road, a road controlled by the Taliban. The decision to bring charges under the circumstances makes no sense, unless explained within the context of the political prosecution for paying homage to the Afghans for the Kandahar massacre.

After intelligence officers intercepted the radio traffic of a pending ambush, results of intercept were transcribed into a SIGACT report.

Here is what the SIGACT report said about radio traffic intercepted from the Taliban in the 41 minutes prior to the beginning of Clint's mission:

> *Summary: 02 Jul 2012 JOCWATCH ENTRY 0184, NSI RC (S) 3 FURY RC (S)*
>
> *At 0619D* C-Troop CAV received ICOM Chatter indicating a pending ambush on a combined patrol moving toward an INS position. The ICOM chatter lasted for nearly 90 minutes.*

In the above SIGACT, C-Troop CAV refers to Charlie Troop or Charlie company, Cavalry Scouts, which was Clint's company, commanded by Capt. Swanson. Notice the phrase, "a *pending ambush on a combined patrol* moving toward an INS position."

That combined patrol is Clint's patrol, combined with the Americans of First Platoon, and a handful of ANA soldiers out front. Of course, 40-some minutes later, the motorcycle with Taliban bombmakers charged Clint's platoon, and Clint ordered his men to open fire. The acronym INS means insurgents. So, according to the Army's own intelligence, Clint's patrol was heading toward an insurgency position—right into an ambush.

This appeared to be the first step of the "pending ambush" predicted in the significant activity report. With the Taliban on the radio waves saying that they were about to ambush Clint's patrol, what was he supposed to do?

But the prosecution's decision to hide the SIGACT report from the defense and the jury is yet another travesty in Clint's case. As with the biometrics evidence, the SIGACT report was never turned over to the defense. So, the prosecution tries to make the fabricated claim that the motorcycle riders were civilian casualties, while at the same time, sat on a report showing that the Taliban was planning to ambush Clint's patrol at the very time and that Clint's men opened fire on the motorcycle charging his platoon from a Taliban-controlled road.

The military prosecutors against Clint, in an unrestrained zeal to obtain a conviction, deliberately hid this piece of evidence from the defense, depriving the defense of its right to submit this evidence to the military jury.

One of the issues in Clint's defense involved the reasonableness of his order to have his men fire on the motorcycle-riding bombmakers, under the circumstances. Knowledge that his platoon was under a threat of a "pending ambush" by the Taliban, is a highly relevant factor to the reasonableness of Clint's decision to open the fire under these circumstances. A juror, fully understanding all the facts that Clint's men fired into a combat zone, in which the Taliban was actively threatening to the ambush the platoon, under circumstances in which the Taliban was using suicide bombers by motorcycle to kill Americans, would certainly conclude that Clint's actions in ordering his men to fire was his only reasonable choice.

But in a hideous act of prosecutorial misconduct, both biometrics evidence proving that the motorcycle riders were bombmakers, and this Significant Activity Report, which showed that Clint's patrol was about to be ambushed, were hidden from the defense, and thus, unavailable to the military jury in deciding Clint's fate.

The president of the United States should use his power as commander in chief of the Armed Forces, and order the Army to vacate Clint's sentence. He should also order Clint immediately released from the U.S. Disciplinary Barracks at Fort Leavenworth. And, finally, the president should restore Clint to his proper military grade is an officer in the U.S. Army with back pay for the time that he's been incarcerated.

American lives matter.

CHAPTER 53

BRIGADIER GENERAL BERGER
JUDICIAL MISCONDUCT FROM
THE ARMY'S HIGHEST-RANKING JUDGE

After John N. Maher discovered exonerating biometrics evidence, showing that the motorcycle riders fired on by Clint's men were, in fact, Taliban bombmakers, and that Clint's men had not fired on innocent civilians, and after he notified Clint's command at Fort Bragg and the Judge Advocate General of the Army, Lt. Gen. Flora Darpino, Clint's case made its way to the Army Court of Criminal Appeals, located at Fort Belvoir, Va. The Army Court of Criminal Appeals did not challenge the authenticity of the biometrics evidence, but instead, totally disregarded the biometrics evidence by claiming that Clint could not have known in advance that the motorcycle riders were enemy insurgents.

Of course, to spew out such warped reasoning, the Army Court, led by Brig. Gen. Joseph B. Berger, III, had to ignore the fact that a) Clint was charged with shooting civilians, but these riders were wartime combatants and thus not civilians; b) the motorcycle came down a road (Old Chilliwack Road) controlled and used only by the Taliban; c) the platoon had been ambushed by sniper fire from that road less than 24 hours earlier; d) U.S. helicopters saw military-aged males gathering in the northwest corner of the village; e) Sgt. Herrmann's men spotted Afghans with ICOM radios on the west side of the village; f) Clint had only a few seconds to react and gave the order from the bottom of an irrigation ditch between grape berms, unable to see anything other than an 8-foot-high wall of baked mud and grape leaves; g) suicide-by-motorcycle had become the murder tactic de jour by the Taliban for killing Americans and American-friendly Afghans; and h) the blimp operator at Combat Outpost Sia Choy observed three Taliban members, up armed with weapons and ICOM radios, shadowing Clint's platoon on July 2 during the entire operation.

The SIGACT, which stated that Clint's patrol was headed into a "pending ambush," was not raised before the Army Court at the time because the defense team did not discover it until June of 2018, sometime after the initial interaction with the Army Court of Criminal Appeals.

After ignoring all of the facts, and blinding itself to overpowering evidence against the prosecution and favoring the defense, the Army Court of Criminal Appeals went on to dismiss the biometrics evidence as irrelevant, on the legally cockeyed theory that Clint could not have known in advance that the motorcycle riders were enemy combatants.

But every member of the Taliban in Afghanistan looks like a civilian. They all wear farmers garb, civilian and Taliban alike. That's part of the Taliban's game plan—to blend in with civilian farmers. The Taliban doesn't wear military uniform. Following the Army Court's demented logic, every American soldier who killed a Taliban terrorist in the war on terror should be prosecuted. Thousands of the Taliban have been killed. None wore uniforms.

Please.

Clint had to react on the best evidence he had within a split second. And thank God, he did act. The Army court was not able to reconcile its position with the plain fact that Clint was charged with shooting civilians, even though these guys simply were not civilians but were enemy combatants.

So if you're going to charge Clint with shooting a poor civilian, he has a right to prove they were not civilians. But the Army hid evidence that Clint could have proved to show they were not civilians, but were enemy combatants.

At this point, in October of 2017, after it became obvious that the military justice system, through the Army Court of Criminal Appeals decision, which could be explained only by 1) extreme intellectual laziness or 2) a continuation of the prosecutorial railroad job designed to keep Clint's scalp on a platter, John N. Maher decided to expand the defense firepower. Maher searched out and found two of the most prominent ex-military JAG officers in the nation, Kevin Mikolashek and David Bolgiano. Both agreed to join the defense team.

Mikolashek served for eight years as an Army officer, where he was as a prosecutor and legal advisor to combat commanders. He would later go on to serve 10 years as an assistant United States Attorney with the Department of Justice. Years later, during the internationally publicized prosecution of former Trump campaign Chair Paul Manafort, Mikolashek would be sought for interviews and quoted for his expertise as a former DOJ prosecutor by national media organizations such as NPR, the *Washington Post*, and *Newsweek*.

David "Bo" Bolgiano was a former member of the 82nd Airborne Division who transitioned to U.S. Army Special Forces, where he won a Bronze Star before later becoming a JAG officer in the U.S. Air Force, rising to the rank of lieutenant colonel. Bolgiano is a nationally acclaimed rules-of-engagement expert, and became deputy general counsel for the Department of Defense.

With the additional two more heavy-hitting ex-JAG officers to the Lorance defense team, in Mikolashek and Bolgiano, lead counsel John Maher had begun to assemble what might be described as a "military legal dream team," with a core component of some of the best military law specialists in the nation.

But even still, the Army remained undeterred in its determination to scapegoat an innocent officer, in Clint Lorance. Take, for example, the recklessness displayed by Chief Judge Brig. Gen. Joseph Berger III made to the Washington, D.C., think tank, the Center for International and Strategic Studies, on March 15, 2018.

As will be seen, Brig. Gen. Berger, the Army's chief judge, made public remarks that day that appeared to be designed to poison Clint's appeal. Without delving too deep into the weeds of military appellate procedure, the U.S. Court of Appeals for the Armed Forces made its final decision to reject Clint's claims on Dec. 19, 2017. Under federal habeas corpus law, Clint had one year from Dec. 19, 2017, until Dec. 19, 2018, to file a petition for habeas corpus in the federal court in Topeka, Kan.

That meant that Clint's case, from a legal standpoint, was still alive up until at least Dec. 19, 2018, and possibly beyond, with the 19th being Clint's deadline for filing a petition for habeas corpus. In fact, between December of 2017 and December of 2018, Clint, through his legal team led by John N. Maher, had appealed to the Secretary of the Army to vacate Clint's conviction. The case, at the time of Berger's remarks, was before the Secretary of the Army for consideration.

Put another way, there is a ladder in the military appeals system, and the habeas corpus system for federal review of military cases. At the point that Brig. Gen. Berger, the chief judge of the Army, decided to insert himself, essentially as a prosecutor, Clint's case had taken only one step up the ladder, and that was Brig. Gen. Berger's court. But there were many steps of the ladder still to be climbed, all the way up to the U.S. Supreme Court.

It appears, as will be seen, that Berger wanted to taint all the steps of the ladder above his court, to ensure that his court would never be reversed, and that true biometrics and other facts that exonerate Clint would never see the light of day.

At the time of Berger's remarks, the case was being considered by the Secretary of the Army, and it was possible that the case might be vacated altogether by the Secretary of the Army. It was also possible that the case might be sent back for another trial. Other possibilities existed as well.

Regardless, under almost every judicial canon in the United States, including judicial canons that govern the conduct of military judges and federal judges, under no circumstances is it ever proper for a judge to make public comments about a case that is still pending within the legal system, particularly if that case could come before the judge again, or if other decisionmakers are currently reviewing the case. And it is not proper to make comments that could be prejudicial to a party's case, given that the judges public comments might influence subsequent legal or factual determinations by other judges or persons in authority over the case.

But on March 15, 2018, while Lt. Clint Lorance's case was pending before the Secretary of the Army on a petition by defense counsel to vacate Clint's conviction, and while it was still eligible for potential habeas corpus later on, depending on the outcome of the Secretary of the Army's decision, the chief judge of the Army Court of Criminal Appeals, Brig. Gen. Joseph Berger, decided to publicly abandon his role as a judge in this case, to throw his obligations under the judicial canons into the trashcan, and by all accounts, to position himself as an advocate for the prosecution in a public forum.

General Berger, who was the chief judge the Army Court of Criminal Appeals, the very court that rejected Clint's initial appeal and ignored the new biometrics evidence that showed that Clint's men were firing at Taliban bombmakers, made a speech, in full uniform, to the Center for International and

Strategic Studies in Washington, D.C., on March 15, 2018, about the My Lai massacre. And Berger, in the middle of a talk about the My Lai massacre, which was the designated topic for the symposium, decided to throw a firebomb in the middle of it all.

In the middle of a speech about Capt. Calley and the My Lai massacre, Berger brought up and inserted the topic of Clint Lorance, likening Clint to a war criminal, and falsely claiming that Clint had violated the rules of engagement, even though Clint had been acquitted of all charges related to the rules of engagement.

In what can be interpreted as nothing other than an effort to intentionally sabotage Clint's case, which at that time was before the Secretary of the Army, who had the power to dismiss it, Berger called Clint a "bad apple" in front of hundreds of people, with the media present, and said Clint had gone "off the rails," likening him to Lt. William Calley, who was accused of the mass murder of 109 South Vietnamese civilians and convicted of mass murder of 22 South Vietnamese civilians.

Naturally, Berger concealed in his speech the fact that biometrics had shown the motorcycle riders to be Taliban bombmakers and thus enemy combatants, or that the SIGACT report showed radio intercepts 40 minutes before the platoon "stepped off" that the Taliban planned to "ambush" Clint's platoon. Remember, this unnecessary public blab-rupture came from the chief judge of the U.S. Army, who decided that he wanted to act like an out-of-control prosecutor, while Clint's case was still pending before the Secretary of the Army, who had the power to dismiss it.

Clint's case was unresolved when Berger blabbed publicly, unlike Lt. Calley's case, which ended in 1974 when Calley's sentence was commuted to time served, some 45 years before. But Clint's case was as active as a hot potato when Berger went on the offensive with his unfortunate Clint-bashing spree, when at that very time, the case was under consideration by the Army Secretary for possible vacation of the conviction and sentence.

When, in the middle of his speech about Calley, the chief judge went off track and turned into a prosecutor, this shows the extent of the Army's vengeful efforts to railroad Clint by hiding evidence and continuing to disseminate a false misrepresentation of facts.

Brig. Gen. Berger said, "We get bad apples from time to time," and then immediately referred to Clint as a "bad apple." Then, Berger said, "We do not always weed them out in enough time. So, you can take a case like First Lt. Clint Lorance. So I will take you to June 2012 in Afghanistan. First Lt. Clint Lorance comes down from the staff to take over a platoon. Clint Lorance was a very aggressive lieutenant, who had his own ideas about how the war in Afghanistan should be fought. Those ideas were not in alignment with the rules of engagement. And that's the fundamental fact that starts us off the trail here. And off the rails. Lorance gives his soldiers guidance that is not in accordance with the ROE."

Unbelievable.

Berger calls Clint a "bad apple," calls him a "very aggressive lieutenant," says he "goes off the rails," and makes false claims about Clint violating the rules of engagement. In fact, Clint was not convicted of any rules of engagement violations and was acquitted of all ROE related charges. Berger doesn't reveal the full truth about that, though.

But Brig. Gen. Berger (who is also the Army's highest-ranking judge) did not let those facts pointing to Clint's innocence get in the way of his false, politically motivated spin on the story. Perhaps he figured that because he was a one-star general in uniform, who happened to be the Army's highest-ranking judge, that people would swallow his toxic potion, hook, line, and sinker, without questioning him.

If he thought that, he engaged in serious miscalculation.

The rules of engagement claim by Brig. Gen. Berger, suggesting that Clint violated the rules of engagement, was flat-out false.

It also shows that Clint would never get a fair trial, as the chief judge, Brig. Gen. Berger, with Clint's case still pending, makes comments about an active case that has been before his court, and was at the moment of his comments under consideration by the Secretary of the Army, with the power to override his court.

By calling Clint a "bad apple," suggesting he had gone "off the rails," and comparing him to Capt. Calley, who was accused of murdering 109 people and convicted of murdering 22 people, Berger's motive was clear—to publicly influence the Secretary of the Army not to vacate Clint's sentence, and also, to poison the well against Clint for any future federal judges who might hear his case. With his blabbing motormouth in 10th gear, with any sense of judicial temperament churning at the bottom of the garbage disposal, Berger became a public hotdog advocating a political cause.

Why else would he make such judicially reckless statements, about a case still under review, if his intent were not to influence the Secretary of the Army against vacating Clint's sentence, or to influence subsequent federal judges who might look under the cover at say, the substance of the biometrics evidence that he inexcusably chose to ignore? Put another way, why else would he drop this bombshell about Clint in the middle of a speech about the My Lai massacre if his purpose was not to influence the decision? There is no other credible explanation.

So, we have a chief judge of the Army Court of Criminal Appeals making false statements, when he should not have been commenting at all about the case because it was still active in the military and federal courts system. Berger claimed that Clint went off the rails. But Berger is the one who went off the rails, abandoning his duties under the judicial canons, and tainting Clint's case with his vengeful comments so much that now, Clint cannot get a fair shake on appeal.

Berger's reckless public statements appear to have worked. On June 14, 2018, 91 days after the general's biting remarks, the Secretary of the Army's designee took final action on Lorance's case, taking no favorable action and ordering Lorance be dismissed from the Army.

Brig. Gen. Berger has violated every judicial canon by inserting himself as a public advocate against Clint, ostensibly trying to influence the Secretary of the Army and subsequent federal courts who might reverse the decision of the Army Court of Criminal Appeals.

Let's review a few of the judicial canons that Berger made a mockery of that day, when he decided to become an open advocate of the prosecution.

The American Bar Association model Judicial Cannon 210 is titled, "Rule 2.10: Judicial Statements on Pending and Impending Cases." The first prohibition under that rule is set out as follows:

> (A) A judge shall not make any public statement that might reasonably be expected to affect the outcome or impair the fairness of a matter pending* or impending* in any court, or make any nonpublic statement that might substantially interfere with a fair trial or hearing.

Question, does calling Clint a "bad apple" and suggesting that he went "off the rails" possibly impair the fairness of the matter then pending before the Secretary of the Army? Of course it does!

Another judicial canon governing federal judges in the federal court system. And we start by looking at Canon 3, which states, plainly, that "A Judge Should Perform the Duties of the Office Fairly, Impartially and Diligently."

Question. Was Brig. Gen. Berger demonstrating judicial impartiality when he called Clint, in public, a "bad apple?"

That comment, in and of itself, constitutes a violation of Judicial Canon 3 of the Federal Judicial Canons for judges.

Consider what the Federal Judicial Canons say about judges making public comments about cases. Rule 3(A)(6) of the Federal Judicial Canons is clear, stating, unequivocally that, "(6) A judge should not make public comment on the merits of a matter pending or impending in any court."

The word "impending" means "about to happen." So even though Clint's case was before the Secretary of the Army, technically not a court, if the Secretary of the Army did not grant relief, then it would go to the federal court in Topeka, Kan., on a habeas corpus petition. So the matter was "impending," that is about to go before a federal court, and Berger ignored and violated that rule, too.

There is no ambiguity here. Berger should have kept his mouth shut about the Lorance case, period. But he made a public comment, and he flat-out violated rule 3(A)(6).

Berger decided to hot dog it, and went off the railroad tracks himself by attacking Clint in a public forum, and in so doing, violated every relevant canon governing his conduct as a judge, and caused so much damage to Clint's case that it is now seemingly impossible for Clint to get a fair hearing on appeal.

Finally, while U.S. Army looks to the model ABA rules and federal rules for guidance on how its judges should act, it also has its own code of judicial canons governing its judges. It's called the Code of Judicial Conduct for Army Trial and Appellate Judges.

One of the most important rules governing Army judges is Rule 1.2, titled "Promoting Confidence in the Judiciary."

Rule 1.2 of the Army's Rules Governing Judges conduct provides that, "A judge shall act at all times in a manner that promotes public confidence in the independence, integrity, and impartiality of the judiciary, and shall avoid impropriety and the appearance of impropriety."

Question: When Berger called Clint a "bad apple," claimed that Clint had "gone off the rails," falsely accused him of violating the rules of engagement, and refused to disclose any exonerating evidence on biometric links to bombmakers, or the pending ambush of Clint's patrol by the Taliban—all which should have cleared Clint—does that sound like a judge who was impartial, or independent, and is that the type of language to promote confidence in the integrity of the Army's judicial system?

Or how about Rule 2.3 (B) of the Rules Governing Army Judges? That rule provides that, "(B) A judge shall not, in the performance of judicial duties, by words or conduct manifest bias or prejudice, or engage in harassment."

Question: Do the general's public comments, appearing as the chief judge of the Army, made on March 15, 2018, suggest he is impartial? Or do those comments, by calling Clint "a bad apple," and suggesting that he had "gone off the rails," and falsely claiming that Clint violated rules of engagement, suggest the judge might have some sort of bias against Clint?

These questions, of course, are rhetorical. The judge's comments about a pending case, which was still before the Army Secretary for a possible vacation of the sentence, makes a mockery of the Army's judicial system and totally undermines public confidence in the system. His words show bias against Clint, violate all judicial prohibitions against speaking in public about a case that is still pending, undermines confidence in in the Army's judicial system, and poison the well to the point that it is now questionable that Clint can get a fair shake as his case moves up the appellate ladder.

After these comments were made public, Clint's lawyers wrote Brig. Gen. Berger, and respectfully, in a polite manner, requested he consider his comments, consider the evidence, and please correct the record publicly. Gen.

Berger at first agreed to have a meeting with counsel to discuss his comments. But then, Berger postponed the meeting, postponed it again, postponed it again, and finally put the meeting off altogether. Perhaps he realized he had something to hide and did not want to be confronted by it.

Berger knew damn well that his comments as a judge were out of line. If he did not know, and he was that reckless, he should have been relieved of his duties immediately by the Secretary of the Army.

Remember, Berger came to speak about the Calley case from some 40 years ago, but voluntarily interjected his comments about Clint Lorance, in an obvious attempt to influence the Secretary of the Army not to vacate Clint's sentence. Or perhaps the good general wanted to influence the federal court, if the case got filed on habeas corpus, the 10th Circuit Court of Appeals in Denver, or the U.S. Supreme Court.

It's time to right this wrong.

CHAPTER 54

LINED-OUT STATEMENTS & WITNESSES PRESSURED

Before closing, we should consider what appears to be pressure against witnesses, by the Army, to change statements that would have helped Clint.

On, Aug. 3, 2012, one month after the motorcycle incident, the CID interviewed First Lt. Dominic V. Latino, the previous platoon leader who had been medically evacuated from the field after an IED exploded and wounded him.

Latino was recovering from his injuries sustained in combat. In a typed sworn statement, Latino related that during his tenure as platoon leader, he would never let a motorcycle near First Platoon because of the deadly risk they posed. Specifically, Dominic V. Latino wrote, "We would not let a motorcycle into close proximity of our element due to current tactics, techniques, and procedures of enemy forces." A review of Lt. Latino's sworn statement, however, shows that the portion about not letting motorcycles near his platoon was later struck or lined out.

Lt. Latino clearly swore under oath that he too, as platoon leader, would never let a motorcycle near his platoon—for obvious reasons, the Taliban was killing Americans with motorcycles. And then later, that sworn statement gets lined out? How would a sworn statement get lined out, if not under suspicious circumstances. It appears that someone with an agenda, an agenda to secure a conviction at all costs, got to Latino.

That statement—that Latino would not let motorcycles anywhere near his platoon—helped Clint's defense, because it showed that another platoon leader of this very platoon, First Platoon, also considered these motorcycles charging at platoon patrols to be a dangerous threat.

Of course, they were bigtime danger. Despite the prosecution's determined attempt to hide the fact, everybody knew that the Taliban was killing Americans, and America-friendly Afghans, with suicide-by-motorcycle tactics. Undoubtedly, this is why Latino made his statement to begin with.

This raises the question: Why was it lined out? Or, who insisted upon lining out Latino's statement?

It appears that someone did not want Latino's statement to make its way to the military jury.

Latino is no longer in the Army. When Clint's defense team contacted him to ask him why the sworn statement about motorcycles had been lined out, he did not wish to comment. Interesting.

Then there is a mysterious situation involving Pvt. First Class Zachary Wayne Thomas.

Recall that two soldiers, the ones closest to the front of the platoon, gave statements indicating that the Afghan National Army fired first at the motorcycle first. These soldiers were Spec. Reyler Leon, and Pvt. Zachary Thomas. These soldiers initially gave sworn statements to Army investigators in the days following the incident.

Leon, who was the mine hound, replacing Cpl. Hanes, who was gunned down a few days earlier, never backed off of his statement that the Afghans fired first.

This sworn statement, that the Afghans fired first, is highly relevant on two points. First, it shows what a hot battle zone that First Platoon was operating in, and that the Afghans also considered the motorcycle to be a threat.

It also raises questions as to whose bullets actually killed the Taliban operatives who were bomb-makers, and riding the motorcycle. Perhaps an Afghan bullet, and not an American bullet, had caused the deaths, meaning it would be impossible to charge Clint with anything.

Even though Leon did not back off his statement that the Afghans fired first, the prosecutors deliberately did not ask him about it at Clint's trial, and then carefully kept it out of evidence, out of earshot of the jury. The defense attorney, Mr. Womack, tried to get it into evidence at trial, but when the prosecutor objected, the military judge sustained the objection.

The defense counsel did not put up much of a fight after that, on the issue of Leon's statement, although he had other grounds under which he could have gotten the evidence admitted, had he pressed the right buttons. It is possible that the lead defense counsel at trial simply did not know what to do when the judge sustained the prosecution's objection. We will never know.

Thus, the strongest defense witness on this point, Spec. Leon, was silenced by the prosecution on the most important point that he (Leon) could have made, that the Afghan National Army fired first.

The military jury never heard about it.

Pvt. Thomas's statement is a little bit different. Thomas, who was also closer to the front of the unit, and thus, in a better position to see than the other paratroopers, made this sworn statement on the day after the shooting:

"My best guess is around 4 to 6 people fired, but was to my knowledge, a mixed ISAF/ANA."

So, Thomas claimed, under oath, in a written statement, that both the Americans (ISAF) and the Afghans were initially firing at the same time at the motorcycle.

This is also significant, because it shows, as previously pointed out, that the Afghans also considered the motorcycle to be a threat.

But despite the sworn statements of Leon and Thomas, the prosecutor looked at the military jury and claimed the Afghans did not fire. Here is what the prosecutor, Capt. Otto said, specifically, to the military jury, during his opening statement at the beginning of Clint's trial:

"The ANA are forward with a different vantage point coming up to the road. The ANA can see. The ANA do not engage."

Otto made this claim, that "the ANA do not engage," despite knowing about the sworn statements of both Leon and Thomas, that the ANA fired, and according to Leon, the ANA fired first. Otto hid the ball. The jury would never know because the prosecution did not want them to know the full facts.

But like the questionable circumstance behind Lt. Latino's statement, there is a fishy smell when it comes to what happened with Pvt. Thomas's statement. Here's why.

After Thomas made the initial sworn statement that a mix of both Afghan National Army and Americans fired first, he was interviewed three more times by high-ranking investigators within the same month after the shooting. By the end of July 2012, after investigators talked to Thomas the fourth time, Thomas walked back his statement about the Afghanis shooting first. By July 31, 2012, he had gone from saying under oath that it was a "mix of Afghan National Army and ISAF" forces firing first, to saying that he could no longer be sure who fired.

It appears someone pressured him into walking his statement back. Of course, the closer a witness is in time and space to an event, the more likely that their recollection is still be accurate. The farther away in time and space, the less likely that recollection of the event will be accurate. But criminal investigators kept beating on Thomas, until he finally said, one month after the fact, that he could no longer be sure who fired first, even though he was sure the day after the fact.

Then, at trial, on cross-examination by Mr. Womack, Clint's civilian defense counsel, Thomas admitted his original sworn statement, that a "mix of Afghan and ISAF" forces fired first, was correct.

For some reason, defense counsel at trial never hammered or argued the significance of this point to the military jury, and never pushed very hard to have Spec. Leon's statement admitted.

Nevertheless, Lt. Latino's statement being lined out (motorcycles not allowed to approach platoon) and Pvt. Thomas changing his statement from that a mix of ANA and ISAF fired first, to he was no longer sure who fired first, suggests that someone was manipulating statements in a way that would help secure a conviction. Given everything else that has happened in Clint's case, from hiding biometrics evidence by the prosecution, to hiding the Significant Activity Report, to Brig. Gen. Berger's off-the-rails comments before the Center for International and Strategic Studies, all smack of prosecutorial interference—individuals bound and determined to secure a conviction, come hell or high water, regardless of the fact that the motorcycle riders were bombmakers.

Even if the mysterious changes in the statements of Lt. Latino and Pvt. Thomas were simply coincidental and not orchestrated, and there is not a snowball's chance in hell that the changes in either case were coincidental, *the fact remains that the prosecution hid from the military jury evidence that the two soldiers closest to the action both gave sworn statements to investigators that the Afghans fired first.* The prosecutor's actions in hiding this fact deprive Clint of his rights to a fair trial under the due process clause of the Fifth Amendment, and his right to confront witnesses under the confrontation clause of the Sixth Amendment.

Prosecutors hid other things, too. They hid evidence of the shootings, by Staff Sgt. Hermann's squad, on the west side of the village. They hid the full extent of radio reports that an attack was brewing on the west side of the village. They hid from the military jury the SIGACT report, showing intercepted messages some 40 minutes before Clint's patrol commenced their mission that morning, that Clint's patrol was likely to be ambushed. They hid biometrics evidence, proving that the motorcycle riders were Taliban bombmakers.

And they claim all this is not relevant?

When you're trying to second-guess an officer's actions in the midst of a red-hot war zone, where Americans have died and been blown up in the last few days, a pending ambush isn't relevant? To try and blow all that off as "not relevant," because you're trying to paint the impression that the patrol was on a peaceful stroll out in Never-Never Land, where no reasonable person would ever fire a gun at a motorcycle rider, is about as disingenuous as the decision to hide the evidence from the defense and from the jury to begin with.

The prosecution's actions are reprehensible. The president of the United States should vacate Clint's conviction by disapproving the findings of the court-martial, and restore Clint to active duty immediately, to the rank that would be consistent with his current time in grade.

American lives matter.

CHAPTER 55

THE EYE IN THE SKY
MORE EVIDENCE HIDDEN BY THE PROSECUTION
LATE 2018

Several months after Gen. Berger's speech at the Center for International and Strategic Studies in Washington, D.C., more evidence surfaced that underscored even more cover-up activity by the prosecution in its zeal to convict Clint.

Kevin Huber had worked as a civilian Aerostat operator at Combat Outpost Sia Choy in 2012. In other words, Mr. Huber was a blimp operator, the same type of military blimp with high-powered cameras that Clint had seen along Highway 1 when he transferred from Pasab, ultimately to Payenzai. Not all of the combat outposts in Afghanistan had blimp operators assigned to them. Most remote outposts, such as Clint's post at Payenzai, did not even have drones, unless someone pulled strings as Clint did in this case, let alone the Aerostat blimps.

However, Combat Outpost Sia Choy, as the squadron headquarters for the 4/73 Calvary, did have an Aerostat flying overhead to monitor activities on the ground.

The Aerostat operators, who controlled the floating blimps, were generally either civilian contractors or active duty military. At Sia Choy, Mr. Kevin Huber, a civilian contractor operating out of Fort Bragg had been sent to Afghanistan to operate a 22-Meter (72 feet) Aerostat stationary airship, with a powerful MX-15, fully digital, high-definition camera system with a high- magnification, step-zoom-spotter lens. The powerful camera aboard the airship was capable of up-close, positive identification of people at a distance up to 5.5 kilometers away. It also streamed of continuous 1080-pixel, high-definition video. The camera system was among the best on the market, and it could identify targets, track targets, and do just about anything that the Army wanted it to do.

With the detailed information captured from aerial surveillance, Huber and his group shared information with the Army intelligence officers, ground commanders, the CIA, or with any other American agency in need of the photographs taken by the cameras.

Mr. Huber's immediate area of responsibility was to scan the landscape around Sia Choy, for Taliban activity, and especially for bomb planting in the grounds around the outpost.

Just before 7 o'clock in the morning of July 2, 2012, Huber was operating from the command and control shelter at Sia Choy. Huber had already begun the tedious process of aerial surveillance of his immediate area of operations, right around Sia Choy, when one of the sergeants, who worked as a radio operator, a Sgt. Watson, came into the CNC (command and control) shelter.

Here is how Huber described the moment to the author:

"We had a Sgt. Watson, who was part of the fires group, come into CNC shelter and say, 'We need you to swing over to east. We have a movement out there being shadowed with guys with ICOMs. They needed me to visually ID with camera.'"

Although Huber did not realize it at the time, Watson was referring to Lt. Clint Lorance's patrol, which had just stepped off from Payenzai. The fires team, which is the radio team, of which Sgt. Watson was a member, had intercepted messages that Clint's squad was about to be ambushed by a Taliban attack. "They wanted to get some aerial surveillance on the squad," he said, "to see what was actually going on."

As an experienced Aerostat operator, Huber knew all the remote combat outposts in the region, and knew Payenzai, which the Aerostat operators referred to as "The Dorito" on their navigational charts.

Huber brought the airship down from an above-ground altitude of 2,100 feet to around 1,600 feet, for a closer look, and positioned the powerful MX-15 camera out to the east, aiming it toward the grape fields to the south and to the west of the Strong Point.

Within just a matter of seconds, he had a positive identification on the American patrol. They were crossing from their Strong Point, across a road, and into a field just south of the village of Payenzai.

Almost immediately, he saw three Taliban members shadowing the American patrol at a distance of about 300 meters. The three insurgents carried AK-47 rifles and ICOM radios. The Taliban insurgents were moving along the back wall of the village, toward the direction of the American position. From what he was observing, it did not appear that the American platoon had yet seen the Taliban. Nonetheless, the Taliban presence presented a hot and dangerous situation for the American platoon.

Mr. Huber had scouted this area many times through his powerful camera on the Aerostat, and knew it to be a constant hot battle zone.

Mr. Huber reported that there was a centralized mosque nearby, in which the Taliban which stored their weapons, including components for IEDs, because they knew that the Americans would not attack the mosque. Mr. Huber, however, had been able to identify the mosque through the Aerostat cameras.

Most likely, the weapons and the ICOM radios that these three Taliban members were carrying as they were scouted the American position had been filtered through that mosque.

Although Sarenzai was outside of his area of operations, Huber had nonetheless conducted aerial surveillance over the village several times, and was conducting surveillance this morning at the request of another unit.

But from the times he had scouted village of Sarenzai, he had become familiar with Old Chilliwack Road.

Mr. Huber verified to the author what several of the soldiers had already testified to at Clint's the court-martial, that Old Chilliwack Road was a known route of entry used by the Taliban, and controlled by the Taliban.

Not only did Mr. Huber verify that Old Chilliwack Road was a Taliban bastion, but he also verified that signs were placed along Old Chilliwack Road—and along all the roads in the area—warning civilians to stay off the roads. Therefore, the three motorcycle riders charging down Old Chilliwack Road were clearly defying the warning signs to keep off the roads, except police or U.S. or Afghan military. This fact made their presence more suspicious and more disconcerting to the American patrol, and obviously, to the Afghan National Army also, which opened fire before the Americans did, according to the sworn written statements of Spec. Leon and Pvt. Thomas.

Recall that Clint had only been in the actual battle space for two days in the time of the shooting incident involving the motorcycles. Clint was still in the process of learning the geography of the area, including the placement of signs on the roads. Mr. Huber, however, in watching this area for a number of months with a super-powerful camera on the Aerostat, had a greater familiarity with the geography than anyone on the ground.

Huber conducted aerial surveillance of Clint's patrol for several minutes that morning, prior to the shooting. He was pulled off of the surveillance of Clint's patrol, just before the shooting, and assigned to another area to surveil. Therefore, he did not see the motorcycle approach down Old Chilliwack. However, Huber reported his observations to the military chain of command, that Clint's patrol was being shadowed by a hostile, armed Taliban group of three insurgents with ICOM radios and weapons.

Mr. Huber, however, who is clearly the most significant non-military witness to the situation on the ground on the morning of the shooting, was never even interviewed by the Army's CID agents, nor was he called as a witness at the trial.

Of course, he was not. His testimony undercuts the prosecution's "Sunday stroll in the park" theory, and shows that Clint's order to have his men fire in self-defense was fully justified. On the afternoon after the shooting, Mr. Huber heard information in the scuttlebutt that some "L.T." had been pulled off the field and detained.

"Later that afternoon, I had just heard a report, tribal talk," he said. "Some LT was arrested and had his weapon taken. I thought it was bizarre."

Most likely, the insurgents that Mr. Huber saw took their ICOM radios with them in the field to shadow Clint's position in order to report information back to their comrades. All this shows evidence of coordination between Taliban forces in the east, west, and now the southern part of the village.

In retrospect, it is likely that the ambush was thwarted by Clint ordering his men to open fire both on the east and the west side of the village. It is a reasonable inference, given the evidence of a very hot battle zone that the prosecution suppressed, that Clint's order to open fire probably saved American lives that morning by putting the Taliban back on these defensive.

Mr. Huber did not fully "put two and two together," that he had been watching Clint Lorance's patrol, until August of 2013, when he saw media coverage of Lorance's court-martial in North Carolina. Based upon the location and the time of the incident, as reported in court, Huber knew precisely that it was Lorance's he had been watching, because he had been instructed to surveil the area around the village of Sarenzai, in the early morning hours of July

2, 2012. Clint's platoon was the only platoon patrolling the area at that time and place.

Huber knew that what he had witnessed, was beneficial to the defense, and that Clint was getting railroaded for having his men opening fire in a hostile battle zone. Huber tried several times to reach out to Lorance's civilian defense attorney, Mr. Guy Womack. He sent emails to Womack's law offices. But Mr. Womack did not respond.

Huber then attempted to reach out to the local media, and notably the *Fayetteville Observer*, which had been covering the court-martial. In a series of emails with Fayetteville Observer reporter John Ramsey, Huber outlined what he saw that morning outside the village of Sarenzai:

Here is what Mr. Huber wrote to reporter John Ramsey on Sept. 27, 2013, six weeks after the completion of the court-martial.

> **From:** Kevin Huber <krhuber13@yahoo.com>
>
> **To:** «ramseyj@fayobserver.com" <ramseyj@fayobserver.com>
>
> **Sent:** Friday, September 27, 2013 10:56:12 AM EDT
>
> **Subject:** RE: Lt. Lorance
>
> …. I was asked to look for his element because he was being followed by guys with a radio (ICOM) and binos. I guess it depends on what the actual ROE was on that day… and it changed fairly frequently. But in trying to find out about all this, I also reached out to his lawyer. If "spotting" or "scouting" with ICOM was deemed hostile intent under the ROE on that day, then he was justified… everything else that preceded that and whether or not he lied about anything before or after is irrelevant to me.

Mr. Huber is correct in his analysis. As we have already pointed out, and consistent with testimony from several of the soldiers Clint's court-martial, the presence of ICOM radios alone was considered to be a hostile act in Afghanistan, as only the Taliban use these types of radios to coordinate their military movements and paramilitary attacks against American troops. The presence of ICOM radios alone allowed American troops to go ahead and open fire, even in the summer of 2012.

But this Taliban scout party did not just have ICOM radios. They all carried guns, and Huber could see the gun so clearly that he could identify them as AK-47 military assault rifles. All this amounted to one thing—as Huber pointed out—that under the circumstances, Clint had every right to be concerned about being in danger, and to open fire when the motorcycle charged his position.

But in addition to what he saw on the ground, with the hostile scout party shadowing Clint's patrol, Mr. Huber dropped another bombshell in his emails: Hamid Karzai had visited Sia Choy only two weeks before the incident.

Consider these remarks from Mr. Huber, to reporter Ramsey, in that same email of Sept. 27, 2013, about President Karzai's visit.

> Another point worth mentioning is that 82nd's command (as a whole) wasn't really welcomed in the AO when they arrived. They were kinda viewed like cowboys because they didn't really have to answer to brigade brass positioned out of FOB Pasab, they answered to their Col. This made them extremely effective in getting things done. So I wonder which brass pushed this event to trial. Lastly, a few weeks prior there was a Civ-cas right outside my COP where a 5/20 Scout sniper killed a father and his son. This prompted a visit by Karzai

within a day or two. I just really wonder if this Lt. is getting the shaft.

This portion of the email is eye opening. Note that the 82nd Airborne element was headquartered at Sia Choy. The brigade headquarters, where Clint was initially stationed, at Pasab, was not an 82nd Airborne command, although the paratroopers were working under their direct control and supervision.

Earlier, we pointed out that Clint's head has been served on a sacrificial platter, in part because of the civilians who were shot in the Kandahar massacre. But now, Mr. Huber points out what is apparently another civilian casualty incident, in what an accidental shooting by an American sniper, which drew the personal attention of the president, apparently in the June timeframe of 2012. So, in addition to the Bales incident in March of 2012 (the Kandahar massacre), we now have another incident that got Hamid Karzai's personal attention, which leads to even more pressure on the Army and the Obama administration to deliver a head on a platter to prove that the United States would get tough on civilian casualties.

Clint Lorance is that sacrificial scalp.

Even though Mr. Huber filed a report concerning his findings, that Clint's squad was being trailed by the hostile Taliban scout squad, and even though a videotape that Huber took of the Lorance patrol being shadowed by the Taliban Scout squad was available for a number of weeks, the prosecution did not even bother to interview Mr. Huber, and of course, did not disclose his report to the defense.

Mr. Huber's information would not have become available at all, except for the fact that he saw an article about Clint in *Soldier of Fortune* magazine in the winter of 2018. Even though five years had passed, Mr. Huber still felt so strongly about the railroad job against Clint that he reached out to

Clint's current defense team, who in this case, did return his call and conduct a thorough interview with him.

It is impossible to conceive that Clint could have gotten a fair of the trial without this gentleman's testimony, who witnessed the entire movement patrol right up until the moment, the shooting. Nobody was in a better position than the "eye in the sky" to see what was going on.

This evidence, witnessed by Mr. Huber, of the armed Taliban trailing Clint's squad is in addition to what the helicopter team saw, with military-age males congregating on the northwest corner of the village, and is in addition to what Staff Sgt. Herrmann's men saw, that is insurgents operating ICOM radios on the west side—evidence also hidden from the jury. What member of the jury would not want to know that Clint's patrol had been shadowed by armed Taliban right up to the moment of the shooting?

The prosecution's failure to disclose this evidence to the defense, in addition to its failure to reveal crucial biometrics evidence to the defense, and its failure to disclose multiple Significant Activity Reports, further underscores the inexcusable conduct of the prosecution in its zeal to secure a conviction at all cost. Clint's conviction should be overturned immediately, and he should be restored to active duty with full pay and benefits, with promotions commensurate with his time in grade.

American lives matter.

CHAPTER 56

A TRAVESTY OF JUSTICE
THE COMMAND SERGEANT MAJOR SPEAKS
WINTER 2018-2019

In the hierarchy of the U.S. Army, no rank or position is more highly thought of, or in some cases revered, than that of command sergeant major. The rank of sergeant major is the highest noncommissioned rank in the Army. Oftentimes, the very small number of men and women who have reached this distinctive rank have given 30 years or more in service to their country. Command sergeant major means that a soldier holding the high enlisted rank of sergeant major had been given authority over all enlisted troops in a particular command unit.

Command Sgt. Maj. Dan Gustafson, now retired in North Carolina, joined the Army in July of 1982. He gave 36 years and seven months of his life to his country. In July of 2012, Sgt. Maj. Gustafson was the command sergeant major for the 4th Squadron/73rd Cavalry Regiment, deployed to Afghanistan, and was stationed at Sia Choy as command sergeant major. Sgt. Maj. Gustafson served as senior enlisted advisor to Lt. Col. Jeffrey Howard, and knows all about Clint's case. He also knows the terrain and the history of the very difficult situation that the men faced in the Zhari District of Kandahar Province.

When the *Soldier of Fortune* article came out in the winter of 2018, like Kevin Huber, the Aerostat operator who witnessed a good portion of the platoon's patrol just before the shooting, Sgt. Maj. Gustafson also read that article. And like Mr. Huber, the sergeant major also felt compelled to speak up.

Oddly, just like Mr. Huber, Sgt. Maj. Gustafson was neither interviewed by the Army's CID investigators, nor did the prosecutor bother to speak with him. Nor was he called as a witness in the case.

Of course not.

The command sergeant major's testimony would cut against the government's narrative that Clint was some sort of out-of-control murderer, and would undermine the administration's objective of serving an American scalp on a silver platter to the Afghans, as recompense for the so-called civilian casualties that the Afghans had been complaining about.

The command sergeant major recently discussed Clint's situation with retired Marine Lt. Col. David Gurfein, a 25-year veteran who served in four combat tours. Lt. Col. Gurfein now heads the United American Patriots, the charitable organization dedicated to assisting men like Clint, and others who have been targeted in politically correct and politically motivated rules-of-engagement type prosecutions.

The sergeant major's comments were frank, freewheeling, and show the foolishness of the case against Lorance. A few of his comments are laid out as follows:

On Whether Clint Was Justified to Order the Shots Against the Motorcycle Riders

Lt. Col. Gurfein: "Sergeant major, in the court-martial, it was found that Clint followed the rules of engagement, or at least his orders were consistent with the rules of engagement. And I'm kind of curious. What is your understanding, or what was your understanding with the rules of engagement, especially with regard to three individuals, military-age males, headed towards a platoon, on a motorcycle?"

Sgt. Maj. Gustafson: "In the area, if you get out on Highway 1, yes, you would see motorcycles shooting around and most of them were probably Taliban. *But when you get out in the areas where there are gunfights going on, and everything else, and all the sudden, three guys are up there on motorcycles coming at you, and if in the area they've been seen talking on a radio, or whatnot, yes, I think that you could probably safely assume that they are bad guys.*

"And you know, they engaged the motorcycle, and I think one of the guys they could not find from the motorcycle. So, you know as well as I do, that the enemy has a pretty good SOP (standard operating procedure) and a battle drill in getting their own guys off the battlefield. You can be in a gunfight with them, and shoot at one of them, and I'm amazed at how fast they get those guys off of battlefield, because they can get them off the battlefield quick. So, if you have ever been in a gunfight in Afghanistan, you were going to witness it at some point. How quickly they move those guys. (Often getting them off the field with motorcycles.)

"So, you are in a village, that I would say nine times out of 10 are supporting the Taliban. And given the situation where we've had guy shot there, constant contact, I'm on a walkthrough there afterwards it was kind of quiet, not a whole lot of activity, nobody is out there waving at you, or bringing you anything to drink or anything, so that kind of sets the tone.

"You have a platoon leader that has come off the brigade floor. He has been picked by a brigade commander that leans forward in the saddle on everything. He wants to get out there and get after it, and then *that platoon leader comes down there and you are throwing him right in the hot spot of Afghanistan. Southern Afghanistan. Back then, if anybody checks, I'll bet that Afghanistan was the most dangerous place in the world. And Kandahar Province was probably the most dangerous area in Afghanistan.*

"We were fighting in the birthplace of the Taliban, right down there in the Zhari District. So, it was pretty heated down there."

On the Hot Atmosphere of the Battle Zone Faced by Clint and His Men

Sgt. Maj. Gustafson: "Lt. Lorance was originally working at the brigade headquarters, on the brigade ops floor up there at Pasab. The troop, Charlie Troop, had an incident where they were on a dismounted movement one day, and they lost a soldier, and the platoon leader was injured. Now to give you some kind of…"

Lt. Col. Gurfein: "Sergeant major, when you said it lost a soldier, do you mean a soldier was killed at the same time that the platoon leader was injured?"

Sgt. Maj. Gustafson: "Yes. The same day."

Lt. Col. Gurfein: "Okay, I knew the platoon leader took shrapnel to his face, eyes, and abdomen, but I didn't realize there was another death that day as well."

Sgt. Maj. Gustafson: "Yes. That soldier passed. The platoon leader was injured. It was bad on the ground down in the area where the platoon was. So, they were going in there to replace another platoon that was out there in this COP (combat outpost). The whole area that was down there … *there was plenty of contact (meaning firefights) down in that area. It was a situation where guys are in a gunfight every day. You could get in a gunfight a hundred meters outside of their COP.*

"So, going in there, when that platoon (meaning First Platoon) was moving down to that location, the route was so black at the time (meaning full of landmines and IEDs) that we could not get any vehicles down there because of the IEDs that had been placed.

"So, they brought the route clearance team in there, but it was taking forever (to clear the ground of mines). So, we went in and dismounted (meaning to go in on foot instead of by vehicle)."

Lt. Col. Gurfein: "And just to clarify, you were the command sergeant major for the squadron at the time. Is that correct?"

Sgt. Maj. Gustafson: "Yes. So, my commander and I went down to Charlie Troop, where their troop headquarters were located, and we linked up with the platoon, and we walked in with these guys.

"So, we were going down through grape rows, and *the grape rows were probably six to eight feet tall. So, there were some grape walls that we had to go over, and others, we were able to move around.* During that movement, we also walked through the village that played a big part in this. There weren't a lot of people moving around. There wasn't a lot of activity down there. But we walked down through there.

"Now, this was the same village where Charlie Troop lost a soldier who was evacked out after he was shot in the neck during an operation down there. And this was just prior to Lt. Lorance going down and taking over as platoon leader, and before *the platoon leader that was in place got blown up.*

"So, we finally got down there. But it took us several hours in the darkness to get down there. We waited for the clearance team to finish clearing (the IEDs out of the ground). And then we were able to move back up to where the squadron was set up (COP Sia Choy). So, after that incident with the soldier, and after that incident with the platoon leader with the IED, they needed a (new) platoon leader to come down there. And that's when Lt. Lorance got the nod. And a decision was made that yep, he was going to be the guy."

On the ICOMs as a Threat to the Platoon

Sgt. Maj. Gustafson: "*So ultimately, a guy holding a walkie-talkie, communicating about the American soldiers there, yes that will be taken as a threat. It was a pretty hostile environment down there.* Like I said, those guys could get in a gunfight a hundred meters outside the COP. And you know, they had a platoon leader, then another soldier, who was taken out in an incident with an IED, and then they had another soldier that was shot in the neck in that village, just a few days or so, or a week or so before (referring to Cpl. Hanes).

On Not Being Interviewed or Called as a Witness

Lt. Col. Gurfein: "Sergeant major, let me just interrupt for a second. Were you ever interviewed by CID, or asked to be a witness?"

Sgt. Maj. Gustafson: "No. And the thing that is funny about that, is that we took those guys out of that COP (referring to Payenzai), we stood that platoon down (referring to after the motorcycle shooting incident) and we brought them down to where squadron headquarters was at (Sia Choy), and we had them held up down there. And then we had Lt. Lorance, and the CID guys were going around and around out there.

"And I even drove out with the CID guys, and walked through the village ... but never once did CID say, 'Hey, sergeant major, can we talk to you?'"

On the Status of Troop Morale at the Time of the Shooting

Lt. Col. Gurfein: "Did you see the missions we were going after as being viable enough to the point that you had to stress the troop morale? It seems like you are saying there was a disconnect there."

Sgt. Maj. Gustafson: "So, here's what I will tell you. And I will use another battalion as an example. There was a staff sergeant in one of our sister battalions (squadrons). And he was very frustrated as were several others. And he wrote a note to his wife, and said, 'Hey, there's a lot of stuff going on here. A lot of times we really don't understand what the mission is. They're always wanting us to go out. They are always pushing us to go on and on and on.' So, it was a dangerous environment, and I think he's stressed that.

"So, he sent the letter out. And I think, a day or two before the letter got to his wife, he and the first sergeant were killed during a mission. And it was a pretty rough time."

Lt. Col. Gurfein: "Absolutely."

Sgt. Maj. Gustafson: "And a buddy of mine, who was the battalion sergeant major over there, he was pulling his hair out because he was feeling the same thing I was. And that was because people did not feel that there was a concern for the troopers in the brigade. That it was, 'Hey, we're going to go out here, and we are going to take care of business at any cost.' "

Lt. Col. Gurfein: "Right."

Sgt. Maj. Gustafson: "If a mission is going to make sense, great! If we've got a purpose to be out there, then great. But you know, it doesn't hurt every once in a while, to take your foot off the pedal to give the guys just a little bit of a break.

"I'm not saying take days off or anything. But you know, get them just a little down time to sleep a little. Or let them call home. Or just take care of laundry. Or maybe play some cards or something."

On Clint as the Scapegoat

Sgt. Maj. Gustafson: "I had a lot of time to reflect on it, and now, I'm retired, and I am out of the Army, and I don't have somebody breathing down my shoulder and saying, 'Hey, is that really what you think, sergeant major?'

"*So, we got a kid up there, and he was a platoon leader at the time, and I think he is used as a scapegoat.* And those guys turned against him because they ultimately thought that they were going to be court-martialed with him."

Lt. Col. Gurfein: "Well, they were told they were. They were accused of murder, and then, they were given immunity. We have letters where they were told that they will testify against him."

Sgt. Maj. Gustafson: "Well, I can tell you this. We got back to Fort Bragg, Col. Mennes had left. The brigade sergeant major, he was still there. But my battalion commander had left. So there was no continuity.

"And the new brigade commander called me up to his office, and he said, 'Sergeant major, give me your thoughts on this. We got three, four, or five guys, or however many there were (asking about whether to prosecute men for the motorcycle incident).'

"And I said, 'Look, sir.'

"I told him straight up. I told him I don't think that these guys deserve to get punished for anything. I told him, *'I think it goes higher than Lt. Lorance.'* I told him, *'If Lt. Lorance is getting court-martialed, why isn't the company commander getting court-martialed? How come nothing is happening to the platoon sergeant? How come nothing happened to anybody else, but we are all just hammering on this guy?'*

"Those guys down there ... they were in a gunfight every day. They had a hostile environment. Lt. Lorance went down there, and then they try to say he was out of control. But, no, that's not the way it was. There is more to it."

* * * * *

Command Sgt. Maj. Gustafson, the senior noncommissioned officer in the entire squadron, is clear. Under these circumstances, in the most hostile environment in the world, in a dangerous situation where most motorcycle riders in Afghanistan, in the sergeant major's opinion, are Taliban, Clint had every right to order his men to open fire.

As has been said, the prosecution really did not want to know the answer about whether Clint's actions were appropriate. They only wanted to deliver his scalp on a silver platter. That's why they deliberately turned a blind eye to men like Command Sgt. Maj. Gustafson and Kevin Huber. That's why they concealed biometrics evidence showing that the motorcycle riders were bombmakers. A political conviction meant more than standing by an American paratrooper who put his life on his line for his country.

As the command sergeant major has also stated, Clint was a scapegoat. And as the sergeant major asked, why was the company commander not prosecuted? What about the platoon sergeant? Why weren't the other 10 men in the squad prosecuted?

To be clear, *the command sergeant major does not believe that anyone should have been prosecuted or punished.* He made that point clear in giving his opinion to the new brigade commander when he returned to Fort Bragg. But he asked these questions rhetorically, to underscore his point. Clint was singled out as the one they prosecuted because the powers that be needed a scapegoat.

And the command sergeant major, with his 36 years of service and experience, and probably the most credible expert possible on the rules of engagement and on judging

Clint's actions, was never even interviewed by the prosecution or the CID. The prosecution was not interested in the truth, but needed a single scapegoat to sacrifice to the Afghans. So, they went after the young lieutenant and let everyone else go. No one should have been prosecuted. Not the company commander, not the platoon sergeant, and not the 10 paratroopers they threatened to prosecute.

Above and beyond all that, even aside from the discovery of exonerating biometrics evidence and the efforts to hide evidence from the jury, and above and beyond the Army's threats to prosecute Clint's own men for murder if they didn't throw him under the bus, it is a damn shame that an American paratrooper patrol in the midst of the most dangerous, Taliban-infested section of the world, the Zhari District, Kandahar Province, Afghanistan, would be subjected to interrogation like a bunch of criminal thugs on the southside of Chicago. These guys stick their necks out on the line every day for this country, and are doing the best they can to combat the enemy and stay alive. Not only that, but on the very same day that they are in a firefight, on a combat patrol, that night they are met with bureaucratic criminal investigators, asking probing and intimidating questions, second-guessing their actions on a battlefield where they have placed their necks on the line for our country.

The Army CID bureaucrats asking the questions, unlike the paratroopers they were interrogating, were not out in a Taliban hornet's nest, and were not risking their lives for their country. Shame on the Obama administration for putting this platoon, and others like it, through a criminal shakedown and for forcing leftwing political correctness on our military.

That murder charges were brought against Lt. Clint Lorance is the functional equivalent of a criminal act on the part of the U.S. government, in and of itself.

All that evidence—biometrics showing the motorcycle riders to be bombmakers, witness statements showing the

Taliban fired first, clear warnings from intercepted radio messages that Clint's platoon was about to be ambushed—all that was deliberately hidden from the military jury, by the prosecution, in a hell-bent effort to deliver Clint's head on a silver platter at all costs

The prosecution of Lt. Clint Lorance, truly, is a travesty of justice. The time has come to right this wrong.

CHAPTER 57

BERGDAHL, THE BAGRAM AIRMEN AND 20 MORE YEARS

Immediately after the sentencing of Bowe Bergdahl, President Donald Trump tweeted that, "The decision on Sergeant Bergdahl is a complete and total disgrace to our country and to our military."

The president is correct.

However, the treatment of Clint Lorance, an American hero, is an even larger disgrace, for reasons exactly opposite of the Bergdahl case. With Bergdahl, we had an American traitor, whose family came to the Rose Garden with the father praising Allah to the smiling, nodding delight of the 44th president, with the military justice system then letting the traitor Bergdahl, whose desertion cost the lives of six American soldiers, walk away with no time served.

With Clint, we have an American patriot who stuck his neck out for his men and who brought them all home alive, but who was railroaded by his government to pay homage to the Afghans for the Kandahar massacre and send a message to American troops under Obama, "Don't shoot until you are blown up first."

The treatment of our soldiers in Afghanistan in 2012 was a national travesty.

On the author's final trip to Fort Leavenworth, before completion of this book, they brought Clint into the defense counsel waiting area, where we usually met. He wore a brown jumpsuit—not orange—but brown as is customary in long-term U.S. military prisons. Just above the shirt pocket area, an oblong white patch on the brown shirt displayed Clint's prisoner number.

Long gone were the rows of medals, including the seven Army Achievement medals that he had won and the overseas service medals. Gone were his jump wings as a paratrooper, and his air-assault badge, allowing him to rappel out of helicopters in combat and down ropes to the ground.

The author spent five years active duty in the U.S. Navy JAG Corps, and another 11 in the reserves, and has never witnessed a young officer accumulate so many medals and so many awards, so quickly, as Clint Lorance.

In a symbol of supreme irony, on Sept. 15, 2012, only two months and 14 days after that hot, fateful morning of July 2, the day they relieved Clint of command of First Platoon and pulled First Platoon off the field permanently, the Secretary of the Army, through Clint's Brigade Commander, awarded Clint the Army Commendation Medal.

Think about that. Clint's colonel thought so highly of his service as an officer that during the period of time in which the Army high command would decide to railroad him for murder, Col. Bryan Mennes awarded him the prestigious Army Commendation Medal, approved by the Secretary of the Army. The medal was awarded for meritorious service from March 1, 2012, through Sept. 15, 2012, with July 2, 2012 (the date of the alleged murder) being smack dab in the middle of that meritorious timeframe.

That his commander would think so highly of Clint's work to award him the Army Commendation Medal, while at the same time the high command of the Army would insist upon a court-martial for murder, and with even the chief judge of the Army making false statements to Washington, D.C., think tanks to preserve the conviction, all goes to show what a circus of a political prosecution this had become.

Logic dictates that one does not award an Army Commendation Medal to a murderer in the Army, and especially not for the same timeframe in which the alleged murder took place. But, of course, nothing was ever logical about the prosecution of Lt. Lorance.

His immediate superiors knew that Clint was a great officer. But Washington wanted a scalp on a silver platter.

When Clint and I last met, that last Army Commendation medal was, of course, nowhere to be seen on the brown prison jumpsuit with the white patch. Clint's prisoner number had replaced the chest full of medals he once had.

Sometimes in prison, a man regurgitates in his mind life-changing dates on the calendar that will never be forgotten. And that was true for Clint, too.

Clint and I discussed a lot of things that day. And he wanted me to know that his mind had never wandered far from Afghanistan, never far from the men and women who are still left behind and still in harm's way, and his mind had never wandered far from the events of July 2, 2012. He had replayed those events, over and over again, almost every day, since the day that it happened.

His mind also had also gone back, a thousand times, to the evening of Aug. 1, 2013, the night that his country turned on him, branded him as a murderer, and stripped him of his uniform as an officer, only for taking action to protect his men, all who were American paratroopers. Even five years after the fact, the shock of that verdict had never worn off.

The sounds and images of that night would never leave him. He recalled the shocked look on the face of his civilian defense counsel, Guy Womack, who looked like someone punched him in the stomach when the jury pronounced him guilty. Womack had advised Clint and his parents over and over again, that, "There is no way they will convict you over this. No way. This is a battlefield incident. No way they will come back with murder."

Womack was right about that, at least. This was a battlefield incident. He was wrong about the rest.

What had gone wrong? Of course, at the time, Clint was not yet aware of all the evidence that the government had hidden, including the biometrics evidence showing that the motorcycle riders were American-killing bombmakers. And he was not aware of the Significant Activity Report showing that his platoon was about to be ambushed. The government hid all that from him.

Still, Womack had been so confident in an acquittal that after conferring with counsel, Clint had decided to not testify on his own behalf. "You are going to win this thing," his lawyer repeatedly assured him. Testifying would only give the prosecutor an opportunity to try to twist his words.

Five years later, if there were any one decision he could have back, he would have insisted upon taking the stand. Clint Lorance was, always has been, and still is his own best witness.

Then, in addition to July 2, 2012, and Aug. 1, 2013, there was yet a third date that had invaded Clint's consciousness, and he had been unable to shake it. It happened on a Monday morning, the 21st day of December in 2015, four days before Christmas.

Clint was about to serve his third Christmas in Leavenworth, away from family and friends. But back in Afghanistan, the suicidal rules of engagement that had gotten so many of his buddies killed, had not gotten any better. If anything, they had only gotten worse.

That morning, outside the huge Bagram Air Base, not far from where John Maher had served as special counsel leading an international team of lawyers in the State Department's secret supervision of Afghan prosecutions of Taliban terrorists, six U.S. Air Force members were on security patrol outside the main gate of the air base.

They were all part of the Air Force Office of Special Investigations, which is an Air Force law enforcement agency. They had been on foot patrol that morning, outside the base, conducting routine security operations.

Then, the Taliban motorcycle rider spotted them.

After Clint had been prosecuted for murder, the word had spread, loud and clear among U.S. forces in Afghanistan. "Protect yourself against suicide motorcyclists at your own risk. If you are wrong, they will prosecute you for murder."

Against this backdrop, the airmen could do nothing but watch as the Taliban motorcyclist revved his engine charged their position in front of the air base. The airmen could not fire—in self-defense—because they would be prosecuted for murder if they did. The fact that other American servicemen had been attacked and killed in this very manner, suicide-by-exploding-motorcycle, did not matter to the American chain of command, at least not under the Obama administration.

Some of them had spouses and children at home. Maj. Adrianna Vorderbruggen had a 4-year-old son back home in Washington, D.C. Staff Sgt. Michael A. Cinco had a wife, Veronica, waiting for him in San Antonio. Staff Sgt. Peter W. Taub, 30, of Philadelphia, left behind a pregnant wife and a 3-year-old daughter.

Staff Sgt. Chester J. McBride, 30, of Statesboro, Ga., left behind two parents, a sister, and a brother-in-law. McBride had spoken at his old high school, in October, before he left for Afghanistan, and had given words of encouragement to the student body.

Technical Sgt. Joseph G. Lemm, 45, of Bronx, N.Y., left a wife and two children. Staff Sgt. Louis M. Bonacasa, 31, of Coram, N.Y., who was serving his fourth and final tour in Afghanistan, had a wife and a 5-year-old daughter.

The blast from the motorcycle rider shook the earth, sending blood, metal and debris in a thousand directions. People screamed and ran and cried. The blast had been so powerful that all six Americans were killed instantly, four days before Christmas, leaving their spouses and children and mothers and fathers with deep, irreparable holes in their hearts.

Clint heard the news of the airmen that evening, while watching the nightly news broadcast from inside the prison walls at Leavenworth. As he watched the coverage, it felt like someone stabbed him in the heart with a sharp knife, and twisted his stomach in knots, all at once.

Because the Army high command had used him as a scapegoat, and prosecuted him for murder to make a political point, no American soldier in Afghanistan could ever protect themselves from this type of suicide attack, unless they were willing to face prosecution and serve 20 years or more in prison. What an impossible predicament!

In some strange way, Clint felt responsible for the lives of these six airmen. Perhaps if he had won his court-martial, the airmen would've had the courage to defend themselves. Then again, there should never have been a court-martial to begin with.

Ironically, if Clint Lorance had been the platoon leader of that Air Force security detail at Bagram, there was a good chance those airmen would be alive. Clint would have opened fire.

As we sat there together, that cold November morning in the defense holding room in the military prison at Fort Leavenworth, Clint spoke of the six Air Force airmen, who he never knew, and would never know. But he spoke of them as if they were family.

It was something that only a veteran could understand. For anyone who has ever served in the American Armed Forces, there is an innate kinship with anyone else who has ever served, whether we know one another or not, or whether we served together, or not. Whether we're Army or Marines, Navy or Air Force, or Coast Guard. Whether we have met or not, we are all family.

As Clint talked about the airmen, he felt the kinship, and he felt it hard. His eyes began to water as he thought of them dying, so unnecessarily, left in a foreign land with no ability to defend themselves.

Then, he made a statement that opened a window into his soul.

"If I could bring them back, alive again, I would gladly do another 20 years."

We sat in silence, for moment, thinking.

A moment later, our conversation turned back to the morning of July 2, 2012. And then came more words that will never be forgotten.

"If I had to do it all over again, I would do it the same way I did it that morning. If something had happened to one of my men because I did nothing, I could never live with myself. If one of them had died, because I did nothing, I would be living in a permanent prison far worse than the prison I'm in now."

In the end, after all the hell that he had paid for his decision, one thing remained.

Every one of Clint's men came home alive.

Every one.

They came home to their mothers, to their fathers, to their wives, and children and girlfriends and fiancées. They came home to hugs, kisses and tears of joy—just as Clint promised they would. Reunions, birthdays, Christmases, weddings, graduations, movies, football games, parties, school and all the joys of life that all his men still had before them, all because their lieutenant, loved in some corners and scorned in others, took a stand for them.

Every one, alive.

Even in prison, vindication.

American lives matter.

THE END

SPECIAL THANKS

Special thanks and recognition are due to the following good people and organizations for making this book possible.

To Steve Jackson and the great staff at WildBlue Press for providing a great forum for telling Clint's story.

To my brilliant literary agent, Chip MacGregor, and his staff at MacGregor Literary, for their sublime professionalism, and for making great things happen, always.

To the great lay editors who conducted first reviews and editorial assistance with this manuscript, including U.S. Army veteran Jack Miller of La Mesa, Calif.; Mary Lynn Landry and Rebecca Anthony of Charlotte, N.C.; and A.J. Flick, the great line editor at WildBlue Press.

To the United American Patriots, who take a stand for American heroes in uniform, men like Clint Lorance, who all too often become targets on the basis of policies that place governmental political agendas over standing with the American serviceman.

And in closing, still believing the words of Ronald Reagan, that for America, "the best is yet to come."

God bless America.

Don Brown
Charlotte, N.C.
March 15, 2019

For More News About Don Brown,
Signup For Our Newsletter:

http://wbp.bz/newsletter

Word-of-mouth is critical to an author's long-term success. If you appreciated this book please leave a review on the Amazon sales page:

http://wbp.bz/toja

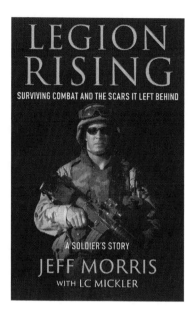
Prologue

Spring, 2007
Baghdad, Iraq
I refused to acknowledge myself in the mirror as I began washing the crimson smears of a dying man's blood from my arms and face. I moved methodically, as if it would clear

the fog of shock that encompassed me. I tried to silence the sound of his agonizing screams that still echoed in my head.

A burning sensation on my face caused me to pause. I leaned closer to my reflection and saw a gash, running across my cheek, under my right eye. I stood still for a moment, trying to imagine what could have caused the cut.

And then I realized.

The skin on my face had been torn by fragments of another man's skull. Fragments that were embedded into the flesh of my own hands.

And in that instance, I stood frozen, feeling the image searing itself into my memory. My mind couldn't process the horror I felt, but I knew that I would never be the same again.

Chapter 1

*"Boys do what they want to do, men do what
they have to do."—Steve Williams*

Destin, Florida

December 1998

As soon as the frigid water touched my ankles, I knew the next minutes were going to be very uncomfortable. During most of the year, a swim in the Gulf in beautiful Destin, Florida, would be the perfect way to spend a Saturday. The white sand beaches usually offer a stark comparison to the brilliant green-blue water of the Emerald Coast. But here now, in the dead of winter, the colorless sand barely contrasted the gray expanse ahead of me. The shoreline lay empty, void of the usual beach goers who were undoubtedly driven off by such a cold, bleak day.

I gritted my teeth and waded farther in, staring ahead at the horizon of flat gray water that extended until it touched the flat gray skies. A little shiver ran through my body, but hardly registered in my mind. The water enveloped me until my feet could barely touch the sand without submerging my mouth and nose. I drew a deep breath before plunging downward, the icy water slapping my face, and began to swim. A full mile lay ahead. Only two thoughts ran through my mind:

Why the hell am I doing this?

and

Don't quit.

So began this phase of my self-imposed training regimen, one I had followed for months prior and would pursue until the day came to take the Navy SEAL Fitness test. I was going to be a SEAL, there was no question in my mind. But I knew that following this path would push the bounds of my mental and physical toughness, and I aimed to be prepared. The dream consumed me.

I hadn't grown up in a military family. In fact, this dream in its earliest form began in high school as the credits of *The Silence of the Lambs* poured down the screen and I watched from my seat with one thought in my head: "I'm going to be in the FBI someday." When I enrolled at Samford University, a few paths led towards federal law enforcement: an accounting degree, a law degree, or service in the military. Something in my blood felt diametrically opposed to being an accountant, and I thought that a law degree would serve me well, so I chose to pursue law school. I studied hard and paid attention, and it seemed a good fit for me, even enjoyable. But even so, I found myself deeply drawn toward the history classes where we studied and discussed war, victory, defeat, and the great men who brought it all about. Thick history books weighed down my backpack, and I pored over the pages in my dorm. My interest in the military was like a kindled flame burning just under the surface, waiting to alter my life's course.

And it did. It happened the day I took the L-SAT. I had studied hard and by every indication was positioned to do well. But as I sat there at my desk, staring at the pages of the test, a restlessness overtook me. I blinked and stared harder, wrestling my focus back to the present. But an overwhelming feeling welled up in me, and with it emerged the urges that lay beneath the surface, ones I had tried to suppress. The pieces all suddenly connected in my mind... my captivated interest every time someone shared a personal experience from the military, the way something in me came to life when I watched a war movie, the deep pull I felt toward beefy history books and the autobiographies of great generals. There in the quiet of that testing room, on that cold, flat desk seat, I finally allowed myself to face the desire that had only burned stronger. Somehow, it was clear now that becoming a lawyer or an FBI agent would not satisfy me. I knew with certainty that day that I would join the military. I tried to finish the test to the best of my ability, but my heart and mind were far from those pages. When I received a less-than-ideal score on the test, it prompted neither surprise nor disappointment in me. And that's when I made a pact, along with a close friend of mine, that we would not only join the military, but we would become Navy SEALs. This dream became my one and only pursuit, and I wanted to immerse myself in it and push myself as far as possible. I wanted to chase the greatest challenge I could find, and becoming a Navy SEAL promised to deliver that.

When I filled out my application, I didn't check any of the boxes except for the ones beside Navy SEALs. I had heard all about BUD/S: Basic Underwater Demolition/SEAL training, the six-month SEAL training course held at the Naval Special Warfare Training Center in Coronado, California. I heard all the horror of burning lungs, complete physical fatigue, and pain that came from the kind of training and tests that an individual must endure to become a SEAL. People told me stories of men coming out of the ocean, exhausted after a lengthy swim, and running through the thick sand that covered the beaches, and how those tiny, gritty grains slowly cut the soft skin of the inner thighs amidst the friction of running. But I wasn't going to allow these things to take me by surprise. Not if I could help it.

I would be prepared.

After swimming that cold, hard mile in the gulf on that wintry day, it took a minute to catch my breath. When I could stand, I jogged against the heavy water until I was back on the beach. Once there, I plunged my hands into the gritty sand and grabbed two fistfuls of it. I pulled open the waistband of my wet shorts and threw the sand in. Against my cold, wet skin it instantly coated my inner thighs and legs. Once it did, I took off running. I wanted to be prepared for the pain I would surely experience one day. The gray sky remained mercilessly dreary, and with each step forward the only sounds were my feet thudding against the earth, my rhythmic breathing, and the light brush of friction as my legs passed one another. With each print my feet left behind, the sand ate my skin raw. But I kept putting one foot in front of the other.

And I thought of my mom.

When most people hear that you grew up in Destin and went to Samford University, they get ideas about your upbringing. But my childhood was much different from any preconceived notions based on just those pieces of my life. My early memories took place in a tiny apartment, and by the time I was six years old, my parents had divorced. In many ways that was a good thing, as the majority of my memories of their time together are not ones I care to re-live. They left me strongly protective of my mom, even at a young age. In many ways, those memories were the match that struck inside of me... the beginning of my burning desire to protect and defend, to combat anything or anyone who would overpower or take advantage of those weaker than themselves.

After the divorce, my mom worked hard to make ends meet. My older brother and I came home by ourselves after school. He was eight and I was six. My mom was working as a bartender, which meant she didn't return home until late into the night. When dinnertime came, I might pull out a small skillet and dump raw ground beef in it, patting and tossing the meat until it looked brown. I'd open a can of spaghetti sauce and mix it with the beef as water began to boil for the pasta noodles. Even at six years old, I knew how to make meals for our little family. Everyone had to pitch in if we were going to make it, and I understood that. Sometimes it was a struggle. Even though I was the youngest, I learned to pick up on the signals—that look on Mom's face or the fact that we were eating canned SPAM at the dinner table again or living with no electricity until we could pay the bill. Whether or not the situation actually called for it, I believed that I had to be the man of the family and made it my mission to help my mom in every way possible.

Many nights she got home late from work and woke up her sons not long after. The three of us would dress and hurry to the car to deliver newspapers on the paper route she ran to make a little extra money. There in the dark backseat of the car, my brother and I would roll the newspapers and hand them to her as she threw them into the dewy yards, in front of the quiet houses where other mothers and children lay peacefully unaware and fast asleep in their beds. But we didn't complain. When you're a child, whatever your daily life holds seems completely normal to you. I learned through watching my mom what it meant to work hard, to never give up when things are tough. There must have been times when she looked at piling bills and felt overwhelmed. There must have been days when her alarm clock rang in the middle of the night, calling her to work when she ached to stay in her bed for just a few more hours. But she never gave up. Watching her taught me what resilience looks like, how to persevere when things get hard. And that would be a lesson I would carry with me when facing many challenging circumstances throughout my life. Even when I wanted to give up.

And that fueled me as I pushed ahead on that icy beach. Step after step. Breath after breath.

***

As a boy, I never wanted my performance in school to be one more thing my mom had to worry about, so I studied hard and made good grades. I saw how hard my mother worked and felt responsible for her. When she picked up odd jobs, I would rush to her side and try to help as best I could. My mom eventually remarried, making my baseball coach, Dennis, my stepfather. Dennis was ten years younger than my mom. At the age of twenty-two, he not only became a husband but also stepfather to two young boys. Dennis never tried to replace our father and he didn't inappropriately try to be our friend. He was simply there to be whatever we wanted or needed him to be. And we appreciated that. Dennis never shied away from hard work, either. He was a fireman, but always worked multiple other side jobs on his off days. He continued to coach our baseball teams and always sacrificed his own time for our family, showing me another example of a diligent work ethic as he demonstrated what it takes to be a man in this world.

Because he was older and could understand things on a much deeper level, the divorce had a greater impact on my brother as a child. He did not excel in school as I did and occasionally was the target of bullying. Whether or not he wanted me to, I made it my goal to protect him and stand up for him. It helped that as a young kid, and through middle school, I was tall for my age. If kids picked on my brother, I charged to his defense. I had no trouble putting myself right in the middle of an intense situation, if it meant sticking up for someone in need. Once, during a fight at the bus stop after school, one kid was easily getting the best of the other. He kept going after him even after the other kid had obviously conceded and laid curled up on the ground. As he moved in again, I stepped in and told him if he wanted to inflict any more punishment he would have to go through me first. Our eyes locked and he eventually backed down.

But for all that bravado and bravery, I never felt strong enough to stand up for myself. Running to the defense of someone else came without hesitation, backing up my position with whatever means were necessary. And yet when it came to personal matters, when no one was affected but me, I froze. Something soft and weak overtook me, making me feel powerless. I hated that part of myself. I remember being thirteen and proudly walking into school with a light gray and blue Billabong jacket my dad had given me. I didn't see my dad all that much, but we lived in the same town so we had some contact. He poured on the presents and treats when we were together, perhaps trying to make up for all that our relationship was missing at the time. And this jacket was one of my favorite gifts of all. Not long after I began wearing it to school, one of my bigger, more intimidating classmates stole it and kept it for himself. It was no secret who did it; he wore it every day, right in front of me, as if taunting me to do something about it. But I never did. I couldn't find the words to stand up for myself. And even more than hating the fact that my prized possession was stolen, I despised whatever it was inside of me that cowered in the face of a personally hard or uncomfortable situation. I saw it as weakness and detested it. I vowed to purge myself of that part of me. But as it turned out, it wasn't so much me who did the purging. It was a football coach.

Football was actually never really my thing. Baseball was, all the way from middle school into high school. I was lanky, thin, and fast, which serves you well on the baseball diamond. I showed a lot of promise in the sport and had the hope of getting drafted some day. But everyone I knew kept pushing me to try out for football since I was athletic and quick. Finally, in my junior year of high school, I decided to follow their advice. It was a gamble and far outside of my comfort zone. At that point in my life, I hadn't taken many risks. In my insecurity, I worried about being shown up as not having what it takes, or exposed as weak. So I went for things that were easily within my reach. When it came to the school dance, you would never find me asking out the girl that seemed out of my league. It was too likely she might turn me down. I went for the good friend who was sure to agree. And baseball was like that for me. It was safe, calculated. I was good at it and didn't have to worry about failing. That's why the decision in my junior year of high school to give football a try was such a significant one. I went out that spring.

And I hated it.

http://wbp.bz/legionrisinga

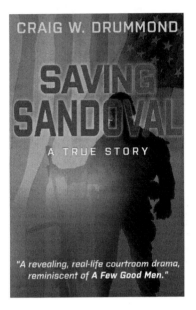
ONE – THE ARREST

"The sniper must be able to calmly and deliberately kill targets that may not pose an immediate threat to him. It is much easier to kill in self-defense or in the defense of others than it is to kill without apparent provocation."
~ ***"Sniper Training," U.S. Army Field Manual 23-10 (1994)***

On 26 June 2007, two United States Army Criminal Investigation Command (CID) Agents quietly approached the front door of a home in Laredo, Texas, and knocked. Their mission: to arrest U.S. Army sniper, Specialist Jorge Sandoval, Jr.

Specialist Sandoval recalled in a 2016 interview:

"It was only a few days after my twenty-second birthday when the agents showed up. I was home on leave from Iraq and excited to be home to spend my birthday with my family. I was at my mom's house, doing some push-ups and working out. Mom was in the kitchen making lunch. It surprised me to hear a knock on the door because I hadn't heard any vehicles approaching the house.

I answered the door and was greeted by two gentlemen wearing polo shirts and cargo pants. They identified themselves as Army CID Agents and asked me, "Are you Specialist Jorge Sandoval, Jr.?"

"Yes." I said, "What is this about?" I stepped outside and that's when I saw two vehicles—an unmarked vehicle and a police vehicle with lights flashing.

"We need to ask you some questions related to an incident that occurred while you were in Iraq. We will need you to accompany us to the police station for questioning."

"Fine. Just let me go inside and get dressed," I said.

I quickly changed my clothes, and when my mom saw that I had changed, she asked me where I was going. "*Adonde vas, mijo?*"

I responded in Spanish, saying, "Look, I don't know… some people want to talk to me. I don't know what it's about. When I find out what's going on, I'll let you know… but I must tell you, I don't know if I'm coming back.'

As the agents were escorting me away from the house I thought, *Maybe something happened with one of my friends in Iraq.* I assumed I was getting into their unmarked vehicle with them so I began to move toward the car door to open it.

"No," they said, stopping me. "You're not going to ride in this vehicle."

Two local police officers blocked off both sides of the road, put my hands behind my back, put me in handcuffs, and put me into the back of a squad car.

That was the moment I first started to realize that I was in some type of custody. *Okay, so this definitely has something to do with me,* I thought, *not one of my friends. What could have happened? Why am I being taken into custody? Did I do something wrong?*

As I tried to get a grasp of the situation, all sorts of things were going through my mind. I traveled back in my memory to Iraq, quickly flipping through my recollections of various dates, trying to get a sense of what was happening to me. I thought back to the events that led to me and a few friends of mine finding ourselves in sniper positions in the U.S. Army.

As the squad car pulled away from my mom's house with me inside, I thought, *This is terrible timing! Michelle's waiting for me, and she's going to think I stood her up.* Michelle was a childhood friend and we had just recently reconnected and started dating. I knew I couldn't text her from the squad car.

http://wbp.bz/savingsandovala

 WILDBLUE PRESS

See even more at:
http://wbp.bz/tc

More True Crime You'll Love From WildBlue Press

Made in the USA
Middletown, DE
20 July 2019